D1563016

PERSON–ENVIRONMENT PSYCHOLOGY AND MENTAL HEALTH

Assessment and Intervention

PERSON–ENVIRONMENT PSYCHOLOGY AND MENTAL HEALTH

Assessment and Intervention

Edited by

William E. Martin, Jr.
Northern Arizona University

Jody L. Swartz-Kulstad
University of Wisconsin–Superior

2000

LAWRENCE ERLBAUM ASSOCIATES, PUBLISHERS
Mahwah, New Jersey   London

Lawrence Erlbaum Associates, Inc., Publishers
10 Industrial Avenue
Mahwah, New Jersey 07430-2262

Cover design by Kathryn Houghtaling Lacey

Library of Congress Cataloging-in-Publication Data

Person–environment psychology and mental health : as-
sessment and intervention / edited by William E. Martin,
Jr., Jody L. Swartz-Kulstad.
     p. cm.
 Includes bibliographical references and indexes.
 ISBN 0-8058-2953-9
1. Ecopsychiatry. 2. Mental health counseling. I. Martin,
William E. (William Eugene) Jr. 1948– . II. Swartz-Kulstad,
Jody L.
RC489.E26P47 2000
616.89—dc21   99-32763
                                             CIP

Printed in the United States of America
10 9 8 7 6 5 4 3 2 1

I dedicate this book to my family: Susan, Neil, Kurt, Carol, and my mother and father, Thelma and Bill Sr.

—Bill

To Mike and Herb, my most valuable supporters, and to my mother and father, for it is through them that I truly appreciate the importance of a "good fit" in raising healthy adolescents and promoting optimal functioning in adults.

—Jody

Contents

PART IV: CONCLUSION

I

Introduction

An Introduction
to Person–Environment Psychology
and Mental Health: Assessment
and Intervention

William E. Martin, Jr.
Northern Arizona University
Jody L. Swartz-Kulstad
University of Wisconsin-Superior

No person exists in isolation from the influences of the environment; few if any mental health professionals would argue with this position. In recent years, focus has been on the person as embedded in the environment. Person–environment (P–E) variables are often pointed to as causal or related factors in the development of mental health problems across the life span. The crucial questions, however, are whether and how we can draw from P–E theory to go beyond mere *study* to develop effective assessment and intervention strategies for adolescents and adults.

DEVELOPMENT OF PERSON–ENVIRONMENT
THEORY

Dawis (chap. 5, this volume) maintains that P–E theory is "a paradigm that can encompass the many differing theories and the multitude of disparate facts that have characterized counseling psychology—and psychology—to this point" (p. 108). Furthermore, he asserts that "It is the paradigm that can generate the puzzle-solving activity that is the hallmark of normal science" (p. 108). P–E theory has permeated applied psychology since the turn of the century. In 1909, Parsons proposed that vocational satisfaction can be achieved through knowledge of both individuals and environments, not merely one or the other. Kantor (1924), suggested that the unit of study in psychology should be the individual as that individual interacts with the contexts that produce behavior. The breadth of P–E theorists influence on psychology is illustrated in a matrix we developed (Swartz & Martin, 1997). The matrix provides a classification of theorists based on whether their contributions focused on behavior as a function of Person (individual or group) x Environment (perceived or actual). For example, Kurt Lewin's (1935, 1951) theory is classified as Person (individual) x Environment (perceived). He maintained that individuals' behavioral environments are the result of their subjective experience of the objective physical environment. By contrast, Roger Barker's (1968) contribution is characterized as focusing attention on more objective characteristics of the environment, Person (group) x Environment (actual). He demonstrated that settings call forth certain types of behavior from the individuals who inhabit them such that, when in school, students "behave school" and when at home, they "behave home."

UNDERSTANDING THE IMPACT OF PERSON–ENVIRONMENT INTERACTION

As individuals develop, the number and variety of environments in which they function increases. It follows then, that as children move into adolescence, a period of time where family, school, and peer systems vie for influence, life becomes more complex. Consider also that individuals have basic learned and inborn abilities that they bring into each environment. Each environment calls on the individual to possess certain skills and abilities; if they do not, then there is a P–E mismatch. Each individual needs certain things from the environment; if these are not received, a mismatch occurs. The greater the degree of mismatch, the greater the potential for psychological distress. Thus, it is clear, in situations where P–E mismatch occurs, neither blaming the victim or the circumstance achieves clinical success, but treating the mismatch will.

Certainly, when we accurately assess influencing factors of the individual, environment, context, and their resulting interactions, we can more fully understand mental health behavior and implement effective mental health interventions. The purpose of this book is to present P–E assessment and intervention models that can be used to improve delivery of mental health services to adolescents and adults. Next, we provide an overview of the chapters in the book.

In chapter 3, Horton and Bucy articulate an ecological and P–E fit model and apply it to assessing adolescents. These contributors establish a developmental contextual perspective that integrates identity formation, cognitive and moral development, and changes in family power. This perspective then permeates their discussion of roles of parents, peers, school, and work in an adolescent's life. Horton and Bucy conclude by identifying assessment techniques that assist in understanding the contexts of adolescents. The assessment techniques covered include interviews, eco-maps, self-report objective measures, projectives, and observations.

Munger (chap. 2) also takes an ecological perspective as he presents a comprehensive needs-based assessment model to discover the social ecologies of children. He begins his chapter instituting a strong case that community-based children's mental health should be a national priority that requires a paradigm shift. He provides support for this position by identifying empirical underpinnings of this multicausal and multidimensional approach. Munger then presents a comprehensive needs-based assessment template predicated on normalization that focuses on the strengths and needs of adolescents by systems. These systems include levels of the individual, family, peer, social, and neighborhood or community. Munger applies the comprehensive needs assessment template in relation to a person's fit to his or her setting ("ecological niche") using the Environmental Status Exam (ESE) concept identified by Moos (1976). In part, ESE involves the manipulation of time use, places, activities, and people that are elements in a person's life that are core to ecological environmental intervention. Additionally, Munger presents a comprehensive needs-based assessment checklist.

In chapter 4, Koehly and Shivy present methodology to assess individual behavior in situ with specific focus on the interpersonal context in which behavior is embedded. The methodology of Social

Network Analyses (SNA) has evolved in sophistication since Moreno (1938) first spawned the method of sociometry in the 1930s. SNA offers a way for P–E psychologists to advance an understanding of behavior by providing indices of relatedness among individuals to produce representation of social environments. Koehly and Shivy illustrate the practical use of SNA by providing an example of conflict among adolescents in a group home setting. Additionally, these authors identify computer and inferential tools that can be used by practitioners to enhance their use of SNA.

Borduin, Heiblum, Jones, and Grabe argue that antisocial adolescents consume much of the resources of the children's mental health, juvenile justice, and special education systems in chapter 6. Furthermore, they state that current treatments do not address multiple and changing needs of youth and often are delivered in settings that have little relation to problems being addressed. These authors present five promising models that attend to real-world conditions. First, they discuss research that points to correlates and causes of serious antisocial behavior in adolescents. Borduin et al. review findings as they relate to individual adolescent characteristics, family relations, peer relations, school and academic performance, neighborhood context, and multidimensional causal models. Then, they discuss promising intervention models that are Behavioral Parent Training (BPT), Functional Family Therapy (FFT), Individualized/Wrap-around Care, Family Ties, and Multisystemic Therapy (MST). They conclude with a discussion of the qualities needed in order for treatment models to be effective at reducing serious antisocial behavior.

In chapter 5, Dawis provides a historical and theoretical foundation for the tradition of a P–E perspective in counseling psychology that complements his article entitled, "The Individual Differences Tradition in Counseling Psychology" (Dawis, 1992). He traces the evolution of P–E psychology including contributions of trait and factor theory, vocational guidance, and counseling psychology. Additionally, Dawis describes the scientific development of "goodness of match" methods between persons and environments. These methods include "psychographs" and commensurate measurement.

In chapter 7, Swanson and Chu relate the importance of work activities to psychological well-being throughout the life span by stressing that mental health and vocational issues reciprocally affect one another in an individual's life. They detail the components of two of the most researched and used P–E matching paradigms in applied psychology; Holland's Model of Vocational Personalities and Work Environments Theory and the Theory of Work Adjustment (TWA). Swanson and Chu present two examples that demonstrate how P–E fit theories apply in individual interventions.

In chapter 8, we assert that mental health professionals have not lived up to their good intentions to effectively integrate ethnocultural factors in the provision of mental health services. We suggest that a P–E approach may indeed be the most likely model to actually improve mental health services to persons from various ethnocultural backgrounds. We present a P–E fit model that focuses on an individual's psychosocial adaptation to settings based on cultural and contextual correspondence.

Following the presentation of chapters, we discuss the focal points that emerged in the book that apply P–E psychology to the establishment of effective mental health strategies for adolescents and adults.

CONCLUSION

No longer do mental health professionals place the "responsibility" for mental health on the shoulders of the person, alone. It is understood that problems arise from the unique interaction between person and environment. Service providers must and are beginning to view the person in context. Although the greatest amount of attention has been paid to educational and work settings, it is clear that *all* of the individuals' life settings contribute meaningfully to positive psychosocial adaptation and each must be considered. The following chapters explore the ways in which taking a person–environment perspective, deepens our understanding of theory and research on the one hand, and practice with adolescents and adults in context on the other.

REFERENCES

Barker, R. G. (1968). *Ecological Psychology: Concepts and methods for studying human behavior.* Stanford, CA: Stanford University Press.

Dawis, R. V. (1992). The individual differences tradition in counseling psychology. *Journal of Counseling Psychology, 39*(2), 7–19.

Kantor, J. R. (1924). *Principles of psychology* (Vol. 1). Bloomington, IN: Principia Press.

Lewin, K. (1935). *Dynamic theory of personality: Selected papers*. New York: McGraw-Hill.

Lewin, K. (1951). *Field theory in social science*. New York: Harper & Row.

Moos, R. H. (1976). *The human context: Environmental determinants of human behavior*. New York: John Wiley.

Moreno, J. L., & Jennings, H. H. (1938). Statistics of social configurations. *Sociometry, 1*, 342–374.

Swartz, J. L., & Martin, W. E., Jr. (1997). Ecological psychology theory: Historical overview and application to educational ecosystems. In J. L. Swartz & W. E. Martin, Jr. (Eds.), *Applied ecological psychology for schools within communities*. (pp. 3–27). Mahwah, NJ: Lawrence Erlbaum Associates.

II

*Person–Environment Psychology
and Mental Health: Assessment
Strategies*

2

Comprehensive Needs-Based Assessment With Adolescents

Richard L. Munger
Blue Ridge Center, Asheville, North Carolina

Developing community-based systems of child mental health care is now seen as a national priority, and communities across the country are working toward establishing such systems (Stroul & Friedman, 1986). The "system of care" philosophy is built around the concept of individualizing services. Implementing a program of individualized care requires an ecological approach. To think ecologically is to concentrate on the interrelationships between all levels that comprise an organism and its environment. In the case of a child, this means the child-as-individual (e.g., biological, intrapsychic, cognitive factors), as well as intra- and extrafamilial, peer, school, neighborhood, community, and overarching institutional factors. An effective individualized program must begin with a comprehensive, needs-based assessment—one that examines all domains in the child's environment to discover the social ecology of the child's behavior (Burchard & Clarke, 1990).

Like the assessment, the intervention itself must touch the child's whole world. A typical individualized program is a creative combination of all types of services, resources, and supports needed by a child and the child's family. The comprehensive, strength-based assessment becomes the key factor in the development of the individualized service plan for the child and family (Katz-Leavy, Lourie, Stroul, & Ziegler-Dendy, 1992).

To be truly individualized, a program must provide services that meet the specific needs of the child and family. This concept stands in direct opposition to the practice of merely plugging a child into a particular categorical label and intervention model. This is not to say that individualized interventions never involve traditional services such as psychotherapy, foster care, and medication. It does mean, however, that these services are brought into a program only when they can be tailored to help satisfy the specific need of the child or family (Burchard, Burchard, Sewell, & VanDenBerg, 1993). It also means that appropriate nontraditional strategies, for example, hiring a special friend for the child, arranging for a staff member to live with the family, fixing the family's car or washing machine, or providing the family with a telephone, will be critical elements of the program.

The assessment and planning process for individualized care involves examining needs across all life domains. These include (a) residential (the need for shelter), (b) familial (may be a surrogate family), (c) social (the need for friends and contact with other people), (d) educational and/or vocational, (e) medical, (f) psychological/emotional, (g) legal (e.g., for children with juvenile justice needs), (h) safety-oriented (i.e., the need to be safe), and (i) other life domain areas such as cultural or ethnic needs and community needs.

Although individualizing services provides a good model, it offers the practicing clinician few blueprints to follow. It is not enough to encourage professionals to use individualized, child, and family needs-based methods. They must be introduced to the theory and shown how to apply the interventions required by the approach. Lack of such concretenesss increases the probability that they will either reject the approaches or apply them in an ineffective manner. Changing the focus of the service system to an individualized approach requires more than hard work and good intentions—it requires a complete paradigm shift (Olson, Whitbeck, & Robinson, cited in Katz-Leavy et al., 1992).

Munger and his colleagues (1998) have been using the applications developed by Henggeler and his colleagues (1998) to train clinicians in individualized, comprehensive needs-based assessment and intervention. To facilitate this necessary paradigm shift, the training of mental health professionals emphasizes the role of the child's total ecological system in bringing about worthwhile change. We are finding that clinicians are receptive to the conceptualizations and can translate the model into viable interventions. The approach, which is consistent with widely adopted child mental health policy, lacks the threat of a competing technology, yet provides clinicians with the tangible skills to use in the therapeutic universe (Munger, Donkervoet & Morse, 1998).

EMPIRICAL UNDERPINNINGS OF ECOLOGICAL THEORY

There is considerable evidence in the scientific literature showing that disturbed behavior in childhood and adolescence is related to important characteristics of the individual youth, family, peer system, school system, and community (for comprehensive reviews, see Borduin et al., chap. 6, this volume; Henggeler, 1989; Kazdin, 1987; McMahon & Wells, 1989; Quay, 1987). For example, the results of causal modeling studies of delinquency (for a review, see Henggeler, 1991) explain the multidimensional and multicausal nature of antisocial behavior in adolescents as well as the interactive relationships among family factors, the constellation of the adolescent's peer group, the adolescent's personal and social abilities, and criminal behavior. Depression in children and adolescents has been associated with multiple characteristics of youth and of the environments in which they live. Common precipitants of adolescent suicide are family disruption, parental rejection, isolation, lack of support, and depression (Hawton, 1986). And although adolescent psychosis is likely caused by brain dysfunction, there is compelling evidence that psychosocial factors contribute to its precipitation (Graham & Rutter, 1985), and family relationships clearly affect treatment outcomes (e.g., Leff, Kuipers, Berkowitz, Eberlein-Vries, Sturgeon 1982; Vaughn & Leff, 1976).

To summarize, results from the empirical literature point to the fact that the types of problems precipitating serious emotional disturbances in youths are multidetermined. Thus, it is concluded that effective treatments should consider children's characteristics as well as key factors in the multiple systems in which youth are embedded.

WHAT IS A COMPREHENSIVE,
NEEDS-BASED APPROACH?

Comprehensive approaches address multiple risk factors in an integrated fashion, and therefore, intervene in multiple contexts—including youth cognitive processes, the family system, the peer network, the school or vocational arena, and the neighborhood (Henggeler, 1997). Dunst and his colleague (1994) defined *need* as "a judgment or indication that a resource (information, advice, assistance, etc.) is required or desired in order to achieve a goal or attain a particular end" (p. 94). Comprehensive assessment focuses on normalization. *Normalization* has been defined by Wolfensberger and Nirje (1972) as the use of culturally normative means for achieving personal behaviors that approximate that which is culturally normal. Normalized needs are those basic human needs of persons of like age, grade, gender, community, and culture (Eiber, 1996). Thus, the expectations for the child are based on those for typical children in the the child's immediate environment. The assessment focuses on the child's needs on the basis of a profile of the child whose skills are typical in each setting. Identification of the child's needs is based on the question: "What does a child who is successful in this setting look like?"

Although it might be possible to collate all the information from a comprehensive assessment in one session, typically it takes several sessions. As the clinician learns more about the family from new sources (e.g., teacher, peers), problems might need to be reconceptualized and new directions for interventions developed. The organization of information from a comprehensive assessment will reveal how particular problems are sustained in the youth's systemic context; this will provide a logical direction for therapeutic intervention (Henggeler & Borduin, 1990).

Figure 2.1 presents a template for the clinician to conceptualize behavior problems within a framework that considers the many individual, family, and extrafamilial variables that might be linked with problems. Clinicians should not assume that any one system is the most important target. An excessive emphasis at any one level, or commitment to any one intervention modality, will present a barrier to understanding the case. The clinician's task is to identify existing strengths of the various systems that can be used to promote

	Strengths	Needs
Identified Child		
Family		
School		
Peer		
Neighborhood/ Community		

FIG. 2.1. Comprehensive needs-based assessment.

change (Henggeler & Borduin, 1990). The clinician also considers a broad range of needs that may be related to the child's problems. A fundamental principle is that other systems may need to change to help maintain improvements in the targeted system.

Individual Level

It is impossible to understand any child behavior in isolation from its context. Even if a problem is the result of a biological abnormality, environmental circumstances would still influence the clinician's conceptualization of the problem. Although the contextual view of behavior problems is primary, an ecological approach acknowledges that individual characteristics of a child can contribute uniquely to behavior problems. Relevant individual characteristics include, for example, genetically determined tendencies, biological variables, intellectual ability, medical conditions (e.g., severe physical handicap), neuropsychological influences, pharmacological agents, intrapsychic forces, cognitions, reinforcement contingencies, gender-role development, and affective states. Although individual characteristics should not be viewed in isolation, they do have distinct implications for the understanding of behavior problems.

Family Level

Many behavior problems are associated with transactions among family members and the interrelations of family subsystems. Although the complexities of any family system make comprehensive analysis challenging, four domains are particularly salient: (a) parent–child relationships, (b) marital relations, (c) nonnuclear family issues, and (d) instrumental issues.

There are certain styles of childrearing that promote appropriate behavior as well as problem behaviors. For example, parents who are warm but structured with consistent rules and high expectations for behaviors, often referred to as authoritative in style, have children with better conduct as well as better social competence with peers and academic achievement (Masten & Coatsworth, 1998). Other important elements of parent–child relationships include the following: (a) parental control strategies, (b) intraparental consistency, (c) sibling relationships, (d) barriers to effective parenting, (e) parental knowledge or skill deficits, (f) facilitation of activities and supervision of children, and (g) the social support networks of parent and child.

Certain styles of marital interaction promote competence, whereas other styles evoke conflict. Some elements of marital relationships that are particularly relevant include the following: (a) conflict over parenting, (b) sexual problems, (c) infidelity, (d) parental psychopathology, (e) parent substance abuse, and (f) domestic violence.

Nonnuclear families are now as prevalent as the traditional family unit. It is essential to understand the issues surrounding family disruption and reconstitution. Primary are the single-parent family, the step-family system, the surrogate-parent family, conflicts between ex-spouses, and the extended family system.

Finally, instrumental issues weigh heavily in understanding family functioning. Among these elements are financial, child care; housing; medical care; employment; transportation, obligations to family members; and shared responsibilities and expectations for money, household tasks, and parenting tasks.

Peer Level

The older the child is the more important peer influences become. Some problems are related more strongly to dysfunctional peer relationships than to family interactions. Because therapeutic interventions must often involve a child's peer group directly or indirectly, a careful assessment is necessary. Some parameters of the evaluation are as follow: (a) the child's social relationships in general; (b) acquaintanceships; (c) close friendships; (d) ability to establish friendships; (e) dysfunctional peer relationships (especially involving delinquent behavior, drug use, or sexual behavior); (f) social and intellectual functioning of friends, including reputation; and (g) family–peer linkages.

School Level

School is one of the most important systems outside the child's family. The school environment is a complex milieu that requires thorough analysis in the assessment process. Some of the domains in the school context include: (a) academic performance, (b) vocational needs, (c) sensorimotor problems, (d) youth–adult relationships (e.g., teachers, coaches), (e) how the child responds to authority, (f) adequacy of the learning environment, (g) friends, and (h) extracurricular activities.

A critical aspect of the school influence is the family–school linkage. Here, a clinician must assess a number of issues, for example: (a) Does family dysfunction interfere with school performance or behavior? (b) Is there parental avoidance of school? (c) How much parental contact is there with teachers? (d) Is there parental monitoring by active, daily interest in school activities (e.g., homework, upcoming exams, grades)? (e) Is the parent involved in school-related organizations? (f) Is there a time and place to study at home? (g) Are there contingencies for school performance (grades) and behavior?

Neighborhood or Community Level

The child's larger systemic context is often ignored by clinicians, but researchers have observed that the neighborhood and community often influence family functioning (Henggeler & Borduin, 1990). Many families also are involved with the social service, legal, or medical care systems. Each of these systems may influence the behavior of family members. The immediate neighborhood of the family possesses characteristics (e.g., availability of activities, friends, transportation, and safety issues) that can be used to promote therapeutic gains; other times they can be barriers.

ENVIRONMENTAL STATUS EXAM

Historically, assessment of the client's environment has received minimal attention as compared to the individual level and intrafamilial levels. One reason for this is that clinical training programs have emphasized person-oriented assessments. Another reason may be that whereas the importance of environmental context in human behavior may be given lip service, the environment appears more nebulous, with few practical tools to evaluate its impact. Therefore, this section presents a useful conceptualization for understanding a child's environment, which may be incorporated into a comprehensive needs-based assessment. Moos (1976) referred to this assessment of a person's fit with his or her setting—an individual's "ecological niche," so to speak—as an Environmental Status Exam (ESE).

In conducting an ESE, it is important to find out what the child does, with whom the child does it, and where it is done. The objective here is to acquire an indepth description of the daily contexts that make up the child's life. Knowledge of the various factors involved in each of the environments helps the interventionist construct meaningful environmental interventions with families in a number of ways. Based on the ESE, appropriate actions can be planned to enhance the quantity and/or quality of the family's environmental resources. For example, it might be helpful to augment a family's social network, perhaps by providing volunteers, such as parent aides, to support the family's change efforts. Or perhaps a member of the family could benefit from experiencing more meaningful social connections outside the family. A "big brother" for a school-aged child, an exercise class for a young mother, or a support group for parents of a substance-abusing adolescent might help in this respect (Tracy & McDonell, 1991).

Gump (1984) reported an experience that helped him realize more clearly how the theory and methods of the ecological viewpoint are relevant to the evaluation of a client. A young woman outpatient was assessed by clinicians from a number of different orientations. Each clinician used a particular assessment tool—psychiatric interview, Rorschach test, thematic apperception test, and so on. Gump's strategy was simply to learn about the woman's behavior over a typical weekend. Instead of attempting to discover her personality traits, he wanted to focus on her activities, which she described to him in detail. When all the evaluation results were in, Gump concluded that the woman's behavior could be explained much more thoroughly with the ecological inquiry added to the traditional techniques than with those techniques alone forming the sole basis of the assessment. Gump summarized his findings well in suggesting that the individual is not "sick" so much as his or her lifestyle.

Csikszentmihalyi and Larson (1984) also suggested that the treatment of various disorders require the knowledge gained from a "thick description" of an individual's daily life. Looking "thickly" simply means not stopping with a quick appraisal of what may, on the surface of things, seem to be the problem. Instead, all the different levels of experience must be investigated. Every underlying environmental structure merits observation and consideration, because each fills an important place in the individual's life space. Clearly, more "thick" knowledge is needed about the daily scenarios that make up the lives of depressed, anxious, conduct-disordered, or drug-dependent teenagers. How do they spend their free time? How do the activities and events in their lives affect their experiential states? What inhibits them from participating in the types of leisure activities that play such constructive roles in the lives of other teens?

Lee (1985) introduced a potentially useful concept with her "life space structures." Beginning with the assumption that human beings are basically reinforcement-seeking creatures, she noted that certain patterns of living develop around a person's complex and primitive attempts to maximize rewards. In other words, people develop unique life space patterns, or as Lee called them, "characteristic ways of negotiating time, space, people, and activity in their day-to-day lives" (p. 624). These patterns help individuals cope with and structure their environments for the satisfaction of their needs and desires. The manipulation of these elements in a person's life is the core of ecological environmental intervention. Each—time, space (places), activities, and people—is briefly described here.

Time Use

The pattern of time use is one of the most revealing characteristics of a person or a group. In fact, in trying to understand the differences between people, the most important thing to find out could be how they spend their time. Given approximately 112 waking hours each week (16 or so per day), individuals select, either actively or passively, a unique sequence of scenarios to fill those hours, and these choices help determine what lives are like. The choices made are especially crucial for youngsters, because childhood patterns of time use help set the future course of one's life (Csikszentmihalyi & Larson, 1984).

So, how do interventionists document clients' patterns of time use? A simple way to gather data about a person's daily life is with a

- Classwork
- Homework
- Personal Maintenance (eating, grooming)
- Household Maintenance (chores)
- Talking / friends
- Media
- Sports
- Community activities
- Employment
- Sleeping
- Hobby
- Extracurricular at School
- Church/synagogue

FIG. 2.2. Principal domains of a child's pattern of time use.

time diary. In this method, at a predetermined time (for instance, on the half-hour), every waking hour of the day the client simply jots down a diary entry that addresses these questions: What are you doing? Who is present? Where are you? What is your affective state?

Csikszentmihalyi and Larson (1984) asked a group of youngsters to carry electronic pagers and sheets of self-report forms. Over the course of a week, the youngsters were beeped at 40 randomly chosen moments. The researchers identified 13 principal domains of a child's pattern of time use (see Fig. 2.2). Examining these domains and how they shape children's experiences is a major goal of the ESE. An analysis of a child's pattern of time use presents a rather clear and consistent picture of the life environment of the child.

Places

Behavior settings (places)—the actual physical surroundings in which behavior occurs—have not been readily appreciated as intervention variables. This is unfortunate, because environmental settings can either constrain or enhance the possibility for healthy behavior and development. Five primary behavior settings where children typically spend an abundance of their time are home, neighborhood, workplace, religious institutions, and school.

Clinicians must be aware of the effects of behavior settings. For example, the finding that certain behavior setting arrangements can have a great impact on friendship patterns can have important implications for treatment (Epstein & Karweit, 1983). For example, a clinician who is aware of this fact might ask about the housing arrangement of a teenager who complains of loneliness and depression, instead of diagnosing the problem based solely on dispositional deficiencies on the adolescent. If the teenager is found to be socially isolated, arrangements could be made for him or her to spend more time in behavior settings where interactions with others occur easily and unthreateningly. Such "environmental therapy" is rarely, by itself, a solution to all problems. However, if a predisposing environmental stressor can be eliminated or circumvented, the intensity of the problem can often be diminished (Heller & Monahan, 1977).

Activities

From Grades 1 through 12, approximately 40% of a child's time is discretionary, that is , not spent in school or involved with essential activities such as eating and sleeping. In today's society, this discretionary time is increasingly unstructured and unsupervised, particularly for adolescents. It must be kept in mind that the manner in which free time is spent has either a positive, negative, or neutral effect on a child's personal development and well-being (Larson & Kleiber, 1993). For adolescents, many risks are associated with unsupervised time, and many positive effects can be gained from participation in constructive activities. Larson and Kleiber (1993) found that although some unstructured time for adolescents is essential to healthy development, many young teens need more structure and support than they are now receiving.

Putting together a ribbon-winning 4-H project, working the school yearbook, and playing guitar in a neighborhood band can all be significant activities in a child's life. Families that become involved in neighborhood Little League baseball or basketball, Girl Scouts, or Boy Scouts, soccer, swimming, football, dance recitals, and other such activities within the community are providing healthy physical outlets and social connections for their children. Although it is not clear whether the correlation between such activities and better mental health is causal or not, youth who are actively involved in such activities are less likely to be depressed and more likely to have better self-esteem than their peers who are not involved (Maguire, 1991).

Out-of-school activities can provide adolescents with valuable opportunities to develop self-direction, self-expression, and self-motivation. The term *transitional activities* refers to activities that not only are enjoyable and self-motivating for adolescents, but that also provide challenges that foster development into adulthood. Participation in sports and involvement in art or hobby organizations stand out as some of the more beneficial activities a youth can undertake.

Clearly then, appropriate leisure activities are important to the development and adjustment of healthy teenagers. Unfortunately, clinicians have traditionally all but ignored this aspect of the adolescent ecology. As with environmental therapy in general, recreational therapy, which deals with this part of adolescents' lives, is too often slighted as a legitimate and effective intervention tool.

Little data exist on how adolescents in different clinical categories use their free time and on how the activities they choose are interrelated with their psychopathology. The scant research that has been done on this topic indicates that individuals with emotional disturbance are less involved in the more favorable types of free-time experiences (sports, social interaction, and organizations) and tend to spend more time in solitary activities, such as watching television. Using their free time for such meaningless activities hurts these at-risk youths in two ways: It hinders their struggle to get through each day, and it deprives them of a wide variety of experience that is important to their psychological development. For some, drug use and delinquency might represent antisocial efforts to fill time and experience the enjoyment that others find in more prosocial activities (Larson & Kleiber, 1993).

Unfortunately, in today's society many adolescents' free-time schedules are filled with developmentally "empty" activities. Clark (1988) compared this activity imbalance to an imbalanced diet, and the results are analagous also. Twinkie-chips-and-candy-type activities do not promote healthy psychosocial development.

People

Focusing on people as elements of environmental assessment simply means identifying individuals who are important in a child's life and bolstering their ability to act as supportive resources. The support they provide often comes through informal or unstructured means, such as providing advice or emotional support. The goal here is to maximize the potential of others to be of help and to ensure that they have the skills and resources they need to provide the assistance and support the youth needs. In other words, it is all about strengthening the adolescent's social support system.

Research has consistently revealed the benefits of a well-developed and reliable social support system. For youth, a particularly critical component of this support system is their peer group. The peer group is a major social setting within which youth seek to find an identity as they grow up and make the transition from childhood to adulthood. More specifically, the quality of peer social support on youth may well have an important effect on their adaptive success. The fact that many children today spend more time with agemates than with other people increases the significance of peer relations.

To summarize, clinicians must extend the same dynamic examination to a child's environment that standard theories have traditionally accorded to individual and intrafamilial functioning. The ESE is a tool to conceptualize the complexities of the extrafamilial system and beyond by looking at the family's use of time across the places, activities, and people in their life space.

Approaches have been developed to assist clinicians in providing more supportive environments. The strategies of intervening directly in these areas—time, places, activities, and people—have been described elsewhere (Munger, 1998); specific practice principles are outlined to guide therapeutic efforts in evaluating and modifying both the social and nonsocial environments of a child's home and broader settings.

A major goal of environmental intervention is to put the child on a positive trajectory regarding social relations and to give the family and other principal members of the child's life the motivation and ability to support that trajectory. The array of environmental strategies available to professionals can be compared to a cafeteria menu—various combinations of items can be selected to find the right mix, thereby, enabling critical environmental trajectories in the child's life (Henggeler & Borduin, 1990).

SPECIALIZED ASSESSMENTS

Although a comprehensive needs-based assessment attempts to assess all relevant variables that may ultimately help explain a child's behavior, clearly there will be issues that are identified by the assessment but require further, specialized assessment. Many, although not all, specialized assessments are conducted by clinicians with specialized skills or background. Figure 2.3 lists some areas of specialized assessment. There are many other areas that could be considered for specialized assessment, however, generally these assessments do not require unique skills, but rather they require a clinician with familiarity and experience treating the disorder; for example, eating disorders, fire-setting, and attention deficit hyperactivity disorders.

The one assessment in Fig. 2.3 that may be unfamiliar to some clinicians is the cultural assessment. Because so many of those who

- Psychological Testing
- Neuropsychological Testing
- Academic/Learning Disabilities Assessment
- Developmental Assessment
- Sex Offender Evaluation
- Parental Capacity Evaluation (including custody)
- Sex Abuse Evaluation
- Forensic Evaluation (capacity to stand trial)
- Mental Status Evaluation (including suicidal/homicidal)
- Crisis Assessment

FIG. 2.3. Specialized assessments.

provide services are from the majority culture, it is incumbent on clinicians to recognize the need for cultural assessments of families and clients. Bloch (1983) and others have identified a number of variables and factors that should be addressed in a cultural assessment. These include level of ethnic identity; values orientation; migration experience; current socioeconomic status and view about the role that ethnicity plays; habits, customs, and beliefs that are important to the client; cultural health beliefs and practices; use of informal network and supportive institutions in the ethnic or cultural community; language and communication processes; self-concept and self-esteem; views and concerns about discrimination and institutional racism; educational level and employment experience; importance and impact associated with physical characteristics; and influence of religion or spirituality on the belief system and behavior patterns. Finally, cultural assessments are often useful to help focus on strengths of the client or family rather than deficits and to develop therapeutic interventions based on the strengths.

CONCLUSIONS

Henggeler (1998) argued convincingly that a major reason for historically poor results of treatments for children's behavior problems may be that the methods addressed only a small portion of the factors that contributed to the behavior. There is good reason to believe that the mental health of children can be fortified and that treatment efforts can meet with a much greater percentage of success if assessments consider the broad range of ecological factors. The weaknesses of present mental health approaches and the strengths of an ecological viewpoint proposed in this chapter point to the same conclusion—youth will be better served by a more comprehensive needs-based approach to mental health services.

Finally, this chapter concludes with a Comprehensive Needs-Based Assessment Checklist—a practical tool for clinicians to consider the many needs affecting youth. Although the listing is not exhaustive, it is template to encourage greater comprehensiveness in the assessment of youth with emotional and behavioral problems.

Comprehensive Needs-Based
Assessment Checklist

1. Individual Level

Yes No

- ☐ ☐ The child has or may have an intellectual deficiency.
- ☐ ☐ The child has or may have a learning disability.
- ☐ ☐ The child has a significant (physical) medical problem.
- ☐ ☐ The child has a history of physical abuse.
- ☐ ☐ The child has a history of sexual abuse.
- ☐ ☐ The child has a history of family trauma (imprisonment, crime, death, etc.).
- ☐ ☐ The child has a history of parental divorce.
- ☐ ☐ The child lives in a single-parent home.
- ☐ ☐ The child has a history of significant alcohol use.
- ☐ ☐ The child has a history of significant drug use.
- ☐ ☐ The child has poor social skills.
- ☐ ☐ The child has inadequate self-care skills.
- ☐ ☐ The child has delayed or precocious physical development.
- ☐ ☐ The child exhibits depression.
- ☐ ☐ The child exhibits impulsivity.
- ☐ ☐ The child exhibits excessive anger or aggression.
- ☐ ☐ The child exhibits hyperactivity.
- ☐ ☐ The child exhibits poor reality testing.
- ☐ ☐ The child is taking medication regularly.
- ☐ ☐ The child has a history of falling out (fainting) spells.
- ☐ ☐ The child has sleep disturbance.
- ☐ ☐ The child has an eating problem.
- ☐ ☐ The child has a history of out-of-home placement.

2. Family Level

- ☐ ☐ The child's siblings also have behavior problems.
- ☐ ☐ The marital relationship is problematic.
- ☐ ☐ Relatives are available to assist the family.

❑ ❑ The family has a supportive network of people it can rely on.

❑ ❑ Parental employment creates conflicts in the family.

❑ ❑ The parent–child relationship is problematic.

❑ ❑ The family has no set routine for sharing meals.

❑ ❑ The family has erratic sleeping routines.

❑ ❑ The TV is on most of the time in the household.

❑ ❑ The family has regular rituals in which members spend time together.

❑ ❑ Family members have regular household chores assigned to them.

❑ ❑ The family is having major financial problems.

❑ ❑ The physical environment of the house has deteriorated.

❑ ❑ The family does not have reliable transportation.

❑ ❑ The family has resided in the same home for some time.

❑ ❑ There are consistent family rules with regard to behavior.

❑ ❑ Family members turn to each other for help/problem solving.

❑ ❑ Discipline consists of attention to positive as well as negative behaviors.

❑ ❑ The parent feels successful in discipline efforts/skills.

❑ ❑ One caregiver serves as the primary decision maker/leader in the family.

❑ ❑ One caregiver is responsible for child care/child-rearing.

❑ ❑ Parent(s) feel that they have sufficient time available for the children.

❑ ❑ Parents' discipline efforts compliment each other.

❑ ❑ Parents have discussed or entered into separation/divorce (terminating relationship) at some point in their history.

❑ ❑ The marital bond appears strong and mutually supportive.

❑ ❑ Each adult partner is satisfied with the division of duties/responsibilities within the household.

❑ ❑ Each adult partner is satisfied with the amount of attention they receive from the other.

❑ ❑ The family participates in leisure/recreational activities together (other than TV watching).

❑ ❑ Family members attend church.

❑ ❑ Family members express love and affection for one another.

❑ ❑ Family members appear to enjoy one another.

❑ ❑ Family members appear disconnected from one another.

❑ ❑ One or both parents is consistently employed.

❑ ❑ There are private spaces available for individual family members within the home.

❑ ❑ The parent is always aware of the child's whereabouts.

❑ ❑ The parent is aware of the child's interests and hobbies.

❑ ❑ The family home is a safe environment.

❑ ❑ Physical violence occurs among family members.

❑ ❑ Parent abuses drugs or alcohol.

❑ ❑ The parent effectively monitors a latchkey child's activities by having the child call in or another method of "checking."

3. Peer Level

❑ ❑ The parent directly helps the child get involved with peers (e.g., signs the child up for a club activity and carries the child to meetings; serves as a volunteer in one of the child's activities, etc.).

❑ ❑ The parent usually knows the child's whereabouts.

❑ ❑ The parent directly monitors the child's peer relationships.

❑ ❑ The parent's own network of friends exposes the child to suitable friendship opportunities.

❑ ❑ The child has a sufficient number of friends.

❑ ❑ The child has close friends (chums).

❑ ❑ The child has the social skills that are necessary to make and keep friendships (e.g., initiating conversations, sharing experiences, playing without fighting, acting friendly, etc.).

❑ ❑ The child resists the parent's harsh discipline attempts, and in doing so, gets back at the parent by involvement with antisocial peers.

❑ ❑ The child is involved with antisocial peers, but his or her activities have positive elements that could be substituted (e.g., a challenging part-time job in place of the excitement of being a gang members).

❑ ❑ Places are available for the child to go to where he or she could make friends (e.g., playground, skating rink, swimming pool, etc.).

❑ ❑ Transportation is available for the child to be involved with peers.

❑ ❑ The child's friends at school are the same as his or her friends outside of school.

❑ ❑ The child spends an excessive amount of time with his or her peer group.

❑ ❑ The child has a specific group of children with whom he or she hangs out.

❑ ❑ The child's peer group engages in antisocial behavior.

❑ ❑ The child's peers are involved in illegal activities.

❑ ❑ The child is a follower in the peer group (as opposed to leader).

❑ ❑ The age difference between the child and his or her friends is a problem for the parent or child.

❑ ❑ The parent is opposed to some of the child's primary friends because of their sex, race, religion, or family background.

❑ ❑ The child is involved in quality leisure activities (as opposed to watching too much TV, etc.).

❑ ❑ The child is involved in activities or hanging out in places that are likely to get him or her in trouble.

❑ ❑ The child likes to get involved regularly with peers.

4. School-Level

☐	☐	The child has at least one out-of-school activity that he or she genuinely enjoys?
☐	☐	The child's current academic placement matches his or her academic capabilities.
☐	☐	The child completes or attempts to complete assigned homework.
☐	☐	The child completes or attempts to complete classwork.
☐	☐	The child's academic performance has changed markedly recently.
☐	☐	The child's behavior is generally consistent across activities such as classroom, recess, lunch, and while riding on the school bus.
☐	☐	The child follows or attempts to follow directions of school personnel.
☐	☐	The child generally displays a positive attitude when interacting with school personnel.
☐	☐	The child has an identified peer group at school.
☐	☐	The child's school peers generally engage in pro-social activities.
☐	☐	The child's school peers are generally academically successful.
☐	☐	School personnel report a positive working relationship with the parent.
☐	☐	The parent reports a positive working relationship with school personnel.
☐	☐	There is an adequate place to study at home.
☐	☐	The parent monitors homework.
☐	☐	The parent monitors report cards.
☐	☐	There are negative consequences at home for poor behavior in school.
☐	☐	There are positive consequences at home for academic success.
☐	☐	The teachers' teaching style addresses the child's learning and behavioral style.

❑ ❑   The school personnel generally demonstrate high expectations for this child.

❑ ❑   The teacher–student ratio is sufficient to meet the child's learning and behavioral needs.

❑ ❑   The school has an effective system for providing negative consequences for antisocial behavior other than removal from school.

❑ ❑   The school has specific people, systems, policies or procedures for helping children with special social or behavioral needs other than special education.

❑ ❑   The school has an effective system for providing additional support for students experiencing academic difficulties (e.g., peer tutoring).

❑ ❑   The school is located near the child's home.

❑ ❑   There is public transportation available from the child's home to the school.

❑ ❑   There are prosocial, adult-monitored activities available after school.

❑ ❑   The school addresses the child's access to after school activities.

❑ ❑   There are alternatives to academic-only training for high school age children such as vocational training, on-the-job training or credit for after-school employment.

❑ ❑   The school actively encourages positive peer friendships.

5. Neighborhood Level

❑ ❑   There is evidence of illegal drug sales or use in the neighborhood.

❑ ❑   There is considerable property crime in the neighborhood.

❑ ❑   There is violent crime in the neighborhood.

❑ ❑   Streets are well lighted at night.

❑ ❑   There are safety hazards in the neighborhood.

❑ ❑   There is a city bus service to the neighborhood.

❑ ❑   Most residents of the neighborhood have automobiles.

☐ ☐   There are one or more churches in the neighborhood.

☐ ☐   There are several same-age peers in the neighborhood.

☐ ☐   The child's school is in close proximity to the
neighborhood.

☐ ☐   There are public playgrounds in the neighborhood.

☐ ☐   There are organized children's activities in the
neighborhood.

☐ ☐   There are teen employment opportunities in the
neighborhood.

☐ ☐   There are adequate child-care resources available
in the neighborhood.

☐ ☐   The family has friends in the neighborhood.

☐ ☐   Children are allowed to play freely within
the neighborhood.

☐ ☐   Safe places are available for activities for the child
(e.g., adult supervised, off of street, etc.) in the
neighborhood.

6. Community Level

☐ ☐   The child is engaged in some community activity,
such as 4-H, little League, Boy or Girl Scouts, etc.

☐ ☐   The child has too much unstructured time on his
or her hands.

☐ ☐   The child is exposed to a good adult role model
in a community activity.

☐ ☐   The child is involved in an activity that is enjoyable and self-motivating while generating
challenges consistent with development
into adulthood.

☐ ☐   The child spends an excessive amount of time
watching TV or listening to music.

☐ ☐   The child is involved in taking after-school lessons
(e.g., music, tutoring).

☐ ☐   The child spends most of his or her free time alone.

☐ ☐   The child has a regular hobby he or she engages in.

❑ ❑ The parent actively tries to arrange activities for the child to participate in the community (e.g., clubs, sports, etc.).

❑ ❑ The parent participates in a community activity in which the child is involved (e.g., volunteers in the church youth group).

❑ ❑ There are adequate social services available in the community for the child's family.

❑ ❑ The child used to participate in a community activity but dropped out.

❑ ❑ The child is involved in a community sports team.

❑ ❑ The parent communicates regularly with leaders of activities in which the child is involved (e.g., talks to Cub Scout den mother).

❑ ❑ Transportation is a barrier to the child's involvement in community activities.

❑ ❑ The community lacks available activities in which the child can participate.

❑ ❑ Inadequate family financial resources prevent the child's involvement in a community activity in which he or she would like to participate (e.g., Little League).

❑ ❑ The parent does not keep up with knowledge about activities in which the child could be involved.

❑ ❑ The child is lacking an activity that he or she gets excited about and that can help the child feel good about him or herself.

❑ ❑ The child is involved in an excessive number of activities and does not have sufficient unstructured time.

❑ ❑ The child is involved in an activity that could be strengthened in its helpfulness (e.g., talking to a coach about helping the child with his or her anger).

❑ ❑ The child needs to be involved in an activity that is better fitted with his or her abilities (e.g., child is involved in sports, and is not athletic, but is talented in music).

❑ ❑ The child is involved in a community activity (e.g., planting trees with a youth group) that allows him or her to make a contribution to the community.

❑ ❑ The child enjoys regular participation in a sports team activity.

❑ ❑ The child attends church regularly.

❑ ❑ The child is involved in a community activity that allows him or her to learn important life skills.

❑ ❑ The child has structured, useful activities during the summer when school is out.

❑ ❑ The parent sets clear expectations on the child's time use in out-of-school activities.

❑ ❑ The family utilizes appropriate community services when necessary (medical care, financial assistance, etc.).

7. Agency Involvement Level

Check the formal organizations or programs with which the child or family is involved:

❑ mental health
❑ juvenile justice/Family Court
❑ protective services
❑ health department
❑ legal advocacy
❑ housing authority
❑ AFDC
❑ food stamps
❑ SSI
❑ Medicaid
❑ medical clinic
❑ adult correctional system
❑ substance abuse agency
❑ child support enforcement
❑ self-help group: _____
❑ church-sponsored group: _____
❑ community action agency: _____
❑ other: _____
❑ other: _____

REFERENCES

Bloch, D. (1983). Bloch's ethnic/cultural assessment guide. In E. Randall-David (Ed.), *Strategies for working with culturally diverse communities and clients* (pp. 85–93). Washington, DC: The Association for the Care of Children's Health.

Burchard, J., & Clarke, R. (1990). The role of individualized care in a service delivery system for children and adolescents with severely maladjusted behavior. *Journal of Mental Health Administration, 17,* 48–60.

Burchard, J., Burchard, S., Sewell, R., & VanDenBerg, J. (1993). *One kid at a time: Evaluative case studies and description of the Alaska youth initiative demonstration project.* Washington, DC: Georgetown University Child Development Center, CASSP Technical Assistance Center.

Clark, R. (1988). *Critical factors in why disadvantaged students succeed or fail in school.* New York: Academy for Educational Development.

Csikszentmihalyi, M., & Larson, R. (1984). *Being adolescent: Conflict and growth in the teenage years.* New York: Basic Books.

Dunst, C., Trivette, C., & Deal, A. (1994). *Supporting and strengthening families: Methods, strategies and practices.* Cambridge, MA: Brookline.

Eiber, L. (1996). Restructuring schools through the wraparound approach: The LADSE experience. In R. Illback & C. Nelson (Eds.), *Emerging school-based approaches for children with emotional and behavioral problems* (pp. 135–149). New York: Haworth.

Epstein, J., & Karweit, N. (Eds.). (1983). *Friends in school: Patterns of selection in secondary schools.* New York: Academic Press.

Graham, P., & Rutter, M. (1985). Adolescent disorders. In M. Rutter & K. Hersovl (Eds.), *Child and adolescent psychiatry: Modern approaches* (pp. 351–367). Oxford: Blackwell.

Gump, P. (1984). Ecological psychology and clinical mental health. In W. O'Connor & B. Lubin (Eds.), *Ecological approaches to clinical and community psychology* (pp. 57–71). New York: Wiley.

Hawton, S. (1986). *Suicide and attempted suicide among children and adolescents.* Newbury Park, CA: Sage.

Heller, K., & Monahan, J. (1977). *Psychology and community change.* Homewood, IL: Dorsey Press.

Hengeler, S. (1997). The development of effective drug abuse services for children. In J. Egerston, D. Fox, & A. Leshner (Eds.), *Treating drug abusers effectively* (pp. 253–279). New York: Blackwell.

Henggeler, S. (1991). Multidimensional causal models of delinquent behavior. In R. Cohen & A. Siegel (Eds.), *Context and development* (pp. 211–231). Hillsdale, NJ: Lawrence Erlbaum Associates.

Henggeler, S. (1989). *Delinquency in adolescence.* Newbury Park, CA: Sage.

Henggeler, S., & Borduin, C. (1990). *Family therapy and beyond: A multisystemic approach to treating the behavior problems of children and adolescents.* Pacific Grove, CA: Brooks/Cole.

Henggeler, S., Schoenwald, S., Borduin, C., Rowland, M., & Cunningham, P. (Ed.s). (1998). *Multisystemic treatment of antisocial behavior of children and adolescents.* New York: Guilford.

Katz-Leavy, J., Lourie, I., Stroul, B., & Zeigler-Dendy, C. (1992). *Individualized care in a system of care.* Washington, DC: Georgetown University Child Development Center, CASSP Technical Assistance Center.

Kazdin, A. (1987). *Conduct disorders in childhood and adolescence.* Newbury Park, CA: Sage.

Larson, R., & Kleiber, D. (1993). Daily experience of adolescents. In P. Tolan & B. Cohler (Eds.), *Handbook of clinical research and practice with adolescents* (pp. 125–145). New York: Wiley

Lee, M. (1985). Life space structure: Explorations and speculations. *Human Relations, 38,* 623–642.

Leff, J., Kuipers, L., Berkowitz, R., Eberlein-Vries, R., & Sturgeon, D. (1982). A controlled trial of social intervention in the families of schizophrenic patients. *British Journal of Psychiatry, 141,* 121–134.

Maguire, L. (1991). *Social support systems in practice: A generalist approach.* Silver Springs, MD: National Association of Social Workers.

Masten, A., & Coatsworth, J. (1998). The development of competence in favorable and unfavorable environments: Lessons from research on successful children. *American Psychologist, 53,* 205–220.

McMahon, R., & Wells, K. (1989). Conduct disorders. In E. Mash & R. Barkley (Eds.), *Treatment of childhood disorders* (pp. 73–132). New York: Guilford.

Moos, R. (1976). *The human context.* New York: Wiley.

Munger, R. (1991). *Child mental health practice from the ecological perspective.* Lanham, MD: University Press of America

Munger, R. (1998). *The ecology of troubled children.* Cambridge, MA: Brookline.

Munger, R., Donkervoet, J., & Morse, W. (1998). The clinical ecological viewpoint. In D. Sabatino & B. Brooks (Eds.), *Contemporary interdisciplinary interventions for children with emotional/behavioral disorders* (pp. 323–349). Durham, NC: Carolina Academic Press

Quay, H. (Ed.). (1987). *Handbook of juvenile delinquency.* New York: Wiley.

Stroul, B., & Friedman, R. (1986). *A system of care for children and youth with severe emotional disturbances* (Rev. ed.). Washington, D.C.: Georgetown University Child Development Center, CASSP Technical Assistance Center.

Tracy, E., & McDonell, J. (1991). Home based work with families: The environmental context of family intervention. In K. Lewis (Ed.), *Family systems application to social work: Training and clinical practice* (pp. 93–108). New York: Haworth Press.

Vaughn, C., & Leff, J. (1976). The influence of family and social factors on the course of psychiatric illnesses: A comparison of schizophrenic and depressed neurotic patients. *British Journal of Psychiatry, 129,* 125–137.

Wolfensberger, W., & Nirje, B. (1972). The principle of normalization in human services. Toronto: National Institute of Mental Retardation.

Assessing Adolescents: Ecological and Person–Environment Fit Perspectives

Connie Burrows Horton
Jayne E. Bucy
Illinois State University

Adolescence is a period of transitions: biological, psychological, social, economic. It is an exciting time of life.
— Steinberg (1996, p. 4).

Although adolescence has been defined in numerous ways, this concept of transition, from childhood to adulthood, is central to most definitions. Whether this time of transition is a period of "storm and stress" or a more peaceful transition has been debated for decades (Cobb, 1998) and, to a large extent, likely depends on the individual adolescent and his or her relationships with key systems in his or her life. It has been suggested that some of the psychological and behavioral difficulties commonly associated with adolescence are actually caused by a "mismatch between the needs of developing adolescents and the opportunities afforded them by their social environments" (Eccles, Lord, & Roeser, 1996, p. 47).

Ecological models view individuals as nested within multiple systems of influence (Bronfenbrenner, 1979). In a similar way, person–environment (P–E) fit models recognize the interactional nature of an individual, the contexts, and the relationship between the individual and these systems (Lerner, Baker, & Lerner, 1985). As such, these models are useful perspectives to consider in assessing adolescents in a counseling situation. Understanding the adolescent alone, or the systems alone, will not provide the necessary assessment information for a counselor. Instead, the adolescent–system interactions must be understood (Lerner et al., 1985).

Integrating the unique developmental issues of adolescents with the ecological/goodness of fit models may not be as an easy task for the counselor. "Together the concepts of organismic individuality, of context, and the relationships between the two, *found in a developmental contextual perspective*, are quite complex" (Lerner & Lerner, 1994, p. 161). Developmental issues of identity formation, cognitive and moral development; the role of the peer group and changes in family power are among those most central is the lives of adolescents (Baumrind, 1991) which counselors must integrate into their ecological–P–E framework.

To understand an adolescent's current functioning, counseling needs, and resources, a counselor must understand the adolescent's relationships with the important systems in his or her lives (Caplan, Tripathi, & Naidu, 1985). The context of family, peers, school, and work frequently will be central. Individual adolescents will have other systems (e.g., athletic teams, religious organizations) that are also particularly important for the counselor to understand. This chapter reflects relevant highlights from the adolescent literature related to each of the central systems, focusing on issues that the counselor may need to understand in assessing adolescents. Specific assessment considerations, instruments, and procedures are also suggested.

Parents

Despite the view of some counselors that adolescents do not really "need" their parents anymore, the reality is that the relationship that individuals maintain with their parents may be particularly important during adolescence. Eccles, Lord, and Roeser (1996) noted that this adolescent–parent relationship is critical because of two primary reasons. First, because adolescence is such an intense time of transitions, extra support is needed. Second, good relationships with parents help adolescents make wise choices as their opportunities to engage in risky behavior increase.

Fortunately, contrary to the myth that is portrayed in most popular television shows, books, and movies, and despite the sometimes tragic exceptions that do exist, most adolescents enjoy close, positive relationships with their parents (Larson, Richards, Moneta, Holmbeck, & Duckett, 1996). In fact, many adolescents consider their parents among their most important role models and report trusting their parents' advice most on major life decisions (e.g., career, college, life partners; Fuligini & Eccles, 1993). Although adolescents frequently have developed enhanced arguing skills, conflict is not overwhelming in most families. Counselors conducting assessments, therefore, should assess the degree of closeness and conflict between adolescents and their parents. Counselors should be wary of parents or adolescents who have a tendency to minimize some fairly serious relationships difficulties as, "typical adolescence" or "those inevitable raging hormones."

Although most adolescents do enjoy positive relationships with their parents, that does not mean that the relationships are without some stress in the transition. Relationships between adolescents and their parents are typically changing from reciprocal to complimentary, as adolescents gain more maturity, and ideally, power in the relationship. There is typically an adjustment period as parents and adolescents negotiate this new arrangement. Because perceived versus desired control is an important predictor in "fit," (Conway, Vickers, & French, 1992), adolescents working out the appropriate amount of control over their lives will be quite salient. There is variability in parents' ability to provide a good sense of fit regarding their adolescents' need for autonomy (Eccles et al., 1996). Finding a helpful balance seems to be key. Although a central task of adolescent development is to establish a greater sense of autonomy, there is also a continued need for support and relatedness from significant adults" (Eccles et al., 1996, p. 65). "Parents are caught on the horns of a dilemma—adolescents, in order to become self-regulated, individuated, competent individuals, require both freedom to explore and experiment; and protection from experiences that are clearly dangerous" (Baumrind, 1991, p. 119). Counselors should consider how parents are responding the their adolescent's emerging sense of autonomy as they consider their own values, goals, and behavioral choices.

Parenting style will be an influential variable in understanding the adolescent: parent fit. Counselors may find it useful to assess the parenting style in the families with which they work. Baumrind's (1991) distinction of authoritarian, authoritative, and neglectful style may be useful to consider. Authoritarian parents, those who relate to their children from a, "I'm the parent; that's why; end of discussion" power position may have a particularly difficult time providing the context in which their adolescents can demonstrate their emerging maturity and decision-making abilities. Neglectful parents may not provide the necessary "scaffolding" (i.e., guidance, modeling) that adolescents need to develop their own competence. Authoritative parents will find that balance of providing the warmth and support their adolescents need while supporting their efforts at independent functioning. Balance, once again, seems central. "Adolescents fare more poorly in families that respond to their development either by throwing up their hands and relinquishing control or by cracking down too much" (Eccles et al. 1996, p. 65).

In addition to the parent–adolescent relationship, the family unit and extended family influence adolescent development. Specifically, families also develop a "style" of interaction and a unique sense of identity that can benefit each member. Family identity is often played out in the families ritual behavior. Most families have developed family rituals that are enacted at regular intervals (mealtimes) or on special occasions (birthday and anniversary celebrations). These family interactions become the basis for a shared family identity and sense of unity among members. Bossard and Boll (1950) referred to family rituals as the "hard core" of family life. For counselors, family rituals provide an open window through which family life may be observed.

Wolin and Bennett (1984) described family rituals as "a symbolic form of communication that, owing to the satisfaction that family members experience through its repetition, is acted out in a systematic fashion over time" (p. 401). Rituals may take many forms, although they tend to fall within three categories: daily interactions, traditions, and celebrations.

Daily interaction rituals provide a context for the family's ongoing daily life. These include how the family shares meals, special greeting and parting rituals, bedtime rituals, and other unique activities that the family finds meaningful and participates in on a regular basis. Family celebrations are those family activities that are culturally driven, although they occur less frequently than daily interactions. Family celebrations including religious and secular holidays are also in this category. Recognition of momentous occasions in the family life such as weddings or funerals are also included in this category. Family traditions are unique to each family.

Families may incorporate rituals to celebrate achievements, new roles for members, and the growing rights and responsibilities of the adolescent. Quinn, Newfield, and Protensky (1985) described rites of passage as having a number of advantages for adolescents including affirming achievement, instilling confidence, and overcoming inertia in the family life cycle.

Therapeutically, counselors may find that families can change their rituals to make them more relevant or meaningful now that their children have become adolescents. Some strategies might include helping families develop new rituals if they are needed, eliminate rituals that no longer have meaning, or change rituals so that they become more meaningful and more regularly practiced (Bennett, Wolin, & McAvity, 1988). Counselors who opt to guide a family's changes in rituals are reminded to carefully respect the family's values, worldview, and religious beliefs (Lax & Lussardi, 1988).

Peers

The central role of adolescents' relationships with their parents and families does not minimize the importance of adolescents' relationships with their peers. In fact, as society has changed, peer groups have become increasingly important to adolescent development. Most adolescents spend more time with their peers than with their parents and more time with their peers than did past generations (Steinberg, 1996).

Key aspects of adolescents peer social life include their best friendships, cliques, and crowds. Close friendships are central to many aspects of development in the adolescent, including self-esteem (Buhrmester, 1990). Cliques are the small close knit group of friends. Some have suggested that cliques may perform critical functions in the lives of adolescents that include providing feedback on new social skills, "coaching sessions" of sorts (Cobb, 1998). Clique membership seems to be nearly a prerequisite for crowd membership (Urberg, Degirmencioglu, Tolson, & Halliday-Scher, 1995). Crowds are the larger social grouping, typically approximately 20, which, in some cases, provide the arena for adolescents to try their new skills whereas at other times there is little interaction but more an affiliation of those with similar status. Male adolescents with athletic abilities tend to have the highest level of status; whereas females' status seems more dependent on involvement in activities (Williams & White, 1983).

Social skills, however, are important predictors of popularity for adolescents of both genders (Steinberg, 1996). Those lackinig in social skills, who are withdrawn, or aggressive are likely to be less popular (Ennett & Bauman, 1996; Steinberg, 1996). Adolescent "isolates" do not enjoy the benefits their peers do of having close friends, cliques, or crowds (Ennett & Bauman, 1996).

To understand an adolescent, a counselor would want to know about key peer relationships, including best friends, cliques, and crowd affiliations. Peers are so central in the lives of adolescents that there are often concerns regarding conformity or peer pressure. Conformity, particularly regarding matters of taste in clothes, hair styles, and music, peaks in early adolescence (Gavin & Furman, 1989). Typically, peer conformity is at an all time high at that point and then declines, even notably by mid-adolescence as teens mature and develop their own individual tastes and style. It is important to note, however, even in the height of peer conformity, regarding matters of serious concern, the values of peers and parents more frequently compliment each other than conflict. Thus, "the relative influence of parents and peers cannot be thought of as a simple tug-of-war with the adolescent in the middle. The values of the friends frequently overlap with those of parents" (Cobb, 1998, p. 276). Peers do however, have an important influence on some deviant behaviors. Although it may be that, in general, adolescents involved in serious deviant or delinquent behaviors "find each other," rather than pressure each other, friends do seem to have a significant influence on one another regarding alcohol and drug use and smoking (Steinberg, 1996; Urberg, 1992).

Counselors should assess adolescents' peer conformity. Questions to consider include the following: Does the degree of conformity seem developmentally appropriate and decreasing? Are parents reasonably accepting of the adolescent's desires to conform to issues of peer perview such as clothes and hair styles? Do parents and peers agree on major life issues? Does the adolescent have a deviant and/or delinquent peer group that is supporting some of the behaviors the counselor hopes to change? Even if the adolescent's peer group is relatively healthy, what are the "norms" regarding alcohol, drugs, and smoking? How able is the adolescent client to assert his or her own choices?

School

Adolescence is a developmental period when individual change occurs on many levels. Many developmental challenges of adolescence are played out within the school. Along with the home, school is a primary social environment of children. The importance of school as a social environment increases as children progress through adolescence. The nature of the fit between the adolescent and the school environment impacts the adolescent's developmental trajectory.

Many changes occur within the child and school environment as the adolescent progresses from elementary school to junior high or middle school, requiring the young adolescent to adjust and cope with these often stressful circumstances. The changes associated with the transition from elementary to junior high or middle school are described by Eccles et al. (1993). They note changes in structure and control, in that teachers emphasize classroom management and discipline. Additionally, decision making falls more to teachers, and students play less of a role in determining their own learning. Students are more likely to be grouped by their ability, and academic and social comparisons are more common. Students are often expected to perform at a higher level and declines in student grades may result.

Adolescence is a time of growing autonomy and self-determination. Unfortunately, schools are generally a mismatch of those needs. Studies show that although young adolescents are granted greater autonomy in upper elementary grades, this is curtailed when students enter junior high (Eccles et al., 1991). Classes often become more teacher-controlled and classroom discipline is valued sometimes over positive relations between students and teachers.

Classroom instructional strategies also change (Eccles et al., 1993). Specifically, grading standards are raised and tend to become normative. Teachers are less effective in meeting the needs of academically at risk students. Teachers prefer whole class over small group or individualized instruction. These factors are cited as causing a decline in student motivation and a deterioration in school behavior and overall mental health (Eccles et al., 1996).

For high school aged adolescents, school size has been shown to be an important issue in adolescent development. Research confirms the often held belief that school size does matter. The positive effects of small school size are not apparent until the school population is below 500 (Garbarino, 1980). Student populations benefit in these small schools through improved social relations, greater involvement, and increased school commitment. These benefits are particularly apparent among students at risk.

School violence is a growing concern in the United States as a result, in part, of recently highly publicized shootings occurring on school campuses. The U.S. Department of Education has issued a copy of *Early Warning, Timely Response: A Guide to Safe Schools* to all of the nation's public and private schools. Fortunately, despite this increased public concern, incidents like these much publicized accounts of shooting sprees are rare. More common, however, are simple assaults, thefts, and vandalism (Furlong & Morrison, 1994). But statistics do not tell the entire story. Also important are students' perceptions of their school climate and their sense of safety when on school grounds. Increasingly, surveys report that students fear being victimized at school or bring weapons to school in order to protect themselves (Everett & Price, 1995). Certain school climates or institutional characteristics such as school size, teacher–student relationships, and level of student participation in decision making may contribute to more classroom disruptions and possibly school violence (Gottfredson & Gottfredson, 1985).

Counselors in school settings should be familiar with the procedures of the school crisis team or help to develop one if none exists (Poland, 1994). Schoolwide programs to prevent violence have also been developed (see Larson, 1994, for a review) as have programs to reduce bullying, which affects one in five students (Batsche & Knoff,

1994). Counselors working in other-than-school settings must recognize the significant stressor or resource that schools can be in the lives of adolescents.

Work

In addition to, or in some cases, instead of, their time at school, many adolescents spend a significant portion of their time at work. In fact, most high school students have at least part-time jobs (Mortimer, Finch, Ryu, Shanahan, & Call, 1996). Adolescent employment is a topic filled with controversy. Whereas some have attempted to simplify the question, asking basically, "is it a good idea or not?," others have pointed out the complexity of the question, noting that adolescents work in a variety of settings, with a variety of coworkers, at different schedules, and so forth. Thus, no one answer applies to all adolescents.

Some advantages of adolescent employment have been discussed. For example, employment can help teach a work ethic and values such as industry, punctuality, and responsibility (Meyer, 1987). Additionally, learning the necessity of work in life, developing in skills in time and financial management might be other advantages. Some have noted that adolescent employment can increase self-esteem as another arena in which to demonstrate competence (Meyer, 1987).

At the same time, some disadvantages have been noted, including higher rates of drug usage and higher rates of delinquency among employed adolescents (Steinberg, Fegley, & Dornbusch, 1993). Perhaps for some, cash to spend is a dangerous thing as it increases the opportunity to engage in risky behavior. Some work settings may also expose adolescents to an older, and in some cases, more deviant, peer group than their clique at school. Additionally, some (e.g., Steinberg et al., 1993) have noted decreased school performance as a critical concern.

The relationship between adolescent employment and grade point average (GPA) does raise some questions. Interestingly, the relation has been found to be curvilinear (Mortimer, Finch, Ryu, Shanahan, & Call, 1996). That is, the nature of the relation varies at different points on the continuum. Put simply, those who work, but not too much (not more than 20 hours per week) appear to have the highest GPAs. Those who do not work, or work more than 20 hours, have lower GPA (Moritimer et al., 1996) Thus, Meyer (1987) concluded that "Counselors working with adolescents who have part-time jobs during high school should be alert to the possible problems of working too many hours … if 15 hours is good, then 25 hours is not necessarily better" (p. 146).

Counselors should assess the role of employment in the lives of their adolescent clients. Questions regarding the employment setting, the number of hours worked, the adolescent's view of the job, the spending patterns of the adolescent, and the effect on school performance should all be considered.

ASSESSMENT ASSUMPTIONS, MEASURES, AND PROCEDURES

Certainly, assessment is critical in counseling. To truly be useful, however, assessments must be consistent with a counselor's theoretical orientation, and therefore, have implications for intervention (Lerner, Baker, & Lerner, 1985). Therefore, counselors from a P–E fit perspective will want to gain assessment information regarding (a) the individual adolescent with whom they are working (including cognitive, affective, and behavioral attributes), (b) the contexts in which the adolescent is functioning (e.g., home, peers, school, work), and (c) the "fit" between the individual adolescent and the various contexts. Likewise, from an ecological perspective, "Assessment in understood as a dynamic, not static process." "concerned about patterns of interaction … reciprocally, and interactively" that are occurring at any point in time (Fine, 1992, p. 10).

Traditional assessment approaches, including IQ tests, personality measures, and behavioral rating scales may address the "individual adolescent" component. To understand the contexts, the fit between the individual and the contexts, and the patters of interaction, counselors may need to consider a variety of other approaches.

Interviews

Counselors, informed by the literature reviewed above, can directly inquire about the key systems in their adolescent clients' lives. By asking their teen clients to discuss their relationships with parents and peers, critical information regarding the potential source of difficulty and/or support may be uncovered for the counselor's use in treatment planning. Understanding the adolescent views of their school and work worlds may also be invaluable in being able to conceptualize sources of stress and strength. Related to each of these contexts, it would be important to understand how the adolescent perceives his or her own attributes, the expectations and demands of the environment, and their own ability to meet those demands (i.e., the "fit between the two"; Lerner, Baker, & Lerner, 1985).

In addition to conducting adolescent client interviews, counselors from a P–E–ecological perspective would frequently be interested in hearing the perspective of significant others in the lives of their adolescent clients. This multi-informant method provides new information to integrate. Although referral concerns, counseling setting, scheduling issues, and other factors might influence specific choices, counselors might consider meeting with the whole family together, with adolescents and parents separately, and/or with teachers or other school personnel. For example, the counselor may very well want to understand the parents' view of their own parenting style, how they view their adolescent's fit with the family's demands, and how they hope to negotiate their adolescent's journey to autonomy. Teachers may also provide valuable information on the adolescent's ability to meet academic and social demands.

By meeting with multiple informants, not only may the counselor gain information to use in individual sessions with the adolescent, but this assessment approach may also lead to other intervention plans. For example, the counselor may discover that the parents could use some support in learning to "let go" of their older adolescent. It may be determined that although this is a bright adolescent and a well-intentioned teacher, the differences in personality and teaching–learning style, and/or an unpleasant history are so great that an instructor change is recommended. The counselor may conclude that rather than simply doing anger management training with an African-American adolescent who has had some outbursts in his all-White school, some classroom-based tolerance for diversity instruction may be provided to the students who have been harassing him.

One tool that may facilitate the interviews of adolescents and/or their significant others is eco-maps.

Eco-maps

Eco-maps provide a diagrammatic view of family life. Developed by Hartman (1978), the eco-map represents the family within the context of their significant relationships with other individuals and institutions with whom the family has contact. The eco-map displays the connections that exist between family and other. Eco-maps provide a comprehensive representation of family life. Although they display relationships that are problematic, they also represent available family resources.

Creating an Eco-Map.   The eco-map is created using pencil and paper and through interview with the family. A circle in the center of the page is first placed to represent the family unit (see Fig. 3.1). This family circle is then surrounded by other circles, each one representing individuals, institutions, and activities that represent the vari-

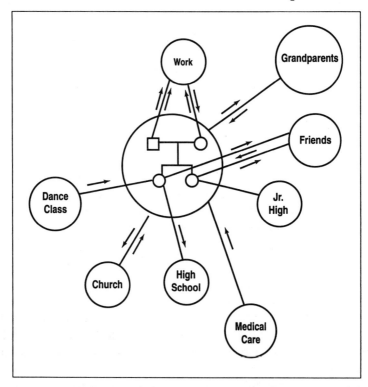

FIG. 3.1. Eco-map of the Lockman family.

ous "systems" that are active in the family context. This might include school, church, workplace, extended family, child-care providers, health care services, mental health or social welfare services, or welfare. Hartman (1978) also suggested a system of different types of lines used to connect the family to each system. These different lines represent the nature of the relationship with the family. Solid lines show a strong connection, whereas dotted lines represent secondary or less substantial relationships. A line with hash marks through it would represent relationships that are stressful or somehow negative to the family. Hartman also advised drawing arrows to indicate how resources or energy flows between the family and the system.

Figure 3.1 is an eco-map for the Lockman family. Notice that the family constellation is represented as a genogram in the center circle. Relationships between the family unit and different systems are shown with the connecting lines. Individual family members may have connecting systems that are uniquely there own and may be shown connections to the family unit.

Eco-maps and the Adolescent.   Eco-maps, used in their typical manner, help the clinician diagram the multiple family systems within which the family resides. With the adolescent client, eco-maps may be a means of accessing the complicated context of the individual. The clinician and client create an eco-map that represents the multiple resources and stressor that are currently at work for the adolescent. The eco-map may help formulate interventions strategies, helping the adolescent to recognize both resources and problem relationships. It also captures the client life at that moment, providing a clear snapshot. Referring back to the eco-map, or drawing another at some later time will document evidence of changes in the adolescent relationships with others.

Self-Report "Objective" Measures

In addition to individually oriented self-report measures that a counselor may choose to administer to assess levels of depression, anxiety, and so forth, self-report measures regarding the contexts in an adolescent's life may be helpful.

For example, the Family Environment scale (FES; Moos & Moos, 1986) is among the most widely used family self-report measure

(Carlson, 1992). The FES is a 90-item true–false measure that includes subscales of cohesion, expressiveness, conflict, independence, achievement orientation, active–recreational, moral–religious emphasis, organization, and control. One advantage of the FES is that it can be completed by adolescents and their parents. Counselors may find it instructive in treatment planning to examine the discrepancies between reports as well as points of agreement (Kronenberger & Meyer, 1996) The manual provides normative data for individual adolescent and parents' scores as well as discrepancy scores. These same authors (Moos & Moos, 1990) developed another measure that helps the counselor examine additional family concerns as well as considering other adolescent contexts and issues. The Life Stressors and Social Resources Inventory–Youth Form includes eight domains: physical health, home and money, relationships with parents, relationships with siblings, relationships with extended family, school, relationships with friends, relationships with boyfriend or girlfriend, and negative life events.

A second example of a self-report family measure is the Family Adaptability and Cohesion Evaluation scales III (FACES III; Olson, Portner & Lavee, 1985). The FACES III is a 20-item rating scale in which respondents rate their answers on a 5-point scale to a variety to questions related to the cohesion and adaptability subscales. Again, adolescents and parents can complete the measure.

Projectives

In addition to asking the adolescent client and/or their significant others direct questions via interview or self-report, at times counselors may choose to use projective techniques to help explore the adolescent's functioning, cognitions, and salient issues. Similar to traditional storytelling cards in the adult version Thematic Apperception Test (TAT) or the child version Child Appercetion Test (CAT), Silverton (1993) published the Adolescent Apperception Cards (AAC). The AAC includes 11 cards to elicit stories regarding key relationships including parents, sibling, and peer. Similarly, the Family Apperception Test (FAT; Sotile, Julian, Henry, & Sotile, 1988) includes 21 cards that portray various family activities, constellations, and situations (Carlson, 1992). In a similar vein, sentence completions may also be helpful. Therapists can tailor the stems to match the particular concern or developmental level (e.g., For me, school is _____.; I think my parents _____. I work because _____.)

Certainly, a clinician using projectives must do so with appropriate cautions. Interpretations should not be based on a single response. Instead, patterns of responses may be helpful in adding explanatory information to what has been gained via other assessment techniques. Motivations, concerns, "issues," and cognitions may be better understood via projective responses. In other cases, projectives allow the clinician to generate hypotheses that are later investigated through other assessment techniques.

Observation

Whereas interviews, self-report measures, and projective techniques may offer some valuable assessment information, perhaps the most critical assessment technique available to the P–E–ecologically oriented counselor is observation. Much of the assessment from this theoretical orientation is done by watching for patterns of interactions between the adolescent and relevant systems in his or her life. There are a variety of forms of observation that may be useful to the counselor working with adolescents.

Family Interaction Tasks

In the Watzlavick (1966) tradition, the family therapy movement has, for decades, used analog observation techniques. Using this method, sometimes called Family Interactions Tasks, families are assigned discussion tasks related to decision making, revealed differences or conflict patterns (Carlson, 1992). The counselor, for example, may give the family instructions to imagine that they have been given a week off in which no one has to go to work or school. The family will be directed to spend 10 minutes planning a family vacation for that week within a certain budget. The counselor observes the family, ideally behind a one-way mirror. If such facilities are not available, the counselor may videotape the family for later viewing (and leave the room once the camera is turned on and left on a tripod) or, as a least preferred option, the counselor can move to a corner of a room and observe the discussion as unobtrusively as

possible. Although this analog approach is certainly somewhat artificial, families frequently do begin to act more like themselves and
almost appear to forget that the counselor is, or will be, watching.
The counselor observes patterns of interactions, including communication styles, handling disagreements, and the ability to compro-
mise. Other scenarios include asking families to discuss the last
conflict they had, how it started, what happened and how it ended
(this one inevitably brings up new conflict so the counselor can get a
glimpse of how the family "fights").

Enactments

Those in the structural family tradition (e.g., Minuchin, 1974) note
that another important form of observation is through naturally occurring incidents, enactments that occur in counseling sessions. For
example, an adolescent may storm out of the room when her father
speaks to her; another may "shut down" when confronted by her
mother. Parents may launch into lectures or be overly accommodat-
ing to an adolescent's requests. Rather than interfering with the
work of therapy, these situations give the counselor a glimpse of
what likely occurs at home. Counselors must use these opportunities to gain information and plan interventions.

Assessments for Intervention Planning

From an ecological and P–E fit perspectives assessments, regardless
of which specific techniques or instruments are used, should give
the counselor information to assist the adolescent in strategies to
modify themselves (e.g., coping skills) or strategies to modify their
context (e.g., change jobs, etc.; Lerner, Baker, & Lerner, 1985). Additionally, in some cases, counselors could consider interventions,
they could make at the systemic–contextual level (e.g., helping the
family change via parenting skills instruction; teaching a classroom-based intervention on diversity appreciation).

Summary and Concluding Thoughts

Truly, adolescence "is an exciting time of life" (Steinberg, 1996, p. 4), a
period of multiple significant transitions. Ecological and P–E fit approaches may help counselors more completely understand the world
of an individual adolescent at that critical developmental stage.

Counselors operating from these perspectives will:

1. Have an appreciation for, and basic understanding of, the relevant contexts in which adolescents operate, including home, school, work, and peer groups and any other systems that are particularly salient for their individual adolescent client.
2. Choose assessment measures and procedures that provide information regarding their adolescent clients, the contexts in which the adolescents are functioning, and the interaction between adolescent clients and salient contexts.
3. Use assessments to plan interventions from an ecological and P–E, viewing the individual adolescent, the context, or both as the potential target for change.

With these perspectives and approaches, counselors may be in a better position to assist adolescents in successfully negotiating the "series of passages from immaturity into maturity" (Steinberg, 1996, p. 4.)

REFERENCES

Batsche, G. M., & Knoff, H. M. (1994). Bullies and their victims: Understanding a pervasive problem in schools. *School Psychology Review, 23*(2), 165–174.

Baumrind, D. (1991). The influence of parenting style on adolescent competence and substance abuse. *Journal of Early Adolescence, 11*, 56–95.

Bennett, L. A., Wolin, S. J., & McAvity, K. J. (1988). Family identify, ritual and myth: A cultural perspective on life cycle transitions (pp. 211–234). In C. J. Falicov (Ed.), *Family transitions: Continuity and change over the life cycle.* New York: Guilford.

Bossard, J., & Boll, E. (1950). *Rituals in family living: A contemporary study.* Philadelphia: University of Pennsylvania Press.

Bronfenbrenner, U. (1979). Contexts of child rearing: Problems and prospects. *American Psychologist, 34*, 844–850.

Buhrmester, D. (1990). Intimacy of friendship, interperpersonal competence, and adjustment during preadolescence and adolescence. *Child Development, 61*, 1101–1111.

Caplan, R. D., Tripathi, R. C., & Naidu, R. K. (1985). Subjective past, present and future fit: Effects on anxiety, depression, and other indicators of well-being. *Journal of Personality and Social Psychology, 48*(1), 180–197.

Carlson, C. (1992). Models and strategies of family-school assessment and intervention. In M. J. Fine & C. Carlson. *The handbook of family school intervention: A systems perspective* (pp. 18–44). Boston: Allyn & Bacon.

Cobb, N. J. (1998). *Adolescence: Continuity, change, and diversity* (3rd ed.). Mountain View, CA: Mayfield.

Conway, T. L., Vickers, R. R., Jr., & French, J. R. P., Jr. (1992). An application of person–environment fit theory: Perceived versus desired control. *Journal of Social Issues, 48*(2), 95–107.

Eccles, J. S., Lord, S. E., & Roeser, R. W. (1996). Round holes, square pegs, rocky roads, and sore feet: The impact of stage-environment fit on young adolescents' experiences in schools and in families. In D. Cicchetti & S. L. Toth (Eds.), *Rochester Symposium on Developmental Psychopathology: Vol. 7. Adolescence: Opportunities and challenges* (pp. 47–92). Rochester, NY: University of Rochester Press.

Ennett, S. T., & Bauman, K. E. (1996). Adolescent social networks: School, demographic, and longitudinal considerations. *Journal of Adolescent Research, 11,* 194–215.

Everett, S., & Price, J. (1995). Students perceptions of violence in the public schools. The MetLife survey. *Journal of Adolescent Health Care, 17,* 345–352.

Fine, M. J. (1992). A systems-ecological perspective on home-school intervention. In M. J. Fine & C. Carlson. *The handbook of family school intervention: A systems perspective* (pp. 1–18). Boston: Allyn & Bacon

Fuligni, A. J., & Eccles, J. S. (1993). Perceived parent-child relationships and early adolescents' orientation toward peers. *Developmental Psychology, 29,* 622–632.

Furlong, M. J., & Morrison, G. M. (1994). Introduction to mini-series: School violence and safety in perspective. *School Psychology Review, 23,* 139–150.

Garbarino, J. (1980). Some thoughts on school size and its effects on adolescent development. *Journal of Youth and Adolescence, 9*(1), 19–31.

Gottfredson, G., & Gottfredson, D. (1985). *Victimization in the schools.* New York: Plenum Press.

Gavin, L. A., & Furman, W. (1989). Age differences in adolescents' perceptions of their peer groups. *Developmental Psychology, 25,* 827–834.

Hartman, A. (1978). Diagrammatic assessment of family relationships. *Social Casework, 59,* 465–476.

Kroneneberger, W. G., & Meyer, R. G. (1996). *The child clinician's handbook.* Boston: Allyn & Bacon.

Larson, J. (1994). Violence prevention in the schools: A review of selected programs and procedures. *School Psychology Review, 23*(2), 151–164.

Larson. R. W., Richards, M. H., Moneta, G., Holmbeck, G., & Duckett, E. (1996). Changes in adolecents' daily interactions with their families from ages 10–18: Disengagement and transformation. *Developmental Psychology, 32,* 744–754.

Lax, W. D., & Lussardi, D. J. (1988). The use of rituals in families with an adolescent. In E. Imber-Black, J. Roberts, & R. A. Whiting (Eds.), *Rituals in families and family therapy* (158–176). New York: Norton.

Lerner, J. V., & Lerner, R. M. (1994). Explorations of the goodness-of-fit model in early adolescence. In W. B. Carey & S. C. McDevitt (Eds.), *Prevention and early intervention: Individual differences as risk factors for the mental health of children. A festschrift for Stella Chess and Alexander Thomas.* New York: Brunner/Mazel.

Lerner, J. V., Baker, N., & Lerner, R. M. (1985). A person-context goodness of fit model of adjustment. In P.C. Kendall (Ed.), *Advances in cognitive-behavioral research and therapy* (Vol. 4, pp. 111–136). Orlando, FL: Academic Press, Inc.

Meyer, K. A. (1987). The work commitment of adolescents: Progressive attachment to the work force. *The Career Development Quarterly, 36*(2), 140–147.

Minuchin, S. (1974). *Families and family therapy.* Cambridge, MA: Harvard University Press.

Moos, R. H., & Moos, B. S. (1986). *Family Environment Scale.* Palo Alto, CA: Consulting Psychologists Press.

Mortimer, J. T., Finch, M. D., Ryu, S., Shanahan, M. J., Call, K. T. (1996). The effects of work intensity on adolescent mental health, achievement, and behavioral adjustment: New evidence from a prospective study. *Child Development, 67,* 1243–1261.

Olson, D. H., Portner J., & Lavee, Y. (1985). *FACES III* (Available from Family Social Science, University of Minnesota, St, Paul, MN 55108)

Poland, S. (1994). The role of school crisis intervention teams to prevent and reduce school violence trauma. *School Psychology Review, 23*(2), 175–189.

Quinn, W. H., Newfield, N. A., & Protensky H. O. (1985). Rites of passage in families with adolescents. *Family Process, 24,* 101–111.

Silverton, L. (1993). *Adolescent Apperception Cards.* Los Angeles: Western Psychological Services.

Sotile, W. M., Julian, A., Henry, S., & Sotile, M. (1988). *Family Apperception Test* (FAT). Charlotte, NC: Feedback Services.

Steinberg, L. (1996). *Adolescence* (4th ed.) New York: McGraw Hill.

Steinberg, L., Fegley, S., & Dornbusch, S. M. (1993). Negative impact of part-time work on adolescent adjustment: Evidence from a longitudinal study. *Developmental Psychology, 29*(2), 171–180.

Urberg, K. A. (1992). Locus of peer influence: Social crowd and best friend. *Journal of Youth and Adolescence 21,* 439–450.

Urberg, K. A., Degirmencioglu, S. M., Tolson, J. M., & Halliday-Scher, K. (1995). The structure of adolescent peer networks. *Developmental Psychology, 31,* 540–547.

Watzlavick, P. (1966). A structured family interview. *Family Process, 5,* 256–271.

Williams, J. M., & White, K. A. (1983). Adolescent status systems for males and females and three age levels. *Adolescence, 18,* 382–389.

Wolin, S. J., & Bennett, L. A. (1984). Family rituals. *Family Process, 23,* 401–420.

Social Environments and Social Contexts: Social Network Applications in Person–Environment Psychology

Laura M. Koehly
The University of Iowa
Victoria A. Shivy
Virginia Commonwealth University

Individual's behavior occurs in situ and, whether the setting is the home, the job, or another of life's many arenas, the importance of contextual factors cannot be denied. In most cases, contextual factors are likely to be synonymous with the ambient interpersonal environment in which a particular individual, or system of individuals, functions.
—Koehly and Shivy (1998, p. 3)

The circumstances in which a particular individual finds her or himself clearly impact on that person's behavior. In the psychological arena, circumstances often seem to amount to the intraindividual variables of self-reported affect, beliefs, or cognitions—in other words, the variables on which clinicians most easily focus and that researchers most expediently study. Despite professional psychology's theoretical acknowledgment of the impact of environmental factors on individuals' behavior, attitudes, and affect, and the recognition that people influence environments, just as environments influence people (Schneider, 1987; Walsh, Price, & Craik, 1992; Wampold, et al., 1995), both researchers and clinicians—in practice—often attend to the person and exclude the environment from active consideration. Although it is no doubt convenient, from a conceptual standpoint, to ignore individuals' interactions within their "personal communities" (Fischer, 1982), the frequency, affective intensity, and duration of these interactions probably result in their being the most meaningful aspects of individuals' lives.

In fact, few clinicians or contemporary researchers would disagree with the premise that most of clients' problems are either interpersonal in nature or have important interpersonal ramifications (Peterson, 1982). This premise is reflected, to a greater or lesser degree, in the current diagnostic nomenclature (APA, 1994) and in our psychotherapeutic theories and interventions (e.g., Kiesler, 1996). Whereas individuals' struggles with intimacy, communication, aggression, loneliness, and insecurity (Peterson, 1982) may indeed play out internally, in the form of conflicted feelings and subjectively felt distress, they also involve and impact on interpersonal relationships. Thus, in order for the clinician or researcher to fully understand individual behavior, he or she must take the time to understand the interpersonal context in which the behavior is embedded.

The study of interpersonal relationships occupies a prominent position in person–environment (P–E) psychology and, as we assert here, the methods associated with social network analysis (SNA) can be used to provide empirical evidence for the theoretical models which underlie P–E psychology. SNA allows one to study the interpersonal transactions among a set of individuals while taking into account both their personal dispositions and other individual characteristics as well as the context within which they interact. SNA provides a general set of methods that use indices of relatedness among individuals to produce representations of the social structure, or social environment, within which a given set of individuals interact. It is, therefore, not only fully consonant with the P–E approach to phenomena, but offers a way for P–E psychologists—clinicians and researchers alike—to significantly advance their understanding of behavior.

A social network consists of a set of individuals, or actors, and the relationships or interactions that exist between them. Examples of network actors might include a group of adolescents living in a youth home, a group of coworkers in highly stressful occupations (e.g., police officers, air traffic controllers, prison guards), or a number of community agencies that combine efforts to provide resources to families in need. The relational patterns of interest to P–E researchers or practitioners might include emotional or informational support, friendship relationships, or task-related communications or advice.

SNA consists of both descriptive methods and inferential methods. These methods focus on characterizing the social network in terms of structural or relational indices, and the unit of the description will depend on the objective of the project. For example, network methods can be used to describe the level of cohesiveness of the network as a whole (*network density*), to identify subsets of cohesive groups or clusters of network members (*cliquing*), to quantify the degree to which given network members initiate interactions within the network (*actor centrality*) or the degree to which a given network member receives interactions or transactions (*actor prestige*), and to assess whether a given network member is separated from all network interactions (*actor as isolate*). The investigator chooses the level of analysis at which to examine network structure; hence, dyadic, triadic, subgroup, or complete group structures can be investigated via SNA. On account of their flexibility, SNA methods allow the research to extend the focus of relational research beyond the dyad, and to the broader social contexts of family, friends, community, or culture.

The network paradigm, as outlined by Galaskiewicz and Wasserman (1994), parallels Kelley et al.'s, (1983) interpersonal process, and the social network perspective is grounded in the following tenets: (a) actors and their actions are necessarily interdependent, (b) relationships, or relational ties, between actors serve as conduits for resources, such as friendship, advice, or support, (c) the structure of the social network, or social environment, can constrain as well as potentiate individual action, (d) network models conceptualize structure as recurrent patterns of interpersonal relationships. Thus, social network research is concerned with studying prolonged and stable patterns of interpersonal relationships and social interaction (Freeman & Romney, 1987). Although SNA researchers focus primarily on the relational patterns among a group of

social actors, actor attribute variables can also be incorporated into
the analysis, resulting in a more complete representation of an individual's behavior in the context of his or her interpersonal relationships and social environment (Kanfer & Tanaka, 1993).
Representative individual differences variables might include age,
gender, attitudes, beliefs, scale scores on a personality assessment
instrument, or any other variable thought to serve as an explanatory
factor for social behavior. The possibility of including such "composition variables" represents an advance in SNA and reflects the increased sophistication of modeling attempts over the last 50 years.
These advances allow the investigator to examine complex questions with respect to an individual's role within his or her social and
interpersonal environment. The social network perspective has
grown in popularity because it enables researchers to study not only
social actors but the social relationships among the actors. Hence, social network methods attempt to explain an individual's behavior
within the context of his or her social environment and, as previously mentioned, the method seems in full accord with the P–E approach. This chapter provides an introduction to the social network
methodology. Specifically, we outline how SNA can be used to investigate an individual within the context of his or her interpersonal
environment.

WHAT IS A SOCIAL NETWORK?

Social Actors

A social network contains two sets of information: social actors or
network members and the relational ties that exist among those actors. The research or practical objective of the study will define the
group of social actors on which relational ties will be measured as
well as the types of relational or interactional information that will
be gathered. Membership rules define the boundaries of the network to be studied and specify how the actors will be sampled.
These rules are used to decide which actors are included in the network under investigation, and which are not. If we are investigating
a bounded group of individuals then network membership is relatively obvious; for example, a researcher might choose to study the
students receiving a particular special education curriculum or the

residents of a youth home. However, there are situations where the boundaries of a network are fuzzy (e.g., McCarty, Bernard, Killworth, & Shelley, 1997; Neyer, 1997; van der Poel, 1993). Consider, for example, the difficulties associated with specifying the network of the homeless and indigent in a large metropolitan area. If the boundaries of the network cannot easily be delineated, then special sampling techniques, such as "snowball sampling," or "small-world" methods, can be used to define the actor set (Erickson, 1978; 1981; Frank & Snijders, 1994; Goodman, 1961; Granovetter, 1976; Snijders, 1992; Snijders & Spreen, 1997; Spreen, 1992; Wasserman & Faust, 1994).

To illustrate social network indices, and facilitate our discussion of SNA methods, we use a hypothetical example. Consider the case of the investigator who wishes to examine the relationships among a set of adolescents who live in a youth home. Perhaps the investigator is particularly interested in the constructs of exhibited aggression or conflict among current residents. In this case, the actors in the social network are the adolescent residents. Figure 4.1 represents the conflict relations among residents of the home. The network members include eight youths: Jake, Chase, Tom, Bill, Beth, Mary, Sue, and Tina, four males and four females, all of whom suffer from some diagnosable mental illness.

Measuring Social Relations

Once the actor set is established, it is necessary to define the social relation(s) that are to be measured. The range of social relations that can be measured is quite broad and depends in large part on the objectives of the research study. In fact, several different relations could be measured on the same set of actors. The substantive questions and theories underlying the research will determine which relational variables to measure. In our example, the investigator was concerned about exhibited aggression among the youth home residents. The investigator might also be interested in friendship relationships among the group, or support relations between residents. The types of relations that an investigator might measure include social or interpersonal evaluations (e.g., friendship, acquaintanceship, dislike), transfer of tangible or intangible resources (e.g., monetary donations, information, emotional support, material aid), observable behavioral interactions (e.g., aggression, playing, hugging), or formal role relationships (e.g., parent–child, supervisor–subordinate).

There are a variety of methods used to measure social relations among network members. The mode of measurement is dictated by the context of the research question, the nature of the network membership, and the social relations(s) under investigation. Paper-and-pencil questionnaires, structured interviews, computerized surveys, direct observation, and archival data (Wasserman & Faust, 1994) have all been used in network research. Questionnaires are most commonly used for data collection when the network members are human research participants. However, face-to-face, telephone, and computerized interviews can increase response rates and decrease the amount of missing data (e.g., Heald, Contractor, Koehly, & Wasserman, 1998; Wasserman & Faust, 1994).

In general, survey methods ask respondents to provide information about their relational ties to other network members. For example, one might ask, "Who do you go to for emotional support during a troubling experience?" "From whom do you seek information about health or social services?" In our youth home example, a suitable question might be, "Who do you hang out with after group?" Respondents may be asked to indicate, from an investigator generated list of individuals, who fits the relational criteria. Alternatively, respondents may be asked to generate their own list of individuals who fit the criteria of interest. Valued relational information may also be gathered. In other words, participants may be asked to rate each network member on the relational variable of interest (e.g., "On a scale from 0 [not at all] to 4 [very often], how often would you go to Karen for emotional support during a routine or minor upset?"). Interviews and questionnaires gather relational data from the perspective of the respondent.

Observational data collection methods might be a more suitable mode of data collection in certain scenarios. For example, if we were studying aggressive behavior among the youth home residents, the investigator might observe the behavior of the residents for a given time period. Observational methods are used in studies involving small groups, when network members are unable to respond themselves, and/or when the relation(s) under investigation necessitate an objective coding for the relational interactions among network members (e.g., Freeman, Freeman, & Michaelson, 1988). Finally, archival records such as newspapers, court records, and financial records can also provide useful relational data.

Measurements of social relations can be dichotomous or valued. Dichotomous relations simply measure the presence or absence of a tie between network members. Valued relations attach a value or strength to the relational ties connecting network actors. For example, familial ties among network members may be measured in dichotomous format, as the members of the network are either related or not. However, valued relations provide more information than merely the presence or absence of the relationship. Aggressive acts can be measured in a number of ways: the frequency of behaviors that initiate conflict or aggression, the degree of aggression received from a particular network member as perceived according to a Likert-type scale, or the presence or absence of aggressive behavior.

Measurement of dichotomous relations are usually coded as a 0 if the relation is absent or a 1 if the relation is present. So, in the case of familial relations, if Jake and Bill are brothers who live in the same hypothetical youth home, the familial tie between them will be coded as a 1. Ties among residents who share no familial relation will be coded as a 0. Valued relations can take on values other than 0 and 1. For example, the investigator may count the number of aggressive actions occurring between residents during a given time period. The value of the exhibited aggression relation will equal the count of aggressive acts occurring between each dyad pair. So, if Jake initiates aggression toward Tom 5 times within the observational period, the investigator would code the aggression relation from Jake to Tom as 5.

Very little work has been done on measurement related issues in social network data. However, Marsden (1990) provided an excellent summary of the literature on psychometric properties of relational data. It is important to realize that social network data are susceptible to the same measurement problems as standard social science data and the investigator should always try to reduce measurement error and increase the reliability and validity of the data.

Often, the nature of the investigation involves integrating actor attributes into the structural analysis. Thus, in addition to relational data, social network data can also include measurements taken on the characteristics of network members. Examples of actor attribute variables, or "composition variables," include gender, ethnic origin, disposition variables, and psychological state variables. Again, the substantive question or theory underlying the research will delineate the attribute variables to be measured. In our example of exhibited aggression among youth home residents, we might be interested in such actor attribute variables as gender, the scale elevations on a personality assessment device such as the MMPI-A (Butcher et al., 1992), or the severity of the resident's psychological diagnosis. We might hypothesize that the nature of a given adolescent's psychopathology might predispose the individual to initiating more conflictual acts or receiving conflict. Furthermore, there may be gender differences, where conflict occurs within gender groups, but rarely crosses gender lines.

Types of Networks

There are three types of social networks that command consistent attention in the literature: complete networks, ego-centered networks, and perceptual networks. In *complete networks*, all members of the network can relate to each other. For instance, in our youth home example, all residents can initiate conflict with all other residents. Thus, we have complete network data. However, some data collection designs and some substantive questions gather relational information on only a subset of actors. For example, an *ego-centered* network consists of a focal actor, or *ego*, and the set of *alters* who are tied to the ego. In this case, relational measurements are made on the ties among the alters. For example, an investigator might examine relationships among individuals who provide support to a specific person who has been diagnosed as "depressed." Here, the depressed individual is designated as the ego. All others who provide support to the ego are called the alters. These potential alters might include family members, friends, social workers, and counselors. In this case, an investigator might want to examine supportive communications between the ego and his or her alters, as well as supportive communications among all alters. Ego-centered networks have been used to investigate the social environments of individuals (Boissevain, 1973), families (Bott, 1957), disease transmission (Morris, 1989, 1993, 1994), communication (Marsden, 1987, 1988), social cognition (Pattison, 1994), and social support (Walker, Wasserman, & Wellman, 1994).

Perceptual networks examine the relational ties among actors as perceived by a given individual or ego. For example, an investigator might ask an individual with a diagnosable mental illness to recreate the communication relations among those alters in his or her support network. The ego's perceptual network would represent the communication relations among the alters, but only as viewed through the eyes of the ego. By using a perceptual networks approach, the investigator could evaluate how well the perceiver's perceptions matched a "true" or consensually agreed on structure. This logic is behind cognitive social structures (CSS), in which network members report on their own relational ties and their perceived relational ties among all network members (Newcomb, 1961; Krackhardt, 1987). A CSS consists of each individual actor's perception of the entire network. Perceptual networks have been studied extensively to understand bias and consensus in individual perceptions of network structure (Banks & Carley, 1994; Heald, Contractor, Koehly, & Wasserman, 1998; Krackhardt, 1987; Kumbasar, Romney, & Batchelder, 1994).

Representations of a Social Network

Social network data can be represented as a sociomatrix or in graphical form. Sociomatrices can be manipulated when computing structural indexes or using inferential methods. Graphs, however, provide a pictorial representation of the relational ties among network actors. Measurements of the social relations among network members are typically represented in a two-way matrix called a *sociomatrix*, which we will denote by X (see Table 4.1). The sociomatrix is a square matrix that conveys relational information among network actors. The matrix is not necessarily symmetric. In Table 4.1, the rows represent the actors sending the relational tie; the columns represent the actors who receive the relational tie. The i,jth entry in the sociomatrix contains a value that represents the strength of the relationship from the ith sending actor to the jth receiving actor. For example, Table 4.1 represents the sociomatrix for the exhibited aggression relation among the youth home residents. During the observational period, Jake and Bill both initiate aggressive behavior toward each other. This is illustrated by the value of a 1 in the 2,4th cell and the 4,2th cell in the sociomatrix; so, $X_{24} = X_{42} = 1$. In this

TABLE 4.1

Sociomatrix for Fig. 4.1:
Conflict Initiation Relations
Among Youth Home Residents

Actor	1	2	3	4	5	6	7	8
	n_1	n_2	n_3	n_4	n_5	n_6	n_7	n_8
Chase n1	-	0	0	0	0	0	0	0
Jake n2	1	-	1	1	0	0	1	1
Tom n3	0	1	-	1	0	0	0	0
Bill n4	1	1	1	-	0	0	0	0
Beth n5	0	0	0	0	-	1	0	0
Tina n6	0	0	0	0	0	-	1	1
Mary n7	0	0	0	0	0	0	-	0
Sue n8	1	1	0	0	1	1	1	-

example, the relational information was measured as a dichotomous variable, either the residents initiated the aggressive behavior
or they did not during the observational period. Most of the SNA indices that are discussed below require that the social relation is measured in dichotomous or categorical format. Thus, if the researcher
measured the relation as the number of aggressive acts exhibited

during the observation period, he or she may have to transform valued information in order to compute relevant network indices.

A social network can also be represented as a *graph* consisting of a set of nodes joined by lines or arcs. The actors in the network membership set are represented as the nodes, or points, in the graph. The node set will be denoted by $N = \{n_1, n_2, \ldots, n_g\}$, where g is the number of actors in the network. Relational ties are represented graphically by connecting two nodes with a line, $n_i \rightarrow n_j$. This indicates that actor n_i "chooses" actor n_j. Figure 4.1 represents the graph for exhibited aggression amongst the set of youth home residents. The nodes in the graph are the residents and these nodes are connected by an arrow representing the direction of the relationship. The direction of the line indicates that an actor initiates some action toward, or "chooses" another actor; for example, Tina (n_6) initiates conflict with Mary (n_7). The information in the graph can be represented in a two-way matrix called an adjacency matrix. For dichotomous relations, the sociomatrix is equal to the adjacency matrix.

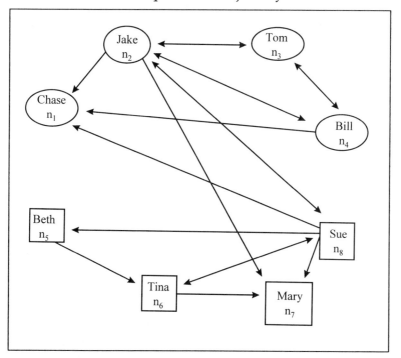

FIG. 4.1. Conflict initiation relations among youth home residents.

The investigator may wish to examine more than one relation among a set of actors. For example, besides conflict initiation, one might want to also investigate supportive relations. If a set of r relations is measured on the same set of actors, then the set of sociomatrices, X_1, X_2, ..., X_r, is referred to as a multirelational network and can be represented as a multigraph. A multigraph consists of a set of nodes with r sets of lines connecting them. Through the use of graphs and multigraphs, SNA offers a way in which to represent the varying relationships among a set of actors graphically and to examine the relationships simultaneously.

We can distinguish between nondirectional relations and directional relations. A nondirectional relation is one in which the sender and the receiver of the relational tie are indistinguishable. The tie is either present or absent between each pair of actors. The sociomatrix for a nondirectional relation is always symmetric and the graph of a nondirectional relation will contain nodes that are connected by lines rather than directed lines. Familial ties are nondirectional. If Jake is related to Bill, then Bill must also be related to Jake. A relation is directional if there is information available that concerns the flow, or initiation, of the relationship. Thus, the orientation of the ties is meaningful. The sociomatrix for directional relations is not necessarily symmetric. The exhibited aggression relation discussed in our example is a directional relation. Directional relations do not imply reciprocation of the relationship; for example, Sue initiates aggression toward Mary, Tina, Beth, and Chase. This relation is only reciprocated by one of these four residents, namely Tina. The term *graph* is used to refer to a graph for a nondirectional relation. A *digraph* is a graph for a directional relation. Because the lines in a digraph are directed lines, we refer to them as *arcs*. Figure 4.1 is an example of a network digraph.

There are important graph structures that are used to define some of the descriptive indices presented here. The *nodal degree* represents the number of ties incident with each node or actor in the graph. For a nondirectional relation, the nodal degree, $d(n_i) = \Sigma_j X_{ij} = \Sigma_j X_{ji}$, is computed by summing across the rows or columns of the sociomatrix matrix for each actor. If the relation is directional, then we can distinguish between the number of ties sent from an actor and the number of ties received by an actor. The *outdegree* of actor i

refers to the number of ties sent by actor i and the *indegree* of actor i refers to the number of ties received by actor i. Mathematically, the outdegree is the sociomatrix row total for actor i, or $d_O(n_i) = \Sigma_j X_{ij}$. The indegree is the column total, $d_I(n_i) = \Sigma_j X_{ji}$. Referring to Fig. 4.1, the outdegree for Jake and Sue is 5; their indegree is 3 and 2, respectively. Chase and Mary do not act aggressively toward any of the residents, so their outdegree is 0. An actor is said to be an isolate if he or she neither sends nor receives any ties. Thus, if $d_I(n_i) = d_O(n_i) = 0$, then node i is an isolate. There are no isolates in the youth home residents example.

A *path* in a graph is a sequence of nodes and lines that connect two particular nodes, n_i and n_j, such that no node or line is included more than once. A *directed path* is a path such that all arcs are "pointing" in the same direction. The number of lines or arcs connecting two nodes is referred to as the *length* of the path, and the shortest path between two nodes is called the *geodesic*; the length of which is called the *geodesic distance*. The geodesic distance between nodes i and j is denoted by d_{ij}. For a nondirectional relation, d_{ij} will necessarily be equal to d_{ji}. This is not always true for directional relations, however, as the geodesic from n_i to n_j may be different than the geodesic connecting n_j to n_i. For example, in Fig. 4.1, Sue acts aggressively toward Beth so the geodesic distance from Sue to Beth is 1; however, Beth does not reciprocate the behavior. Rather, Beth initiates aggression with Tina who then acts aggressively toward Sue. The geodesic distance from Beth to Sue is 2. Thus, in this case, the geodesic distances $d_{8,5}$ and $d_{5,8}$ are obviously not equal. Finally, two nodes are said to be *unreachable* when there is no path that connects them. Thus, the geodesic distance between two unreachable actors is infinite. Mary and Chase are unreachable.

SOCIAL STRUCTURE

We will present some of the descriptive indices most commonly used to describe a social network. Inferential methods will be summarized and appropriate references provided. UCINET IV (Borgatti, Everett, & Freeman, 1992) and STRUCTURE (Burt, 1991) are two computer packages that can be used to compute descriptive indices of network structure and perform basic inferential analyses.

There are also resources on the Internet (see http://www. heinz.cmu.edu/project/INSNA/) that can guide the user to statistical programs for more complex analyses. Graphical displays of a sociomatrix can be created using KackPlot 3.0 (Krackhardt, Blythe, & McGrath, 1994).

Descriptive Indices of Structure

The strength of the SNA approach lies in the fact that, rather than studying the individual as an isolate, the relationships among a group of social actors can be described as well as how these relationships may affect or influence each individual and the larger network. In order to examine these relationships we need to effectively describe social structure. Some of the basic structural properties that can be computed are discussed here. More complex structures are described in Wasserman and Faust (1994) and Wasserman and Pattison (1996). The structures are defined for dichotomous relations; however, extensions to valued relations can be found in Wasserman and Faust (1994). Social network analysis is grounded in graph theory. Therefore, each of the indices presented can be viewed as a property of the network graph. The exhibited aggression example will be used to illustrate the network indices.

Centrality and Prestige

Often a researcher may be interested in evaluating the prominence or importance of each social actor within a group. A prominent actor is one who is well connected to other members of the network, and actor prominence indices indicate an individual's location or role within the network. Measures of centrality and prestige can be classified according to the relational type represented in the network. If the social relation is nondirectional, then we cannot distinguish between ties sent and ties received. Actor prominence for nondirectional relations reflects the number of ties in which the actor is involved and is measured as actor *centrality*. For directional relations, however, we can distinguish between ties sent and ties received. Prominence is measured using indices of centrality and *prestige*. A central actor is one who sends many ties, either directly or indirectly, to other network members. Thus, a central actor can be considered "expansive" (Faust & Wasserman, 1992) or "outgoing."

A prestigious actor is one who receives many ties from others, or is "popular." For a more detailed discussion than the one provided below and mathematical representations of measures of actor prominence, please see Bonacich (1987), Faust and Wasserman (1992), Knoke and Burt (1983), Wasserman and Faust (1994; chap. 5), and Koehly and Wasserman (1996).

Actor Prominence: Nondirectional Relations.   There are several types of centrality for nondirectional relations commonly seen in the literature: degree centrality (Proctor & Loomis, 1951; Shaw, 1954), closeness centrality (Beauchamp, 1965; Sabidussi, 1966), betweenness centrality (Anthonisse, 1971; Freeman, 1977, 1979, 1980; Pitts, 1979) , information centrality (Stephenson & Zelen, 1989), and stochastic centrality (Faust & Wasserman, 1992; Koehly & Wasserman, 1996). Each of these indices of actor prominence accentuates different ways an actor can influence the relational flow within the network. Also, not all of the prominence indices are meaningful for every relation. We focus our discussion on three measures of centrality: degree centrality, closeness centrality, and betweenness centrality. Degree centrality, measured by an actors nodal degree, focuses on the direct links between group members. In our example, an individual who exhibits aggression toward many others has a large degree centrality; one who does not exhibit aggression toward others, will have a degree centrality equal to zero. Jake and Sue have the highest degree centrality index and thus are the most central, most aggressive individuals in the group. Chase and Mary have the lowest degree centrality and are the least aggressive adolescents in the home.

The remaining centrality indices allow for indirect influence of an actor and are easier to understand in the context of communication relations. Closeness centrality takes into account the indirect paths between actors as well as the direct paths by considering the geodesic distances connecting an actor with all other network members. A high closeness centrality index suggests that the actor is "close" to many others. Thus, in the context of communication, an actor with high closeness centrality is one who can relay information quickly to many of the group members. Betweenness centrality considers the number of geodesics within which an actor lies. If an individual falls within many geodesics, he or she will have a high betweenness centrality. Individuals with high betweenness centrality act as a "cut point" person through which information flows; they are central in the sense that they have a high level of control over the flow of information through the network.

Actor Prominence: Directional Relations. For directional relations, we can distinguish between ties sent and ties received. An actor who "chooses" many others is said to be central to the network. On the other hand, actors who are "chosen" often are said to be prestigious. The centrality measures discussed for nondirectional relations can easily be extended to the directional case. Degree centrality will focus on the outdegree of the actor. Thus, we consider only ties sent or choices made. Both closeness and betweenness centrality for directed relations will consider the length of directed geodesics.

Actor prestige focuses on the ties received by an actor. Degree prestige (Alexander, 1963), proximity prestige (Lin, 1976), and rank prestige (Katz, 1953) are commonly reported indexes of actor prestige. Degree prestige is indicated by the indegree of graph nodes; actors who are prestigious are popular because they receive many ties from other group members. In the aggression example, an actor with a high degree prestige index is one who is the "receiver" of aggressions from many others. Chase, Jake, and Mary are the most prestigious adolescents as they are the receivers of most of the exhibited aggressions during the observation period.

Proximity prestige is similar to the idea of closeness centrality in that it focuses on the geodesic distances to an actor rather than the distance from an actor. Thus, an individual with a high proximity prestige can receive information quickly from many others. Rank prestige not only considers the ties received by an actor, but also takes into account the prestige of the actors from whom the ties are received. Thus, an individual with a high rank prestige receives information quickly from prestigious others.

An investigator may want to relate actors' centrality and prestige indices with composition or individual differences variables. For example, is there a tendency for individuals with certain psychological disorders to be more central or more prestigious? Is there a correlation between personality characteristics and tendencies to initiate or receive aggressions? Are there gender differences in exhibited aggressions?

Centralization.   *Centralization* is an index of the variation of the individual centrality and prestige indices in a network. For each index of interest, the centralization is computed by summing the differences between the largest observed index and each individual index. This sum is then normalized by dividing by its theoretical maximum. Wasserman and Faust (1994) provided computational formulas for a number of centralization indices. Centralization can lie between 0 and 1. A value of 0 suggests that all actors have the same value for the index of interest. A value of 1 suggests that one actor completely dominates the other network members. For example, the centralization index for degree centrality in Fig. 4.1 is 0.45. Thus, there is a number of residents (e.g., Jake and Sue) who dominate in initiating conflict among the group.

Density

Another structural property that is of interest is the network *density*, D, which is the proportion of possible ties present in the network. Density is calculated by dividing the sum of all entries in the sociomatrix by the number of possible ties, $D = \Sigma_i \Sigma_j X_{ij} / g(g-1)$. A sparse network, where there are few relational transactions, will have a low density. For our example, the total number of ties in the graph in Fig. 4.1 is 18 (sum of all cells in sociomatrix X in Table 4.1) and the total possible number of ties is 56. The density of this graph is 0.32, suggesting that 32% of the possible ties are present in the exhibited aggression structure. Network density provides a direct measure of group cohesiveness or participation. An investigator can use density to evaluate how cohesiveness or participation changes over time. For example, the investigator might expect that the density will decrease as a function of the residents' participation in group therapy, reflecting a decrease in exhibited aggression.

Reciprocity

A *dyad* is a pair of actors and the possible ties that can occur between the two actors. For a nondirectional relation, there are two states that a dyad can be in: a *null* dyad and a *mutual* dyad. A null dyad is one where there is no tie linking the two dyadic actors. There is a relational tie between the pair of actors in a mutual dyad. In a directional relation, the possible relational states that the dyad can take on become more complex. There can be a null dyad, where there are no ties between the two actors. Two types of *asymmetric* dyads can be defined, $n_i \rightarrow n_j$ and $n_j \rightarrow n_i$. And, finally, the mutual dyad occurs when both actors in the dyad choose each other. If actor i chooses actor j and actor j chooses actor i, then the pair of actors exhibit *reciprocity* of choice. In Fig. 4.1, Chase and Beth illustrate a null dyad as they do not act aggressively toward each other. An example of an asymmetric dyad is the relationship between Sue and Beth; Sue acts aggressively toward Beth, but Beth does not reciprocate the behavior. Jake and Tom reciprocate aggressive behaviors and thus form a mutual dyad. An investigator may be interested in relating these dyadic states to various composition variables. For example, are conflictual relationships more likely to be reciprocated amongst male members? Are null dyads more common when the actors are of different genders?

Balance

An important concept that can easily be investigated using social network methods is the idea of relational or structural balance. Initially, balance was studied in the context of valenced relations (Heider, 1958). Heider argued that people want to believe that those with whom they are friends are friends with each other. Heider's theory is based on a liking relation, where the values of ties are signed. Others have extended Heider's theory to consider directional ties, rather than signed ties (Davis & Leinhardt, 1972; Holland & Leinhardt, 1971, 1976). These researchers suggested that balance is exhibited in network structure through transitive triads.

A *triad* is a triple of actors and the possible ties that can exist between them. Similar to the dyadic states just defined, triadic states can get quite complex. Two types of triads are of particular interest for nondirectional relations. The *transitive triad* will contain all three possible ties between the three actors. An *intransitive triad* occurs when there are only two lines present out of the three possible lines between the triple of actors. For directional relations, we need to take into account the direction of the arc when defining triad types. A triad is transitive when n_i chooses n_k given that n_i chooses n_j and n_j

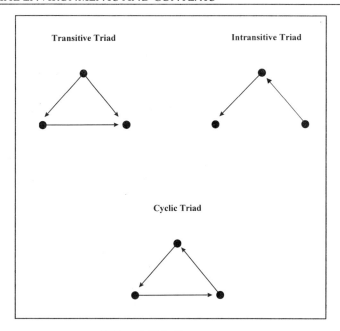

FIG. 4.2. Triadic structures.

chooses n_k. An intransitive triad occurs when n_i does not choose n_k, but n_i chooses n_j and n_j chooses n_k. A third type of triad, called the *cyclic triad*, can be defined for directional relations. A cyclic triad consists of a triple of actors where if n_i chooses n_j and n_j chooses n_k, then n_k chooses n_i. Fig. 4.2 provides a graphical representation of these three triadic structures for digraphs. Note that for nondirectional relations, we cannot distinguish between the cyclic triad and the transitive triad.

Triadic analyses are used to evaluate whether the relationships among a group are balanced. A balanced structure is one that exhibits a large number of transitive triads in comparison to intransitive triads. Referring to Fig. 4.1, the triad formed by Sue, Beth, and Tina is transitive because $n_8 \rightarrow n_5$, $n_5 \rightarrow n_6$, and $n_8 \rightarrow n_6$. The triad formed by Sue, Beth, and Chase is intransitive: $n_8 \rightarrow n_5$, $n_8 \rightarrow n_1$, but n_5 does not choose n_1. The graph in Fig. 4.1 does not appear to be relationally balanced. There are only 11 transitive triads out of a possible 56 [= $(1/6)g(g-1)(g-2)$].

Subgroups

An important application of social network analysis is the identification of cohesive subgroups of actors. In groups, such as our youth home example, subgroup formation is often inevitable and at times can be disruptive. The formation of cohesive subgroups can lead to difficulties eliciting constructive interaction among the adolescents in group therapy. A cohesive subgroup consists of a subset of actors (three or more) among whom there are strong ties. There are several ways to define cohesion when identifying subgroup memberships. Cohesive subgroups have been conceptualized by reciprocity, closeness, or reachability of members, and density of ties within the subgroup as compared to nonmembers (Wasserman & Faust, 1994). Each of these criteria incorporate successively weaker properties for identifying subgroup memberships.

If reciprocity, or mutuality of ties, is used to create cohesive subgroups, then all members of a subgroup must exhibit reciprocal relationships. A cohesive subgroup that fits this definition is said to be a *clique*. A clique is a subset of network members all whom "choose" each other. In Fig. 4.1, there is only one clique: (Jake, Tom, Bill). So, the clique formed by Jake, Tom, and Bill is one in which all three adolescents act aggressively toward each other. A more flexible criteria for forming cohesive subgroups is based on the concept of reachability. The *n-clique* uses the concept of reachability to form cohesive subgroups; the maximal distance (n) between two group members is prespecified. For example, a 2-clique is a subgroup of network members in which the geodesic distance between each pair of actors is at most 2. A 1-clique is a clique as defined above. In Fig. 4.1, there is one 2-clique: (Jake, Tom, Bill, Sue). Note that the members of the clique are also members of the 2-clique, however, Sue has joined the subgroup because the geodesic distance between Sue and Tom and Sue and Bill is 2. Density also can be used to form cohesive subgroups of actors. The objective is to maximize the density within a subgroup of actors while minimizing the density between subgroups of actors. Discriminant analyses could be used to evaluate whether composition variables differentiate subgroup memberships (Arabie, 1984). For example, an investigator might hypothesize that subgroups will form across gender lines. The male adolescents tend to act aggressively toward other males rather than the female residents; similarly, females tend to act aggressively toward the female residents and not the male residents.

Subgroups can also be formed by grouping individuals who have similar positions within the network structure. Individuals who are similar in terms of their position have similar patterns of relational ties with others in the group. *Structural equivalence* refers to network members who have the same relational ties to the same actors in the group. The two therapists in a therapy group may be structurally equivalent during the group process. Each therapist is tied to the same clients. *Regular equivalent* actors share the same pattern of ties to similar network actors, not necessarily the same actors. For example, if we were studying the roles that community agencies play in providing social services to families in need, we might expect that similar agencies in different communities to be regularly equivalent; they interact with different community members similarly.

Inferential Methods

Since Moreno's (1934) foundational work in sociometry, statistical techniques for describing the structure of a network have been evolving. Wasserman and Pattison (1996) have described the evolution of these statistical analyses in terms of three generations of models. All of these statistical approaches to network analysis have focused on describing and examining, quantitatively, the structural properties of social relations and the social actors in a group or network. The first generation, beginning in the late 1930's with the work of Moreno, involves comparing specific network properties to values expected under some null distribution or model (Bronfenbrenner, 1943, 1944, 1945; Moreno & Jennings, 1938). The observed structural property, such as network density or the number of transitive triads, was compared to the expected structural property in a simulated random network where simulation of ties was based on some prespecified distribution or conditional distribution.

The second generation evolved out of the first during the 1980s and increased the sophistication of the statistical tests for various structural effects, assuming the presence of other structural properties. The second generation of models allowed for the simultaneous estimation of parameters that quantify the tendency for various structural effects, such as density and reciprocity. The models proposed by Holland and Leinhardt (1981), referred to as p_1, are *dyadic interaction models*. These models describe the network structure stochastic as a function of four types of structural properties: network density, reciprocity, actor popularity (indegree) and actor expansiveness (outdegree). Thus, the structural unit of interest in p_1 is the dyadic relationship. The p_1 models have been generalized to account for multiple relations (Fienberg, Meyer, & Wasserman , 1985; Wasserman, 1987), valued relations (Anderson & Wasserman, 1995), blockmodels (Anderson, Wasserman, & Faust, 1992; Wang & Wong, 1987; Wasserman & Anderson, 1987), and longitudinal networks (Wasserman & Iacobucci, 1988).

Holland and Leinhardt's p_1 models assume that the dyads, or pairs of actors, are statistically independent. This assumption is rather strong and has been questioned extensively in the literature (Iacobucci & Wasserman, 1990; Wasserman & Faust, 1994; Wasserman & Pattison, 1996; Wasserman & Weaver, 1985). The third generation of models relaxes the assumption of dyadic independence. The work of Frank and Strauss (1986) describes dependencies among actors by utilizing concepts underlying the theory of Markov random graphs. These models postulated by Frank and Strauss were not computationally tractable until the groundbreaking research of Strauss and Ikeda (1990), who defined the models in terms of simple logistic regressions. Wasserman and Pattison (1996) extended the work of Strauss and Ikeda to more complicated network structures. Furthermore, Walker (1996) extended the work of Wasserman and Pattison to ego-centered networks, whereas Koehly (1996) provided a general modeling framework for a set of related perceptual networks. Anderson, Wasserman, and Crouch (in press) provided an excellent introduction to the p^* family of models.

DISCUSSION

We close this chapter with some final thoughts and caveats, but one observation seems in order. We adapted much of our material for this chapter from an article that was recently published in the *Journal of Counseling Psychology* (i.e., Koehly & Shivy, 1998). Our task in that paper was to introduce counseling professionals to SNA methods and to persuade readers that SNA techniques were worth learning about. When we set out to write this chapter, and were charged with a similar task, we felt our job to be similar to that of "preaching to the choir," in that SNA methods seem to be almost tailor-made for the P–E approach to psychology. SNA methods present, perhaps, the most expedient way to simultaneously examine both the "person side" as well as the "environmental side" of P–E correspondence models. Hence, we anticipate considerable interest in SNA methods. However, as with any new methodological approach, limitations must be anticipated, and a number of caveats must be issued. These limitations cross disciplinary lines and seem well worth repeating.

One potential difficulty with SNA and related models (e.g., Marcus & Kashy, 1995) is the need for copious amounts of rating or ranking data from network inhabitants. Earlier in this chapter we noted that the characteristic richness of an SNA stems directly from the fact that the network approach is data-intensive. Some SNA designs indeed require the use of lengthy paper-and-pencil questionnaires or extensive interview procedures. The use of observational techniques or the collection of archival data can ease some of the burden that this places on research participants. However, there is often no substitute for self-report data and, if such data are required by the substantive concerns of the study, then the investigator should take into consideration the willingness of network inhabitants to engage in data collection tasks. Participants' motivation may be enhanced through careful explanation of the nature and importance of the study, or by remuneration. However, incorporating computer technology in the data collection process might also help. For example, visual images of network members, in the form of digitized photographs, could be used as stimuli in lieu of more tedious paper-and-pencil rating and ranking tasks. Regardless of the specific procedure used, data collection issues are likely to arise in an SNA, and should be anticipated.

Another potential difficulty with SNA is related to the fact that the methods are not fully developed. Thus, although many descriptive SNA indices are well-understood and implemented in the form of software packages for network analysis—such as in Borgatti, Everett, and Freeman's (1992) UCINET IV or Burt's (1991) STRUCTURE—the statistical models and software needed to test propositions about network properties are generally harder to find.

Researchers who wish to study complex social phenomena involving multiple relations or longitudinal network data may need to collaborate directly with more quantitatively oriented psychologists or sociologists. In turn, P–E researchers might also offer their assistance, applied researchers are likely to be among the first to discover the gaps in existing procedures and techniques (Wasserman & Faust, 1994).

In sum, it would seem that P–E psychologists have much to gain from social network analysis. SNA methods offer not only a way to go beyond the dyad (Kanfer & Tanaka, 1993; Wasserman & Faust, 1994), but also to look at the reciprocal interactions that take place between two or more actors in a formal or informal social system. Given the sophistication of SNA models, individual differences variables, like gender, ethnicity, age, or diagnosis, can be included in the analyses as explanatory factors (Wasserman & Faust, 1994), resulting in a much more complete representation of individuals' behavior in context. The underlying assumptions of SNA methods parallel Kelley's (et al., 1983) notion of interpersonal process and, hence, are likely to seem immediately familiar to P–E psychology practitioners and researchers. P–E psychologists have long recognized the reciprocal relationships between environments and environmental inhabitants. Despite this, the environment has long been excluded from active examination. With the introduction of SNA methods P–E psychologists may have an elegant means to study individuals' interactions as they take place naturally, within their "personal communities" (Fischer, 1982).

ACKNOWLEDGMENTS

We thank Kari Kempf, William E. Martin, Jr., and Jody L. Swartz for their helpful comments on the manuscript. The characters depicted in this manuscript are purely fictitious and any resemblance to persons living or dead is purely coincidental.

REFERENCES

Alexander, C. N. (1963). A method for processing sociometric data. *Sociometry, 26,* 268–269.

Anderson, C. J., & Wasserman, S. (1995). Log multiplicative models for valued social relations. *Sociological Methods & Research, 24,* 96–127.

Anderson, C. J., Wasserman, S., & Crouch, B. (in press) A p^* primer: Logit models for social networks. *Social Networks*.

Anderson, C. J., Wasserman, S., & Faust, K. (1992). Building stochastic blockmodels. *Social Networks, 14*, 137–161.

Anthonisse, J. M. (1971). *The rush in a graph*. Amsterdam: Mathematische Centrum.

American Psychiatric Association (1994.). *Diagnostic and statistical manual of mental disorders: DSM-IV* (4th ed.). Washington, DC: Author.

Arabie, P. (1984). Validation of sociometric structure by data on individuals' attributes. *Social Networks, 6*, 373–403.

Banks, D., & Carley, K. (1994). Metric inference for social networks. *Journal of Classification, 11*, 121–149.

Beauchamp, M. A. (1965). An improved index of centrality. *Behavioral Science, 10*, 161–163.

Boissevain, J. (1973). An exploration of two first order zones. In J. Boissevain & J. D. Mitchell (Eds.), *Network analysis: Studies in human interaction* (pp. 125–148). The Hague: Mouton.

Bonacich, P. (1987). Power and centrality: A family of measures. *American Journal of Sociology, 92*, 1170–1182.

Borgatti, S. P., Everett, M. G., & Freeman, L. C. (1992). *UCINET IV Version 1.64*. Columbia, SC: Analytic Technologies.

Bott, E. (1957). *Family and social network*. London: Tavistock.

Bronfenbrenner, U. (1943). A constant frame of reference for sociometric research. *Sociometry, 6*, 363–397.

Bronfenbrenner, U. (1944). A constant frame of reference for sociometric research: Part II. Experiment and inference. *Sociometry, 7*, 40–75.

Bronfenbrenner, U. (1945). The measurement of sociometric status, structure, and development. *Sociometric Monographs* (No. 6). Beacon House, NY.

Burt, R. S. (1991). *STRUCTURE, version 4.2*. New York: Center for the Social Sciences, Columbia University.

Butcher, J. N., Williams, C. L., Graham, J. R., Archer, R. P., Tellegen, A., Ben-Porath, Y. S., & Kaemmer, B. (1992). *MMPI-A. (Minnesota Multiphasic Personality Inventory—Adolescent). Manual for administration, scoring, and interpretation*. Minneapolis: University of Minnesota Press.

Davis, J. A., & Leinhardt, S. (1972). The structure of positive interpersonal relations in small groups. In J. Berger (Ed.), *Sociological theories in progress* (Vol. 2, pp. 218–251). Boston: Houghton Mifflin.

Erickson, B. (1978). Some problems of inference from chain data. In K. F. Schuessler (Ed.), *Sociological Methodology, 1979* (pp. 276–302). San Francisco: Jossey-Bass.

Faust, K., & Wasserman, S. (1992). Centrality and prestige: A review and synthesis. *Journal of Quantitative Anthropology, 4*, 23–78.

Fienberg, S. E., Meyer, M. M., & Wasserman, S. (1985). Statistical analysis of multiple sociometric relations. *Journal of the American Statistical Association, 80*, 51–67.

Fischer, C. S. (1982). *To dwell among friends: Personal networks in town and city.* Chicago: University of Chicago Press.

Frank, O., & Snijders, T. A. B. (1994). Estimating the size of hidden populations using snowball sampling. *Journal of Official Statistics, 10,* 53–67.

Frank, O., & Strauss, D. (1986). Markov graphs. *Journal of the American Statistical Association, 81,* 832–842.

Freeman, L. C. (1977). A set of measures of centrality based on betweenness. *Sociometry, 40,* 35–41.

Freeman, L. C. (1979). Centrality in social networks: I. Conceptual clarification. *Social Networks, 1,* 215–239.

Freeman, L. C. (1980). The gatekeeper, pairdependency, and structural centrality. *Quality and Quantity, 14,* 585–592.

Freeman, L. C., Freeman, S. C., & Michaelson, A. G. (1988). On human social intelligence. *Journal of Social and Biological Structures, 11,* 415–425.

Freeman, L. C., & Romney, A. K. (1987). Words, deeds and social structure: A preliminary study of the reliability of informants. *Human Organization, 46,* 330–334.

Galaskiewicz, J., & Wasserman, S. (1994). Introduction: Advances in the social and behavioral sciences from social network analysis. In S. Wasserman & J. Galaskiewicz (Eds.), *Advances in social network analysis* (pp. xi–xvii). Thousand Oaks, CA: Sage.

Goodman, L. A. (1961). Snowball sampling. *Annals of Mathematical Statistics, 32,* 148–170.

Granovetter, M. (1976). Network sampling: Some first steps. *American Journal of Sociology, 81,* 1267–1303.

Heald, M. R., Contractor, N. S., Koehly, L. M., & Wasserman, S. (1998). Formal and emergent predictors of coworkers' perceptual congruence on an organization's social structure. *Human Communication Research, 24,* 536–563.

Heider, F. (1958). *The psychology of interpersonal relations.* New York: Wiley.

Holland, P. W., & Leinhardt, S. (1971). Transitivity in structural models of small groups. *Comparative Group Studies, 2,* 107–124.

Holland, P. W., & Leinhardt, S. (1976). Conditions for eliminating intransitivities in binary digraphs. *Journal of Mathematical Sociology, 4,* 314–318.

Holland, P. W., & Leinhardt, S. (1981). An exponential family of probability distributions for directed graphs. *Journal of the American Statistical Association, 76,* 33–65.

Iacobucci, D., & Wasserman, S. (1990). Social networks with two sets of actors. *Psychometrika, 55,* 707–720.

Kanfer, A., & Tanaka, J. S. (1993). Unraveling the web of personality judgments: The influence of social networks on personality assessment. *Journal of Personality, 61,* 711–738.

Katz, L. (1953). A new status index derived from sociometric analysis. *Psychometrika, 18,* 39–43.

Kelley, J., Berscheid, E., Christensen, A., Harvey, J., Huston, T., Levinger, G., McClintock, E., Peplau, L. A., & Peterson, D. (1983). *Close relationships*. New York: Freeman.

Kiesler, D. J. (1996). *Contemporary interpersonal theory and research: personality, psychopathology, and psychotherapy*. New York: Wiley.

Knoke, D., & Burt, R. S. (1983). Prominence. In R. S. Burt & M. J. Minor (Eds.), *Applied network analysis* (pp. 195–222). Newbury Park, CA: Sage.

Koehly, L. M. (1996). *Statistical modeling of congruence and association between perceptual and complete networks*. Unpublished doctoral dissertation, University of Illinois at Urbana-Champaign.

Koehly, L. M., & Shivy, V. A. (1998). Social network analysis: A new methodology for counseling research. *Journal of Counseling Psychology, 45*(1), 1–15.

Koehly, L. M., & Wasserman, S. (1996). Classification of actors in a social network based on stochastic centrality and prestige. *Journal of Quantitative Anthropology, 6*, 75–99.

Krackhardt, D. (1987). Cognitive social structures. *Social Networks, 9*, 109–134.

Krackhardt, D. , Blythe, J., & McGrath, C. (1994). KrackPlot 3.0: An improved network drawing program. *Connections, 17*(2), 53–55.

Kumbasar, E., Romney, A. K., & Batchelder, W. H. (1994). Systematic biases in social perception. *American Journal of Sociology, 100*, 477–505.

Lin, N. (1976). *Foundations of social research*. New York: McGraw-Hill.

Marcus, D. K., & Kashy, D. A. (1995). The social relations mode: A tool for group psychotherapy research. *Journal of Counseling Psychology, 42*, 383–389.

Marsden, P. V. (1987). Core discussion networks in Americans. *American Sociological Review, 52*, 122–131.

Marsden, P. V. (1988). Homogeneity in confiding relations. *Social Networks, 10*, 57–76.

Marsden, P. V. (1990). Network data and measurement. *Annual Review of Sociology, 16*, 435–463.

McCarty, C., Bernard, H. R., Killworth, P. D., & Shelley, G. A. (1997). Eliciting representative samples of personal networks. *Social Networks, 19*(4), 303–323.

Moreno, J. L. (1934 / 1978). *Who shall survive?: Foundations of sociometry, group psychotherapy, and sociodrama* (3rd ed.). Beacon House, Inc., Beacon, NY.

Moreno, J. L., & Jennings, H. H. (1938). Statistics of social configurations. *Sociometry, 1*, 342–374.

Morris, M. (1989). *Networks and Diffusion: An Application of Loglinear Models to the Population dynamics of Disease*. Unpublished doctoral dissertation, Department of Sociology, University of Chicago, Chicago, IL.

Morris, M. (1993). Epidemiology and social networks: Modeling structure diffusion. *Sociological Methods & Research, 22*, 99–126.

Morris, M. (1994). Epidemiology and social networks: Modeling structured diffusion. In S. Wasserman & J. Galaskiewicz (Eds.), *Advances in social network analysis* (pp. 26–52). Thousand Oaks, CA: Sage.

Newcomb, T. M. (1961). *The acquaintance process.* New York: Holt, Rinehart & Winston.

Neyer, F. J. (1997). Free recall or recognition in collecting ego-centered networks: The role of survey techniques. *Journal of Social & Personal Relationships, 14*(3), 305–316.

Pattison, P. E. (1994). Social cognition in context. Some applications of social network analysis. In S. Wasserman & J. Galaskiewicz (Eds.), *Advances in social network analysis* (pp. 53–78). Thousand Oaks, CA: Sage.

Peterson, D. R. (1982). Interpersonal relationships as a link between person and environment. In W. B. Walsh, K. H. Craik, & R. H. Price (Eds.), *Person–environment psychology: Models and perspective* (pp. 127–192). Hillsdale, NJ: Lawrence Erlbaum Associates.

Pitts, F. R. (1979). The medieval river trade network of Russia revisited. *Social Networks, 1,* 285–292.

Proctor, C. H., & Loomis, C. P. (1951). Analysis of sociometric data. In M. Jahoda, M. Deutsch, & S. W. Cook (Eds.), *Research methods in social relations* (pp. 561–586). New York: Dryden Press.

Sabidussi, G. (1966). The centrality index of a graph. *Psychometrika, 31,* 581–603.

Schneider, B. (1987). $E = f(P,B)$: The road to a radical approach to person-environment fit. *Journal of Vocational Behavior, 31,* 353–361.

Shaw, M. E. (1954). Group structure and the behavior of individuals in small groups. *Journal of Psychology, 38,* 139–149.

Snijders, T. A. B. (1992). Estimation on the basis of snowball samples: How to weight? *Bulletin de Methodologie Sociologique, 36,* 59–70.

Snijders, T. A. B., & Spreen, M. (1997). Segmentation in personal networks. *Mathematiques, Informatique et Sciences Humaines, 137,* 25–36.

Spreen, M. (1992). Rare populations, hidden populations, and link-tracing designs: What and why? *Bulletin de Methodologie Sociologique, 36,* 34–58.

Stephenson, K., & Zelen, M. (1989). Rethinking centrality: Methods and applications. *Social Networks, 11,* 1–37.

Strauss, D., & Ikeda, M. (1990). Pseudolikelihood estimation for social networks. *Journal of the American Statistical Association, 85,* 204–212.

van der Poel, M. G. M. (1993). Delineating personal support networks. *Social Networks, 15,* 49–70.

Walker, M. E. (1996). *Stochastic models for social support networks.* Unpublished doctoral dissertation, University of Illinois at Urbana-Champaign.

Walker, M. E., Wasserman, S., & Wellman, B. (1994). Statistical models for social support networks. In S. Wasserman & J. Galaskiewicz (Eds.), *Advances in social network analysis* (pp. 53–78). Thousand Oaks, CA: Sage.

Walsh, W. B., Price, K. H., & Craik, R. H. (1992). *Person–Environment psychology: Models and perspectives.* Hillsdale, NJ: Lawrence Erlbaum Associates.

Wampold, B. E., Ankarlo, G., Mondin, G., Trinidad-Carrillo, M., Baumler, B., & Prater, K. (1995). Social skills of and social environments produced by different Holland types: A social perspective on person–environment fit models. *Journal of Counseling Psychology, 42,* 365–379.

Wang, Y. J., & Wong, G. Y. (1987). Stochastic blockmodels for directed graphs. *Journal of the American Statistical Association, 82,* 8–19.

Wasserman, S. (1987). Conformity of two sociometric relations. *Psychometrika, 52,* 3–18.

Wasserman, S., & Anderson, C. J. (1987). Stochastic *a posteriori* blockmodels: Construction and assessment. *Social Networks, 9,* 1–36.

Wasserman, S., & Faust, K. (1994). *Social network analysis: Methods and applications.* New York: Cambridge University Press.

Wasserman, S., & Iacobucci, D. (1988). Sequential social network data. *Psychometrika, 53,* 261–282.

Wasserman, S., & Pattison, P. (1996). Logit models and logistic regressions for social networks: I. An introduction to Markov graphs and p^*. *Psychometrika, 61,* 401–425.

Wasserman, S., & Weaver, S. O. (1985). Statistical analysis of binary relational data: Parameter estimation. *Journal of Mathematical Psychology, 29,* 406–427.

III

*Person–Environment Psychology
and Mental Health: Intervention
Strategies*

5

The Person–Environment Tradition in Counseling Psychology

René V. Dawis
University of Minnesota
and The Ball Foundation

Psychological theory in the past can be divided simply, albeit simplistically, into two camps:

$B = f(O)$, and $B = f(S)$,

represented, respectively, by personologism (e.g., Allport, 1937; Murray, 1938) and behaviorism (e.g., Hull, 1943; Skinner, 1938). The first group of theorists held that psychology's goal was to understand behavior in terms of organismic—or person—variables such as traits, dispositions, attitudes, and needs. The second group believed that psychology's task was to identify the stimulus conditions required to predict and explain behavior. That is, the first theoretical school looked for explanations of behavior in the person, whereas the second school looked for them in the environment. Thus, logically speaking, both theoretical camps can be thought of as belonging to the same school:

$B = f(O,S)$ when stated in molecular terms, or

$B = f(P,E)$ when stated in molar terms,

with the first camp holding environment constant in their formulations, and the second camp, person. In this sense, one can say that psychology has always subscribed to the person–environment (P–E) point of view. Actually, some early theorists, notably Lewin (1936) and Tolman (1932), did propose theories that reflected a P–E perspective. But by and large, the P–E point of view was not espoused explicitly in psychological theory until fairly recently (Epstein & O'Brien, 1985; Kenrick & Funder, 1988; Magnusson & Engler, 1977), under the impetus provided by the Mischel (1968) situationism controversy (Bem & Allen, 1974; Bowers, 1973).

Counseling psychology differs from its parent field in that from its very beginnings it had adopted the P–E model as its guiding formulation. Counseling psychology evolved from the vocational guidance movement (Super, 1955; Whitely, 1984; Williamson, 1965). In turn, modern vocational guidance is said to have started (Brewer, 1942; Paterson, 1938) with Frank Parsons, who founded the Vocation Bureau in Boston to "give scientific vocational counsel" to young people. Parsons' (1909) posthumously published book, *Choosing a Vocation*, was the movement's "bible" (Paterson, 1938). In this book, Parsons provided "practical steps that can be taken ... in the selection of a vocation," founded on a formula in which vocational choice is to be arrived at by the matching of person with occupation. This formulation is arguably the earliest version of a P–E model to appear in the counseling psychology literature (or perhaps even in psychology literature). In due course, counseling psychology progressed from the Parsons formulation to the "matching model" to trait-and-factor counseling to P–E fit theory to counseling from a P–E interaction perspective. This chapter recounts counseling psychology's passage from Parsons to P–E fit.

The Parsons Formula

Today, after almost a century, the Parsons formula for choosing a vocation is still very much the method of choice—or the default method—among career counselors. No other proposal has been able to replace it (but see Savickas, 1993). In a much-quoted paragraph, Parsons (1909) stated his formula this way:

> In the wise choice of a vocation there are three broad factors: (1) a clear understanding of yourself, your aptitudes, abilities, interests, ambitions, resources, limitations, and their causes; (2) a knowledge

of the requirements and conditions of success, advantages and disadvantages, compensation, opportunities, and prospects in different lines of work; (3) true reasoning on the relations of these two groups of facts. (p. 5)

At the outset it should be noted that Parsons had the highest respect for the individual's right to choose. "No person may decide for another what occupation he should choose, but it is possible to help him so to approach the problem that he shall come to wise conclusions for himself" (Parsons, 1909, p. 4).

Parsons's procedure, as just stated, consisted of three steps: analysis of the person, analysis of occupations, and putting the two analyses together in the service of a "wise choice." Although the approach appeared to be straightforward, implementing it was not easy. Parsons was well aware that many people—especially young people—would need help with one or more of the three steps. It was for this reason that he wrote his book, as a guide for those who would wish to offer help as would-be "vocational counselors."

Desiring to "give scientific vocational counsel," Parsons looked toward the then-new science of psychology for assistance. Unfortunately, psychology at that time (the early 1900s) was attempting to establish its scientific status, and so the field necessarily focused on basic science or theory-driven questions—slighting the study of practical applications of the science. Finding "the cupboard bare" (Paterson, 1938), the pragmatic Parsons had recourse to the methods that were available.

For the person analysis step, Parsons recommended "self-investigation and self-revelation," assisted where possible by a vocational counselor. He prepared an extensive questionnaire, a checklist, and a structured interview schedule to use in this process. Parsons had full confidence in the efficacy of self-analysis.

For the occupation analysis step, Parsons found little help from the available literature, so he put his efforts toward developing materials that described occupations in some detail: task requirements, settings, compensation, job opportunities, and the like. The vocational guidance movement promptly followed Parsons's lead, concentrating on the generation of occupational information as its main activity. Thus, vocational guidance practice was for a time "arrested in its development" at the level of providing occupational information (Paterson, 1938). To this day, career programs in U.S. high schools see the provision of occupational information as their main function, and school career libraries are largely dedicated to occupational information materials. There even are contemporary career counselors who still see their role solely as being providers of occupational information.

Unfortunately, having good occupational information alone is not enough for wise vocational choice, especially when one relies on self-analysis for information about the person. Self-analysis, it turned out, was seriously flawed because it was based on estimation or judgment rather than on objective measurement. Psychologists, even then, were discovering that the evaluation of person characteristics by self or by others can be influenced by a variety of biasing factors, such as selective memory and social desirability (see, e.g., Hollingworth, 1923). It was not until the 1930s that psychological science finally began to furnish vocational counselors with objective and reliable tools to take the place of subjective and untrustworthy self-analysis.

Even the last of Parsons's three steps turned out to be rather problematic; "true reasoning" did not follow easily on assembling the "two groups of facts." As Alexander (1934) pointed out, if individual analysis is conducted in one set of terms and occupational analysis in another set of terms, the work of fitting the two together is nearly hopeless. What Alexander had anticipated was the need for commensurate measurement.

The Matching Model

The first promising solution to the problem of relating person analysis to occupation analysis was the method of "clinical matching" through the use of a "dynamic criterion" (Viteles, 1936). In this procedure, a vocational choice is evaluated clinically in terms of the person's probable success or failure in the chosen occupation. In other words, the "goodness of match" is ascertained by expert clinical judgment about how the person would fare in the chosen occupation.

To aid clinical judgment, Viteles (1932) introduced a device called the "psychograph." A psychograph was a graphic presentation of (a) a list of relevant person characteristics (e.g., physical and mental abilities, special aptitudes, education and training, specific vocational skills) and (b) ratings of each characteristic made on some scale (e.g., a 5- or 10-point scale). Psychographs could be used to describe the occupation as well as the person. Ratings for an occupation (also called a "job psychograph") were based on the characteristics of successful occupational members as judged by the counselor. If the same list of characteristics were used for both person and occupation psychographs, the person could be compared with the occupation directly—characteristic by characteristic—and a clinical judgment about the "goodness of match" would be easier to reach. This was the precursor of commensurate measurement.

The "matching model" was also used in the evaluation of counseling outcomes. A typical study (e.g., Williamson & Bordin, 1941) would follow up on a group of counselees to determine their vocational status some years after counseling (employment status, occupation, if employed, salary, job satisfaction, etc.). A panel of expert judges (typically experienced counselors) would then evaluate the "goodness of match" between the counselee and the occupation, based on their reading of the counselee's case folder (which contained data from person analysis) and their knowledge of the occupation and its requirements (about which they presumably were "expert"). Thus, many years before "accountability" became an obligatory cliche, vocational counselors who based their practice on psychological science were already evaluating the effectiveness of their practice on the basis of the outcomes their counseling produced.

Trait and Factor Theory

Objective measurement of person characteristics came to counseling psychology through the psychology of individual differences and its collateral development of the psychological test (Dawis, 1992). Following Binet's successful demonstration that intelligence could be measured (Binet & Simon, 1908/1961), early measurement efforts focused on developing tests of general mental ability (g). With World War I and the introduction of group testing, group tests of g were developed, modeled on the Army Alpha (DuBois, 1970). More importantly, the theory of psychological testing (Guilford, 1954; Gulliksen, 1950) evolved rapidly from the foundations laid by Spearman (1904a, 1904b).

With progress in psychometric theory and technology, the construction of psychological tests proceeded apace. In addition to tests of g, tests of special abilities were developed, such as tests of mechanical ability, clerical ability, spatial ability, musical ability, and finger and manual dexterity. These tests correlated positively, but not highly, with tests of g, and therefore contributed unique information. Technical innnovations, such as the multiple choice format, standardized group administration, and machine scoring, combined to make ability and aptitude testing much easier and much more economical to administer (DuBois, 1970).

Other developments in psychological testing, notably in interest, attitude, and personality assessment, rounded out the requirements set by Parsons for person analysis. Interest measurement, in particular, became the special province of vocational psychology. Until the 1980s, research on interest measurement was conducted almost exclusively by vocational and counseling psychologists (Dawis, 1991), resulting in such well-constructed instruments as the Strong Vocational Interest Blank (now the Strong Interest Inventory; Harmon, Hansen, Borgen, & Hammer, 1994) and the Kuder Preference Record—Vocational (now the Kuder Occupational Interest Survey; Kuder & Zytowski, 1991). With these developments in the psychometric measurement of person characteristics, Parsons's person analysis step could now be placed on an objective and reliable footing.

Two other developments are worth special mention: advances in commensurate measurement and in factor theory.

Commensurate Measurement. Taking their cue from Viteles, D.G. Paterson and his coworkers at the Minnesota Employment Stabilization Research Institute proposed describing occupations in terms of "occupational ability patterns" (Dvorak, 1935; Trabue, 1933). An occupational ability pattern was a psychograph in which the list of characteristics consisted of abilities (e.g., general, verbal, numerical, spatial ability) that were measured objectively, that is, by ability tests. The "pattern" was a profile of ability-test means obtained on a sample of satisfactorily performing members of an occupation. A person could then be tested on the same set of ability tests, and the person's test profile compared directly with the occupational ability pattern. This would allow direct quantitative assessment of "goodness of match" with the use of indexes such as average (or total) difference, average (or total) absolute (unsigned) difference, and average (or total) squared difference. Commensurate measurement was finally quantified, thereby enabling the conduct of research using statistical analyses. Much empirical research has backed the validity of occupational ability patterns (see, especially, the *Manual for the USES General Aptitude Test Battery, Section III*, for validity data on several hundred occupations; U.S. Department of Labor, 1970)

Actually, each study done to validate the use of ability tests in academic or industrial personnel selection (and there have been thousands of such studies) results in a description of an environment (school or work) in commensurate terms, that is, in terms wherein person and environment can be measured and compared on the same measurement scale dimensions. Furthermore, such validity has been shown to generalize across differing conditions, thereby enhancing their usefulness for counseling (Schmidt & Hunter, 1977; Schmidt, Hunter, & Pearlman, 1981). Thus, all three Parsons' formula steps are automatically operationalized in a quantified manner when an ability test or test battery is empirically validated.

In the area of interest measurement, different approaches were developed to quantify commensurate measurement. Instead of an "occupational interest pattern" (of scale means), Strong (1943) devised the "occupational scale," which produced a score that indicated how similar a person's interests were to those of an occupational sample. The responses of each occupational sample were used to develop a separate scoring key for each occupation (i.e., different occupational scales were scored on different sets of items). Strong's method was a primitive version of discriminant function analysis, in which a subset of items was identified that maximally differentiated the occupational sample from a reference group (separate "men-in-general" and "women-in-general" groups were used to develop separate gender-referenced occupational scales). Follow-up studies by Strong and others have shown that high scores on an occupational scale predicted staying in the occupation, whereas low scores predicted leaving the occupation (Dawis, 1991; Strong, 1955).

Kuder and his co-workers (Kuder, 1977) developed a different approach occasioned by advances in computing technology. Unlike Strong's occupational scale scores, which were based on selected items and a reference group, Kuder's "lambda coefficient" directly indexed the similarity of the person's responses to the responses of the occupational sample on *all* items—and without needing a reference group (Kuder, 1977, pp. 41–43). Kuder's approach used the person's responses as the scoring key to score the members of each occupational sample, then averaged the occupational members' scores and corrected the average for variability in the sample. The validity of Kuder lambda scores has also been studied extensively (see, e.g., Zytowski, 1976a, 1976b).

Factor Theory. Factor theory, a development indigenous to the science of psychology, originated with Spearman (1904b), who showed mathematically how the intercorrelations among ability tests (variables) could be reproduced by assuming that individual differences (variance) on each test resulted from two factors, a general factor common to all tests and a specific factor unique to each test. Even earlier, Pearson (Harman, 1967) developed a method, the method of principal axes, that could be used to reduce an intercorrelation matrix to a smaller matrix with fewer columns, each column representing a principal component (axis) that enters into the linear composition of each variable. (This development, however, would need to await advances in computing technology before it could be used.) But it was Thurstone (Harman, 1967) who discovered that the rank of the matrix determined the number of common factors, enabling the generalization of Spearman's method to the method of multiple factor analysis. These landmark contributions paved the way for the development of factor theory.

The emergence of factor theory was a turning point for psychological science, which has to deal with intangible entities. Factor theory allows the psychologist to measure an hypothesized, unobserved variable (a "latent" variable) by using a set of observed ("manifest") variables. In a sense, the manifest variables are used to "triangulate" and "locate" the latent variable. Thus, items with differing content can be used to measure the same hypothesized trait or factor. Personality "traits" and ability "factors" are typically measured in this fashion. Furthermore, first-order traits or factors (i.e., derived from sets of items) can be used to measure higher order traits or factors, as was done in the case of the Big Five in personality assessment (Digman, 1990; for a fuller treatment of the "trait" construct, see Tellegen, 1991.)

Latent variables, therefore, are truly "operationally defined" by the manifest variables used to infer and measure them. But latent variables are new variables, different from their constituent manifest variables, and thus should be subjected to the usual psychometric tests of reliability and validity. Counterintuitively, latent variables can be (and often are) more reliable and more valid than the manifest variables used in their measurement, as, for example, in the case of g.

Factor theory is the basis for trait-factor theories of personality (Hall & Lindzey, 1970), such as those of Cattell (1950) and Eysenck (1953). Proponents of such theories propose that factor analysis, a "rational and largely objective procedure," be substituted for the "intuitive and usually unspecified manner" in which most variables in the personality domain have been formulated. They believe that factor analysis is a completely independent and objective means of "confirming or denying" proposed personality traits. Thus, in vocational counseling, trait-and-factor theory substituted "objective procedures" and "factor analytically confirmed traits" for Parsons's largely subjective list of characteristics in self-analysis.

Trait-and-Factor Counseling

Trait-and-factor counseling evolved in four "stages," according to its leading exponent, E. G. Williamson (Williamson & Biggs, 1979). In the first stage, the major concern was for objectivity in differential diagnosis—the key step in counseling—via the development of objective measures of person traits and the commensurate measurement of person and occupation. In the second stage, models for the counseling process were developed and differential diagnosis was extended to include other counselee adjustment problems besides the educational and the vocational. In the third stage, factor analysis was applied extensively to both predictor and criterion data, and new knowledge about traits and factors emerged on which to base counseling. In the fourth stage, trait-and-factor counseling collided with Rogerian counseling, leading to a philosophical and theoretical reexamination of the trait-and-factor approach to counseling. One might now want to add a fifth stage, in which trait-and-factor counseling has evolved into P–E fit counseling (Chartrand, 1991).

Trait-and-factor counseling is founded on four sets of presuppositions (Berdie, 1972; Williamson & Biggs, 1979):

1. Concerning individual differences—that people differ in their standing on any given trait; that a person's standing may differ on different traits; that the duration (and sometimes even sequence) of developmental stages may differ for different individuals; and that even if many people are similar on some traits and some people are similar on many traits, no two individuals—not even identical twins—are the same on all traits. The obvious implication of individual differences is the requirement that counseling has to be individualized, inasmuch as no single approach will work for all (or even most) counselees.

2. Concerning data and research—that decisions and plans made during counseling are only as good as the data that inform such decisions and plans; that the most dependable (reliable, valid) data are those that have been subjected to or are based on scientific research; that research-based data are always to be preferred to speculation or hypothetical construction, no matter how imaginative or intelligent the latter may be; that one of the primary counseling tasks is to gather sufficient relevant data; and that knowing and ascertaining the relevance and dependability of data should be one of the primary skills of the counselor.

3. Concerning measurement—that quantification via measurement does not demean the person but, to the contrary, greatly enhances the ability to describe the person as an individual; that quantification opens the door to the power of mathematical analysis, thus greatly enlarging the capability for differential diagnosis, the key counseling procedure; that the most useful data are obtained through measurement via competently constructed instruments; that state-of-the-art psychological measurement (psychometrics) has demonstrated the superiority of the trait-factor construct over other alternatives; and that training in measurement should be one of the requirements for a professional counselor.

4. Concerning values—that the counselee's values are always to be fully respected; that counseling cannot escape being based on values; and that among the values counseling should be guided by are the following: (a) freedom for individuals, (b) freedom requires opportunity to make choices, and (c) social organization and social

control are required to provide for individual freedom and individual opportunity (Berdie, 1972, p. 9).

Trait-and-factor counseling can be summarized briefly as follows (Williamson & Biggs, 1979):

1. The purpose of counseling is to teach counselees effective decision-making skills. Such skills require accurate self-knowledge and the relating of this self-knowledge to significant social and psychological criteria. Self-knowledge is most accurate when based on scientifically produced information rather than on "common sense."

2. The major counseling "process" occurs in the counseling interview, which has four important uses: collecting information, assessing potentiality, remediating problems, and facilitating development. The counseling process involves cognitive and rational problem solving techniques as well as interpersonal relationship techniques. The basic assumption of trait-and-factor counseling—individual differences—requires individualization of the counseling process. The case study approach helps provide for such individualization.

3. A special feature of trait-and-factor counseling is the use of social comparison to help the counselee gain realistic self-knowledge. Social comparison is effected through the use of "norm" (normative) groups provided in the manuals of well-constructed tests. A crucial task of the counselor is to select the norm groups that are appropriate for the particular counselee. Another important task is to help the counselee "internalize" (understand and accept) social comparison data and integrate them in the counselee's knowledge of self.

4. The goals of counseling differ for each counselee and depend on the particular counselee's needs. The final decision is the counselee's, but the counselor's influence should be used to persuade the counselee in the direction of "arete" as the goal of personal development. "Arete," the conception of excellence or successful performance, is defined by socially significant criteria. Such criteria are formulated by both individual and society—ideally, with both views harmonizing and neither view dominating. Helping the counselee achieve such a balance between individual and social criteria is another important task of the counselor.

About Rogerian Counseling. In the 1950s, trait-and-factor counseling was unfavorably compared with Rogerian counseling (Rogers, 1942, 1951), a development with roots in then-emerging humanistic psychology. Rogerian counseling was "nondirective" compared with "directive" trait-and-factor counseling. Rogerian counseling paid attention to the affective side, whereas trait-and-factor counseling was overly cognitive and rational. Rogerian counseling was "client-centered," implying that trait-and-factor counseling emphasized societal or institutional concerns more than the counselee's needs. Unfortunately, these criticisms were based on erroneous constructions and outright caricatures of trait-and-factor counseling, as Rounds and Tracey (1990) and Chartrand (1991) have so decisively shown.

Like all counseling, Rogerian counseling can be construed from the P–E point of view. The key concept in Rogerian theory is congruence between P—self—and E, the rest of the "phenomenal field" (the person's perception of the situation). In Rogerian counseling, the closer the congruence between P and E, the better the mental health of the person. Mental illness and mental health problems are attributable to a lack of P–E congruence.

From a P–E perspective, it might be said that Rogerian counseling was more concerned about the internal environment, whereas trait-and-factor counseling was more concerned about the external environment. Thus, Rogerian counseling dealt more with the emotive and subjective side of things, and trait-and-factor counseling more with the rational and objective side. Rogerian counseling focused on the person's satisfaction, whereas trait-and-factor counseling focused more on the person's satisfactoriness (the external environment's evaluation of the person).

The two schools held diametrically opposed views about counselee assessment. For Rogerian counseling, assessment was not only unnecessary but worse, destructive of rapport and progress in counseling. For trait-and-factor counseling, differential diagnosis was of the essence. A corollary difference was that Rogerian counseling eschewed the evaluation of counseling outcomes, whereas trait-and-factor counseling considered it indispensable.

P–E Fit Theory

Chartrand (1991) showed how P–E fit theory is a "direct descendant" of trait-and-factor theory. She mentioned three basic assumptions inherited by P–E fit theory from trait-and-factor theory: (a) that people are capable of making rational decisions; (b) that people and environments differ in reliable, meaningful, and consistent ways; and (c) that the greater the "fit" between person and environment, the greater the likelihood of "success." Moreover, according to Chartrand, P–E fit theory has moved beyond simple trait-and-factor "matching" to the view that the P–E encounter is a "dynamic reciprocity."

Two theories best represent P–E fit theory in counseling psychology: the Holland theory (Holland, 1966, 1985) and the theory of work adjustment (Dawis & Lofquist, 1984; Lofquist & Dawis, 1969).

Holland's Theory.   Holland has proposed what is arguably the most robust theory in counseling psychology. The number of research studies supporting this theory runs in the hundreds. The theory's robustness might be attributed in part to its formal simplicity and the consequent ease of putting the theory to the test as well as into practice.

Holland proposed that personality development results in six recognizable personality types, characterized most prominently by their dominant interests, as follows:

1. Realistic—focused primarily on the "real world," the concrete world of things;
2. Investigative—focused primarily on objective facts, fact-finding, and theorizing about facts;
3. Artistic—focused primarily on the aesthetic, appreciation as well as creation;
4. Social—focused primarily on interpersonal relationships, individual as well as group;
5. Enterprising—focused primarily on risk-taking for gain or achievement; and,
6. Conventional—focused primarily on adherence to convention.

These six personality types are related to each other in a manner that can be depicted by a hexagon, with the types arranged around the points of the hexagon in the order given above (R-I-A-S-E-C). Similarity between types is proportional to their distance on the hexagon (i.e., the adjacent types are most similar, the opposite types most dissimilar).

Personality types are to be thought of more as primary than pure (as in colors), so that particular individuals are rarely of purely one type. However, most individuals would manifest a dominant personality type.

Environments are also recognizable in terms of the same six types (called "environmental models") because environments are "shaped" by the persons in them, and "birds of a feather flock together." The "congruence" or interaction between person type and environment model has predictable consequences. High congruence has positive consequences (e.g., stable vocational choice, job satisfaction, good job performance), whereas low congruence has negative consequences (unstable vocational choice, job dissatisfaction, poor job performance).

The above presentation of Holland's theory is necessarily abbreviated and perhaps even oversimplified, but the important point is that it demonstrates the P–E interaction perspective. Although it has been called a trait-and-factor theory (Osipow, 1983), the Holland theory, unlike its trait-and-factor predecessors, is explicit in its espousal of P–E interaction as the basis for behavioral prediction. P–E "congruence" is central to the theory. Reviews of the research supporting the validity of "congruence" as a predictor of socially significant criteria are given in Assouline and Meir (1987) and Spokane (1985), as well as in Holland (1985).

Theory of Work Adjustment.   Lofquist and Dawis, like Holland, were products of the Minnesota trait-and-factor school. Not surprisingly, their theory of work adjustment (TWA) makes ample use of traits and factors, and, like Holland's theory, makes P–E fit the pivotal concept of the theory.

According to TWA, two areas in personality development are basic: the acquisition of response capabilities (crystallized as skills) and of reinforcer requirements (crystallized as needs). Skills and needs are "surface" traits, hence modifiable. They can be referenced (via factor analysis) on more stable "source" traits, identified as abilities and values, respectively. Patterns of abilities and values constitute personality structure, which is typically stable at adulthood. Personality development can also be indexed on time-denominated variables (collectively called personality style), described in terms of the latency, intensity, pattern, and duration of effort or energy deployment. Personality style is usually stable by adulthood.

To enable commensurate measurement, TWA describes environments in terms of skill requirements and reinforcer capabilities (to match up with person skills and needs), ability requirements and reinforcer factors (matching person abilities and values), and environment style variables (matching personality style). P–E fit can thus be evaluated directly from P and E measurements.

Furthermore, TWA focuses on three dependent variables—socially significant criteria—all measured on P. Two of these are judgment variables: satisfaction (P's evaluation of E and the P–E interaction), and satisfactoriness (E's evaluation of P and the P–E interaction). The third is behavioral: tenure (duration of P's stay in E). According to TWA: (a) satisfaction is predicted from value-reinforcer "correspondence" (fit), (b) satisfactoriness is predicted from ability-requirement corrrespondence, and (c) tenure is predicted from satisfaction and satisfactoriness. Research support for these predictions is given in Dawis and Lofquist (1984) and Dawis (1996).

In TWA, "correspondence" (P–E fit) refers to the coresponsiveness of P and E to each other's requirements (Chartrand's [1991] "dynamic reciprocity"). The fundamental TWA proposition is that P seeks to achieve and maintain correspondence with E (and E with P). Lack of correspondence (discorrespondence) is the trigger for adjustment behavior, which is characterized in terms of two thresholds (for starting and stopping adjustment behavior) and two modes (activeness, wherein P effects change in E, and reactiveness, wherein P effects change in P, self). Changes occasioned by adjustment behavior occur at the level of surface traits (skills and needs), usually leaving the source traits (abilities and values) relatively unchanged.

TWA construes the adjustment process as symmetrical: what holds for P also holds for E (e.g., E has thresholds for starting and stopping adjustment and two modes of adjustment). Even the targets for effecting change are symmetrical: requirements and capabilities of P and E. In other words, P–E interaction in TWA is construed as a system (Dawis & Lofquist, 1978), wherein causation is circular rather than linear.

Counseling From a P–E Perspective

As Rounds and Tracy (1990) pointed out, current P–E fit theories are long on content and lean on process. They do not say how counselor–counselee interaction is to take place. To fill this lack, Rounds and Tracy offered a model of the counseling process based on contemporary psychological science literature on problem solving, information processing, and attitude change. The model sees the individual differences assumption as fundamental. This assumption requires that type of intervention be fitted to the counselee (i.e., the P–E fit principle should be used in determining the treatment of choice). In turn, type of intervention is hypothesized to be a function of the counselee's (a) information processing level, (b) motivation level, and (c) level of progress in counseling. For example, counselees with high levels of information processing skills should need no more than simple presentation of information, whereas those with low levels may need "strong supportive" (i.e., directive) counseling; counselees with high motivation levels should be influenced more by the content qualities of the information, whereas those with low levels may be influenced more by "persuasion cues" associated with the information and less by the content's quality.

Lofquist and Dawis (1991) generalized TWA (above) as person–environment-correspondence (PEC) theory and applied it to the counseling process. According to PEC theory, counselee and counselor each have a P–E view of the counseling relationship, wherein each is P to the other as E. Each has requirements (expectations) and capabilities when they enter into the counseling relationship. Fulfillment of their expectations is mirrored in their satisfaction, and although the counselee's satisfaction is the usual focus of attention, the counselor's satisfaction should not be overlooked.

Lofquist and Dawis' PEC-theory model of the counseling process is a learning-reinforcement model (cf. Krumboltz's social learning model; Mitchell & Krumboltz, 1996). The classic S-shaped learning curve describes the process in its idealized form, with a slow rate of progress at the beginning and toward the end of counseling, and the fastest rate in the middle. Reinforcement is the key to counseling progress, with the counselor's main function being to provide reinforcers. (Recall that in TWA-PEC theory, what is reinforcing is determined by the counselee's needs.)

Reinforcement by the counselor may be guided or unguided, depending on whether goal(s) are set. Unguided reinforcement occurs in "nondirective" counseling, where the counselor's task is to provide a safe environment within which the counselee can explore the phenomenal field to arrive at congruence with self. Unconditional positive regard, warmth, and empathy denote the reinforcers the nondirective counselor uses. Guided reinforcement occurs in a problem-solving or skill-learning situation, where the counselor's task is to help the counselee solve a presenting problem—which solution might call for the learning of skills. In this instance, two classes of reinforcers may be used by the counselor: cognitive reinforcers (such as providing information, coaching), and affective reinforcers (providing unconditional positive regard, warmth, and empathy).

PEC theory sees counseling (the process) as a system, in which the feedback provided by E (the other) is evaluated in the satisfaction of P (the counselee or the counselor). The skilled counselor uses cues about the counselee's current satisfaction as guides for directions to take and reinforcers to use. Counselor training should therefore cover how to identify these cues and what responses are appropriate for different cues.

A reciprocal picture can be painted about the counselor's satisfaction and the reinforcements provided by the counselee and the progress of counseling. Such a picture deserves more careful study by counselor educators. It goes without saying that counselor morale and sense of professional accomplishment depend significantly on counselor satisfaction.

A Final Word

Counseling psychology—and its parent field, psychology, as well—have yet to settle down to what Kuhn (1970) has described as the business of doing normal science: filling in the fullness of detail that is characteristic of a mature science. To accomplish this, we require a governing paradigm, something our diverse counseling psychology—and psychology—textbooks unwittingly show is sadly missing. This chapter's account of counseling psychology's development from the "primitive" Parsons formulation to the elaborate P–E interaction model suggests that perhaps P–E theory is the paradigm we require. It is a paradigm that can encompass the many differing theories and the multitude of disparate facts that have characterized counseling psychology—and psychology—to this point. It is a paradigm that can generate the puzzle-solving activity that is the hallmark of normal science. It is a paradigm worth trying.

REFERENCES

Alexander, W. P. (1934). Research in guidance. *Occupations, 12,* 75–91.

Allport, G. W. (1937). *Personality: A psychological interpretation.* New York: Holt.

Assouline, M., & Meir, E. I. (1987). Meta-analysis of the relationship between congruence and well-being measures. *Journal of Vocational Behavior, 31,* 319–332.

Bem, D. J., & Allen, A. (1974). On predicting some of the people some of the time: The search for cross-situational consistencies in behavior. *Psychological Review, 81,* 506–520.

Berdie, R. F. (1972). Differential psychology as a basis of counseling. *The Counseling Psychologist, 3,* 76–81.

Binet, A., & Simon, T. (1908). The development of intelligence in children. Reprinted in J. J. Jenkins & D. G. Paterson (1961), *Studies in individual differences* (pp. 81–111). New York: Appleton-Century-Crofts.

Bowers, K. S. (1973). Situationism in psychology: An analysis and critique. *Psychological Review, 80,* 307–336.

Brewer, J. M. (1942). *History of vocational guidance.* New York: Harper & Row.

Cattell, R. B. (1950). *Personality: A systematic, theoretical, and factual study.* New York: McGraw-Hill.

Chartrand, J. M. (1991). The evolution of trait-and-factor career counseling: A person x environment fit approach. *Journal of Counseling & Development, 69,* 518–524.

Dawis, R. V. (1991). Vocational interests, values, and preferences. In M. D. Dunnette & L. M. Hough (Eds.), *Handbook of industrial & organizational psychology* (2nd ed., Vol. 2, pp. 833–871). Palo Alto, CA: Consulting Psychologists Press.

Dawis, R. V. (1992). The individual differences tradition in counseling psychology. *Journal of Counseling Psychology, 39,* 7–19.

Dawis, R. V. (1996). The theory of work adjustment and person–environment-correspondence counseling. In D. Brown & L. Brooks (Eds.), *Career choice and development* (3rd ed., pp. 75–120). San Francisco: Jossey-Bass.

Dawis, R. V., & Lofquist, L. H. (1978). A note on the dynamics of work adjustment. *Journal of Vocational Behavior, 12,* 76–79.

Dawis, R. V., & Lofquist, L. H. (1984). *A psychological theory of work adjustment.* Minneapolis: University of Minnesota.

Digman, J. M. (1990). Personality structure: Emergence of the five-factor model. *Annual Review of Psychology, 41,* 417–440.

DuBois, P. H. (1970). *A history of psychological testing.* Boston: Allyn & Bacon.

Dvorak, B. J. (1935). Differential occupational ability patterns. *Employment Stabilization Research Institute Bulletin, 3* (Whole No. 8). Minneapolis: University of Minnesota.

Epstein, S., & O'Brien, E. J. (1985). The person–situation debate in historical and current perspective. *Psychological Bulletin, 98,* 513–537.

Eysenck, H. J. (1953). *The structure of human personality.* New York: Wiley.

Guilford, J. P. (1954). *Psychometric methods.* New York: McGraw-Hill.

Gulliksen, H. (1950). *Theory of mental tests.* New York, Wiley.

Hall, C. S., & Lindzey, G. (1970). *Theories of personality.* New York: Wiley.

Harman, H. H. (1967). *Modern factor analysis.* Chicago: University of Chicago.

Harmon, L. W., Hansen, J. C., Borgen, F. H., & Hammer, A. L. (1994). *Strong Interest Inventory applications and technical guide.* Stanford, CA: Stanford University.

Holland, J. L. (1966). *The psychology of vocational choice.* Waltham, MA: Blaisdell.

Holland, J. L. (1985). *Making vocational choices* (2nd ed.). Englewood Cliffs, NJ: Prentice-Hall.

Hollingworth, H. L. (1923). *Judging human character.* New York: Appleton.

Hull, C. L. (1943). *Principles of behavior.* New York: Appleton-Century-Crofts.

Kenrick, D. T., & Funder, D. C. (1988). Profiting from controversy: Lessons from the person–situation debate. *American Psychologist, 43,* 23–34.

Kuder, F. (1977). *Activity interests and occupational choice.* Chicago: Science Research Associates.

Kuder, F., & Zytowski, D. G. (1991). *Kuder Occupational Interest Survey general manual.* Monterey, CA: CTB/McGraw-Hill.

Kuhn, T. S. (1970). *The structure of scientific revolutions* (2nd ed.). Chicago: University of Chicago.

Lewin, K. (1936). *Principles of topological psychology.* New York: McGraw-Hill.

Lofquist, L. H., & Dawis, R. V. (1969). *Adjustment to work.* New York: Appleton-Century-Crofts.

Lofquist, L. H., & Dawis, R. V. (1991). *Essentials of person–environment-correspondence counseling.* Minneapolis: University of Minnesota.

Magnusson, D., & Engler, N. S. (1977). *Personality at the crossroads: Current issues in interactional psychology.* Hillsdale, NJ: Lawrence Erlbaum Associates.

Mischel, W. (1968). *Personality and assessment.* New York: Wiley.

Mitchell, L. K., & Krumboltz, J. D. (1996). Krumboltz's learning theory of career choice and counseling. In D. Brown & L. Brooks (Eds.), *Career choice and development* (pp. 233–280). San Francisco: Jossey-Bass.

Murray, H. A. (and collaborators). (1938). *Explorations in personality.* New York: Oxford.

Osipow, S. H. (1983). *Theories of career development.* Englewood Cliffs, NJ: Prentice-Hall.

Parsons, F. (1909). *Choosing a vocation.* Boston: Houghton Mifflin.

Paterson, D. G. (1938). The genesis of modern guidance. *Educational Record, 29,* 36–46.

Rogers, C. R. (1942). *Counseling and psychotherapy: Newer concepts in practice.* Boston: Houghton Mifflin.

Rogers, C. R. (1951). *Client-centered therapy: Its current practice, implications, and theory.* Boston: Houghton Mifflin.

Rounds, J. B., & Tracey, T. J. (1990). From trait-and-factor to person–environment fit counseling: Theory and process. In W. B. Walsh & S. H. Osipow (Eds.). *Career counseling: Contemporary topics in vocational psychology* (pp. 1–44). Hillsdale, NJ: Lawrence Erlbaum Associates.

Savickas, M. L. (1993). Career counseling in the postmodern era. *Journal of Cognitive Psychotherapy, 7,* 205–215.

Schmidt, F. L., & Hunter, J. E. (1977). Development of a general solution to the problem of validity generalization. *Journal of Applied Psychology, 62,* 529–540.

Schmidt, F. L., Hunter, J. E., & Pearlman, K. (1981). Task differences and validity of aptitude tests in selection: A red herring. *Journal of Applied Psychology, 66,* 166–185.

Skinner, B. F. (1938). *The behavior of organisms.* New York: Appleton-Century-Crofts.

Spearman, C. (1904a). The proof and measurement of association between two things. *American Journal of Psychology, 15,* 72–101.

Spearman, C. (1904b). "General intelligence," objectively determined and measured. *American Journal of Psychology, 15,* 201–292.

Spokane, A. R. (1985). A review of research on person-environment congruence in Holland's theory of careers. *Journal of Vocational Behavior, 26,* 306–343.

Strong, E. K. Jr. (1943). *Vocational interests of men and women.* Stanford, CA: Stanford University.

Strong, E. K. Jr. (1955). *Vocational interests 18 years after college.* Minneapolis: University of Minnesota.

Super, D. E. (1955). Transition from vocational guidance to counseling psychology. *Journal of Counseling Psychology, 2,* 3–9.

Tellegen, A. (1991). Personality traits: Issues of definition, evidence,and assessment. In W. M. Grove & D. Cicchetti (Eds.), *Thinking clearly about psychology: Vol. 2: Personality and psychopathology* (pp. 10–35). Minneapolis: University of Minnesota.

Tolman, E. C. (1932). *Purposive behavior in animals and men.* New York: Appleton-Century-Crofts.

Trabue, M. R. (1933). Occupational ability patterns. *Personnel Journal, 11,* 344–351.

U.S. Department of Labor (1970). *Manual for the USES General Aptitude Test Battery.* Washington, DC: U.S. Government Printing Office.

Viteles, M. S. (1932). *Industrial psychology.* New York: Norton.

Viteles, M. S. (1936). A dynamic criterion. *Occupations, 14,* 963–967.

Whitely, J. M. (1984). Counseling psychology: A historical perspective. *The Counseling Psychologist, 12,* 3–109.

Williamson, E. G. (1965). *Vocational counseling: Some historical, philosophical, and theoretical perspectives.* New York: McGraw-Hill.

Williamson, E. G., & Biggs, D. A. (1979). Trait-factor theory and individual differences. In H. M. Burks, Jr. & B. Stefflre. *Theories of counseling* (3rd. ed.) (pp. 91–131). New York: McGraw-Hill.

Williamson, E. G., & Bordin, E. S. (1941). A statistical evaluation of clinical counseling. *Educational and Psychological Measurement, 1,* 117–132.

Zytowski, D. G. (1976a). Predictive validity of the Kuder Occupational Interest Survey: A 12- to 19-year follow-up. *Journal of Counseling Psychology, 23,* 221–233.

Zytowski, D. G. (1976b). Long-term profile stability of the Kuder Occupational Interest Survey. *Educational and Psychological Measurement, 36,* 689–692.

6

Community-Based Treatment of Serious Antisocial Behavior in Adolescents

Charles M. Borduin
Naamith Heiblum
Michael R. Jones
Shelly A. Grabe
University of Missouri-Columbia

Violent criminal acts and other serious crimes (i.e., index offenses) perpetrated by adolescents present significant problems at several levels of analysis, and these problems argue for the development of effective treatment approaches. On a personal level, adolescents who commit serious crimes experience numerous psychosocial problems as well as reduced educational and occupational opportunities (Melton & Pagliocca, 1992). Moreover, serious antisocial behavior by adolescents has extremely negative emotional, physical, and economic effects on victims, victims' families, and the larger community (Gottfredson, 1989; Miller, Cohen, & Rossman, 1993). Therefore, effective treatment may not only benefit the youth and his or her family, but may also save many persons from victimization.

On an epidemiological level, adolescents, especially boys, account for a disproportionately high percentage of the arrests for violent and other serious crimes (Federal Bureau of Investigation, 1996), and such arrests greatly underestimate the prevalence of adolescent criminal activity (Elliott, Dunford, & Huizinga, 1987; Loeber, Farrington, & Waschbusch, 1998). In addition, although serious juvenile offenders and their families constitute a relatively small percentage of the population, they account for a large percentage of a community's crime (Farrington, Ohlin, & Wilson, 1986; Loeber et al., 1998; Moffitt, 1993). Thus, if one purpose of treating juvenile offenders is to decrease crime, then serious juvenile offenders and their families are a logical target for intervention efforts.

On a social services level, antisocial adolescents consume much of the resources of the child mental health, juvenile justice, and special education systems (Robins, 1981; Stouthamer-Loeber, Loeber, & Thomas, 1992) and are overrepresented in the "deep end" of these systems (Melton, Lyons, & Spaulding, 1998), with considerable cost to the public treasury and intrusion on family integrity and youth autonomy. Moreover, antisocial youths often have continued contact with the mental health and criminal justice systems well into adulthood (Borduin & Schaeffer, 1998; Kazdin, 1995). Therefore, the development of effective treatments for youth criminal activity may help to free resources to address other important problems of children and their families.

Unfortunately, as numerous reviewers have concluded (e.g., Borduin, 1994; Henggeler, 1989; Lipsey, 1992; Mulvey, Arthur, & Reppucci, 1993), the development of effective treatments for serious antisocial behavior in adolescents has been an extremely difficult task. In part, this difficulty is due to the fact that serious antisocial behaviors, especially those involving aggression, tend to be highly stable in individuals (Kratzer & Hodgins, 1997; Loeber, 1982) and across generations (Huesmann, Lefkowitz, Eron, & Walder, 1984). However, an even more important reason for the general lack of effective interventions for violence and criminality in adolescents is that the treatments now typically available in the juvenile justice and mental health systems do not address the multiple and changing needs of these youth. Indeed, such treatments are generally individually oriented and delivered in settings that bear little relation to the problems being addressed (e.g., group home, training school, psychiatric hospital). Clearly, there is a pressing need to develop effective alternatives to the restrictive and narrowly focused practices that currently dominate mental health interventions for serious juvenile offenders.

The purpose of this chapter is to review some promising models of treatment that can guide the development of effective mental health interventions for serious antisocial behavior in adolescents. Each of these treatment models (or approaches) is community-based and, as such, devotes at least some attention to ameliorating the real-world environmental conditions that led to the youth's antisocial behavior. Although a large number of treatment approaches have been used with juvenile offenders in community settings (see Mulvey et al., 1993), this chapter examines the most promising approaches and conveys what is known about their effectiveness.

As a starting place for consideration of the treatment needs of juvenile offenders and their families, the following section provides a brief review of empirical findings regarding the correlates and causes of violent (e.g., forcible rape, robbery, aggravated assault) and other serious antisocial behaviors (e.g., burglary, motor vehicle theft, arson) in adolescents. Five promising models of community-based treatment for serious antisocial behavior in adolescents are then described. Finally, key issues related to the design and implementation of effective treatments for juvenile offenders are discussed.

CORRELATES AND CAUSES
OF SERIOUS ANTISOCIAL BEHAVIOR

A large number of studies have evaluated correlates of antisocial and violent behavior in adolescents (for reviews, see Henggeler, 1989; Kazdin, 1995; Ollendick, 1996; Thornberry, Huizinga, & Loeber, 1995). In general, these correlates pertain to the individual adolescent and to the key social systems (family, peer, school, neighborhood) in which the adolescent is embedded. A number of other studies have evaluated multidimensional causal models of serious antisocial behavior in adolescents. This section reviews the major findings that have emerged in these areas of research.

Individual Adolescent Characteristics

There is a substantial body of empirical research showing that antisocial and aggressive behaviors in adolescents are associated with lower IQ scores, even after controlling for race, social class, and test motivation (Lynam, Moffitt, & Stouthamer-Loeber, 1993; Stattin & Klackenberg-Larsson, 1993). Research also suggests that there is a substantial discrepancy between the performance IQs and verbal IQs of antisocial adolescents, and that the association between anti-social behavior and overall IQ is due to the relatively low verbal IQs of these adolescents (Quay, 1987). Although some researchers have observed an association between the size of the performance IQ/verbal IQ discrepancy and the seriousness of antisocial behavior in adolescents (e.g., Walsh, Petee, & Beyer, 1987), other researchers have not found such an association (e.g., Cornell & Wilson, 1992; Tarter, Hegedus, Alterman, & Katz-Garris, 1983).

The association of low verbal IQ with antisocial and aggressive behavior might be a result of the linkage between low verbal IQ and the delayed development of higher order cognitive abilities. For ex-ample, researchers have concluded that delinquent youths in gen-eral, and aggressive delinquent youths in particular, have lower moral reasoning maturity than do nondelinquent youths (e.g., Arbuthnot, Gordon, & Jurkovic, 1987; Astor & Behre, 1997), and that aggressive youths have poorer abstract reasoning and prob-lem-solving abilities than do nonaggressive youths (e.g., Dunn, Lochman, & Colder, 1997; Seguin, Pihl, Harden, Tremblay, & Boulerice, 1995).

Researchers have also suggested that social skills deficits are linked with aggressive behavior in adolescents. However, in a re-view of this literature, Henggeler (1989) concluded that findings have been inconsistent, especially when the influences of mediating factors such as IQ are considered. In contrast, studies of sociocognitive deficits in aggressive adolescents and adolescent vio-lent offenders (for reviews, see Akhtar & Bradley, 1991; Crick & Dodge, 1994) have consistently found evidence of hostile attributional biases (i.e., a propensity to infer hostile intentions in ambiguous interpersonal situations). The association between hos-tile attributional biases and aggressive behavior seems to be inde-pendent of verbal IQ, social class, or race (see Dodge, Price, Bachorowski, & Newman, 1990; Graham, Hudley, & Williams, 1992). Interestingly, there is growing evidence that mothers of ag-gressive boys share the propensity to infer hostility in ambiguous situations and may, in effect, model a hostile attributional bias for their sons (e.g., Bickett, Milich, & Brown, 1996; Dix & Lochman, 1990; MacKinnon-Lewis et al., 1994).

Family Relations

Research suggests that the family relations of violent juvenile offenders are more disturbed than the family relations of nonviolent juvenile offenders or nonoffenders. Indeed, a number of studies have demonstrated that violent juvenile offending is associated with low levels of family warmth and cohesion (e.g., Blaske, Borduin, Henggeler, & Mann, 1989; Borduin & Henggeler, 1987) and high rates of marital and family conflict (e.g., Borduin, Pruitt, & Henggeler, 1986; Mann, Borduin, Henggeler, & Blaske, 1990). Likewise, studies using community samples have found that adolescent self-reported antisocial and violent behavior is linked with low parental affection and family cohesion (Gorman-Smith, Tolan, Zelli, & Huesmann, 1996; Haapasalo & Tremblay, 1994; Loeber & Schmaling, 1985; Olweus, 1980; Patterson & Stouthamer-Loeber, 1984) and high family and marital conflict (Jouriles, Bourg, & Farris, 1991; Tolan & Lorion 1988). Evidence also suggests that affective relations in families of female serious juvenile offenders may be even more dysfunctional than those in families of male offenders (e.g., Henggeler, Edwards, & Borduin, 1987).

Lax and ineffective parental discipline (see Henggeler, 1989; Snyder & Patterson, 1987; Weiss, Dodge, Bates, & Pettit, 1992) and poor parental monitoring (Gorman-Smith et al., 1996) have also been linked consistently with aggression and delinquency in adolescents. However, whether these parenting practices lead to aggressive and antisocial behavior or are the result of such behavior is unclear. Indeed, longitudinal research (Vuchinich, Bank, & Patterson, 1992) with preadolescent boys and their parents has indicated bidirectional effects between parental discipline practices and youth antisocial behavior (also see Lytton, 1990; Rutter, 1994).

The effects of witnessing or experiencing family violence on the development of aggressive and antisocial behavior in adolescents have received considerable attention from researchers. Studies suggest that violent delinquent adolescents are more likely to have been physically abused by a parent or to have witnessed violence between their parents than are nonviolent or nondelinquent adolescents (for reviews, see Smith & Thornberry, 1995; Widom, 1989). Studies also suggest that the chronicity of family violence is more strongly linked to later aggression in youths than is the severity of the violence (Widom, 1989). Further research is needed to identify whether the relation of family violence to adolescents' aggressive criminal behavior is direct or is moderated by a third variable known to be associated with adolescent aggression (e.g., parental rejection).

Peer Relations

Peer relations are important to psychosocial development because they provide adolescents with a sense of belonging, emotional support, and behavioral norms. Within peer groups of many adolescent offenders, the sense of belonging and emotional support are evident; however, the group behavioral norms often conflict with societal norms. Moreover, criminal activity, including violence, often serves an adaptive function for these adolescents because it can be collaborative and can elicit continued peer support and acceptance. In fact, a high percentage of assaultive behavior is carried out with peers (Dishion, Eddy, Haas, Li, & Spracklen, 1997; Elliott, 1994; Emler, Reicher, & Ross, 1987; Strasburg, 1978), and the youth's involvement with deviant peers is a powerful predictor of both the frequency and the seriousness of his or her antisocial behavior (e.g., Hanson, Henggeler, Haefele, & Rodick, 1984; Lyon, Henggeler, & Hall, 1992; Smith, Visher, & Jarjoura, 1991; White, Pandina, & LaGrange, 1987).

Although involvement with deviant peers can contribute to serious antisocial behavior, positive family relations and prosocial peer support tend to mitigate the negative effects of deviant peers. For example, Poole and Rigoli (1979) found that high involvement with delinquent peers was strongly predictive of criminal activity under conditions of low family support but only slightly predictive of criminal activity under conditions of high family support; boys who had highly delinquent friends and nonsupportive family relations reported 500% more criminal activity than did boys with highly delinquent friends and supportive family relations. Similarly, other researchers (e.g., Dishion, Patterson, Stoolmiller, & Skinner, 1991) have reported that high levels of parental discipline skill and monitoring can also buffer the negative effects of youth involvement with deviant peers.

School and Academic Performance

Poor school performance (e.g., low grades, special class placement, general reading problems, retention, suspension) and subsequent dropping out of high school have been consistently linked with aggressive behavior (see Hinshaw, 1992) and serious delinquency (see Chavez, Oetting, & Swaim, 1994; Elliott & Voss, 1974). Furthermore, this linkage seems to be independent of pertinent mediating variables such as conduct problems during childhood (Maughan, Gray, & Rutter, 1985) and IQ (Berrueta-Clement, Schweinhart, Barnett, & Weikart, 1987). Academic underachievement and dropping out of school have also been associated with higher rates of criminal activity during early adulthood (e.g., Farrington, 1989; Thornberry, Moore, & Christenson, 1985).

School characteristics also can contribute to serious antisocial behavior. Hellman and Beaton (1986) reported that violent and other antisocial behavior in junior high schools was related to low student attendance and to high student–teacher ratios; violent and antisocial behavior in senior high schools was associated with instability in the student population (i.e., high rates of transfers and new admissions) and with poor academic quality of the school. These relations between school characteristics and in-school antisocial behaviors emerged even after controlling for crime rates in the local communities. Furthermore, organizational aspects of schools, such as inconsistent discipline practices (Mayer, 1995) and unfair school policies (Hawkins & Lamb, 1987), have also been linked with serious antisocial behavior in adolescents.

Neighborhood Context

There is a small but growing empirical literature regarding the influence of neighborhood context on the criminal activity of individual adolescents. One of the most consistent findings in this literature is that witnessing community violence (i.e., seeing someone being shot, stabbed, robbed, or physically assaulted) is positively related to violent criminal behavior in adolescents (DuRant, Cadenhead, Pendergrast, Slavens, & Linder, 1994; Farrell & Bruce, 1997; Fitzpatrick & Boldizar, 1993; Webster, Gainer, & Champion, 1993). Indeed, in neighborhoods with higher rates of crime, youths are more likely to be exposed to a criminal subculture in which adult modeling of violent or other serious antisocial behaviors (Simcha-Fagan & Schwartz, 1986) and ready access to weapons (Webster et al., 1993) and drugs (Burkstein, 1994; Moss & Kirisci, 1995) can contribute to youth involvement in criminal activity. Youths living in high-crime areas are also frequent victims of community violence, and such victimization has been linked to involvement in violent antisocial behaviors (DuRant et al., 1994; Farrell & Bruce, 1997; Fitzpatrick & Boldizar, 1993; Malik, Sorenson, & Aneshensel, 1997).

Multidimensional Causal Models

Although the studies cited here have contributed significantly to our understanding of the different factors associated with serious antisocial behaviors in adolescents, it should be noted that these studies generally possess three important methodological limitations. First, in light of the correlational nature of the studies, it is impossible to determine whether the observed correlates lead to the antisocial behavior, whether the antisocial behavior lead to the correlates, or whether the association is reciprocal. For example, does parental rejection lead to antisocial behavior, does antisocial behavior lead to parental rejection, or are parental rejection and antisocial behavior part of a reciprocal causal structure, mutually influencing one another over time? Second, the association between a particular psychosocial variable and antisocial behavior may be spurious (i.e., the result of their joint association with a third variable). For example, low levels of sociomoral reasoning may be linked with aggression because both sociomoral reasoning and aggression are associated with authoritarian discipline strategies. Third, most of the extant studies have tapped only a small subset of the correlates of antisocial behavior. Thus, it is not possible to examine the interrelations among the correlates of antisocial behavior to determine which variables have direct versus indirect effects on such behavior, or which variables are no longer linked with antisocial behavior when the effects of other correlates are controlled.

To address the inherent limitations of correlational research, several research groups have developed empirically based multidimensional causal models of serious antisocial behavior in adolescents.

For example, Elliott, Huizinga, and Ageton (1985) used a longitudinal design with a representative national sample of adolescents (N = 1,725) to assess the psychosocial determinants of delinquent behavior, including violent and other serious crimes. Path analyses showed that serious delinquency (i.e., index offenses) at Time 1 and involvement with delinquent peers at Time 2 (1 year later) had direct effects on serious delinquent behavior at Time 2, especially for males. In addition, serious delinquent behavior at Time 2 was predicted indirectly by family difficulties and school difficulties, which predicted involvement with delinquent peers. Similarly, in a cross-sectional study using 553 male adolescents and their mothers drawn from 12 New York City neighborhoods, Simcha-Fagan and Schwartz (1986) found that association with delinquent peers, school attachment, neighborhood criminal subculture, and age had direct effects on severe self-reported delinquent behavior (including violent crime). Furthermore, family residential stability, neighborhood organizational participation, and neighborhood residential stability had indirect effects on severe delinquency through their direct association with school attachment. These and other causal modeling studies (e.g., Simons, Johnson, Beaman, Conger, & Whitbeck, 1996) provide consistent support for the view that variance in violent and other serious antisocial behavior is contributed to directly or indirectly by variables at the individual, family, peer, school, and community levels.

It is logical to conclude from the results of the causal modeling studies that serious antisocial behavior in adolescents is multidetermined. It is important to recognize, however, that the determinants of serious antisocial behaviors probably vary according to the developmental stage of the adolescent. For example, individual (e.g., hostile attributional biases) and family (e.g., parental rejection, low family cohesion) variables may represent key determinants of the onset of violent criminal activity among younger adolescents, whereas peer (e.g., association with deviant peers) and school (e.g., low achievement, dropping out) variables may be linked more strongly with continued participation and even escalation in violent criminal activity in middle and later adolescence. Indeed, in a cross-sectional study that included community samples of 12-year-old (n = 122), 15-year-old (n = 138), and 18-year-old (n = 81) boys, LaGrange and White (1985) found considerable differences between age groups in the strengths of the predictors of delinquent behavior. Although the samples in this study were quite small and included few serious offenders, the findings suggest that age is an important mediating variable that should be considered in the development of future causal models of adolescent criminal activity.

PROMISING MODELS
OF COMMUNITY-BASED TREATMENT

The preceding review has several important implications for the development of effective treatments of serious antisocial behavior in adolescents. First, the multicausal nature of serious antisocial behavior suggests that treatments should be comprehensive enough to address the major correlates or determinants of such behavior (e.g., adolescent cognitions, family relations, peer relations, school performance, neighborhood factors). Second, because the psychosocial determinants of serious antisocial behavior can vary on a case by case basis, the nature and intensity of interventions should be individualized and flexible. Third, to optimize the ecological validity of interventions, treatments should be delivered directly within the community-based settings (home, school, neighborhood) that comprise the youth's natural environment and that contribute to serious antisocial behavior.

The following review examines several promising models of community-based treatment for juvenile offenders. Although each of these models has wide appeal, few incorporate each of the aforementioned implications. Thus, it is not surprising that most of the treatments have had little demonstrated success in reducing long-term rates of serious antisocial behavior in adolescents. On the other hand, Multisystemic Therapy, a broad-based and multifaceted treatment approach, has recently demonstrated considerable success in decreasing rates of criminality and violence in adolescents.

Behavioral Parent Training

Behavioral parent training (BPT), or parent management training (see Kazdin, 1998), has been widely used in mental health, social service, and juvenile justice systems in the treatment of youth antisocial behavior (see Serketich & Dumas, 1996). Most BPT programs are based on the assumption that youths' problem behaviors are developed and maintained by inconsistent and unpredictable contingencies provided by parents (Patterson, 1982; Patterson, Reid, & Dishion, 1992). BPT targets those parent behaviors (e.g., poor monitoring) and parent–child interchanges (e.g., coercive discipline) that have been empirically demonstrated to cause or contribute to youth antisocial behavior, and parents are trained to identify, monitor, and respond to the youth's problem behaviors in new ways (Bank, Marlowe, Reid, Patterson, & Weinrott, 1991; Serketich & Dumas, 1996). BPT programs can vary considerably in length (i.e., from less than 10 hours up to 50 or 60 hours) and are usually conducted in an outpatient setting with the parents, who are trained to implement the prescribed procedures at home with the child (Kazdin, 1998).

Although BPT has demonstrated much success in treating aggressive and antisocial behavior in younger children and preadolescents (Miller & Prinz, 1990; Serketich & Dumas, 1996), results regarding its effectiveness in modifying adolescent problem behaviors and parent–adolescent relations have been inconsistent (Serketich & Dumas, 1996). Moreover, no studies have demonstrated the effectiveness of BPT in reducing the short- or long-term arrest rates of serious juvenile offenders (see Bank et al., 1991). Perhaps this is because BPT does not typically address the multiple risk factors (e.g., marital discord, parent psychopathology, socioeconomic disadvantage) that are associated with adolescent behavior problems. As Kazdin (1995, 1997) and others (e.g., Forehand & Kotchick, 1996; Serketich & Dumas, 1996) noted, efforts to address parent and family dysfunction during BPT might lead to improved treatment outcomes with youth characterized by many risk factors. Clinical trials are needed to evaluate this possibility.

Functional Family Therapy

Functional Family Therapy (FFT; Alexander, Holtzworth- Munroe, & Jameson, 1994; Alexander & Parsons, 1982) emphasizes a family systems perspective in which adolescent behavior problems are assumed to reflect maladaptive transactional patterns between family members. Through an integration of cognitive, systems, and behavioral treatment approaches, FFT helps family members to recognize the maladaptive interactions that sustain the adolescent's problem behavior and to develop more constructive communication and support patterns. Treatment sessions include all family members so that the therapist can observe and directly alter maladaptive interaction patterns and reinforce new adaptive ways of responding. Although FFT was originally developed as a clinic-based treatment approach, the model has since been adapted for home-based treatment of juvenile offenders (e.g., Gordon, Arbuthnot, Gustafson, & McGreen, 1988).

The first major evaluation of FFT was a randomized, controlled clinical trial with adolescents who had committed status offenses (i.e., mild delinquent behaviors such as staying out late, not attending school, and running away); results showed that FFT led to improved family relations following treatment and to lower recidivism for status offenses, but not criminal offenses, at a 6- to 18-month follow-up (Alexander & Parsons, 1973; Parsons & Alexander, 1973). More recently, quasi-experimental studies with significant methodological shortcomings (e.g., small sample sizes, nonrandom assignment of participants to treatment and control groups) have supported the effectiveness of FFT in reducing serious antisocial behavior at 15-month (Barton, Alexander, Waldron, Turner, & Warburton, 1985), 28-month (Gordon et al., 1988), and 64-month (Gordon, Graves, & Arbuthnot, 1995) follow-ups. However, controlled evaluations of short- and long-term outcomes must be conducted before more definite conclusions can be drawn about the efficacy of FFT with serious juvenile offenders.

Individualized/Wraparound Care

Although there have been numerous examples of interagency collaboration in the treatment of juvenile offenders since the 1970s, these examples usually involve efforts to "fit" youth into some combination of available programs (or components) and tend to ignore youth needs not addressed by existing services (see Melton & Pagliocca, 1992). However, a newer and more promising model of interagency collaboration, known as "individualized care" or "wraparound services," involves a commitment to complete flexibility in arranging treatment and other services for individual youth and their families (Burchard & Clarke, 1990; Lourie, Katz-Leavy, & Stroul, 1996). In this model, an interdisciplinary team (comprised of the youth, parents, and agency representatives) develops a service plan that addresses both the short- and long-term needs of the youth and family, and service providers are selected on the basis of their ability to meet these needs. Moreover, the team modifies and redesigns the service plan to address changing needs of the individual youth and family. Thus, unlike component service models, which tend to be time limited and lack flexibility, individualized care or wraparound services is intended to provide integrated services to the youth and family for as long as needed.

One notable example of the individualized care/wraparound services model is the Alaska Youth Initiative (AYI; Burchard, Burchard, Sewell, & VanDenBerg, 1993; Melton & Pagliocca, 1992). The AYI evolved from a component services model to an integrative model of care in an effort to better serve adjudicated delinquent youths in their own communities and to prevent out-of-home placements. The principal features of the AYI are as follows (Melton & Pagliocca, 1992):

- Building and maintaining normative lifestyles.
- Ensuring that services are client-centered.
- Providing unconditional care.
- Planning for the long term.
- Working toward lesser restrictive alternatives.
- Achieving provider competencies.
- Maintaining consensus among key decision makers.
- Funding services with flexible budgets.
- Installing a gatekeeper function.
- Developing measurable accountability.

The AYI possesses the flexibility that is needed to address the many factors that may contribute to a given youth's antisocial behavior. Indeed, when relevant interventions do not already exist, the needed services are developed and funded. Moreover, AYI treatment and other needed services are intensive and implemented in the youth's own community. The selection of competent service providers and the emphasis on provider accountability (accomplished through routine monitoring of the performance of service vendors) are also significant features of the AYI.

Available data on referral patterns in the AYI indicate that the project has helped reduce the number of youths placed in residential settings (e.g., psychiatric hospitals or correctional facilities) and increase the number of youths served in their own homes or specialized foster care (Child Welfare League of America, 1992). Nevertheless, controlled evaluations of short- and long-term outcomes are needed before more definite conclusions can be drawn about the efficacy of the AYI or other examples of the individualized care/wraparound services model (e.g., the Vermont Wraparound Care Initiative; Burchard & Clarke, 1990; Yoe, Santarcangelo, Atkins, & Burchard, 1996). In addition, further elaboration of service-planning decisions, treatment methods, and measures of treatment adherence will be needed before this flexible, broad-based model of service coordination and delivery can be replicated and evaluated by other researchers (also see Clarke & Clarke, 1996; Rosenblatt, 1996).

Family Ties

Family Ties is an intensive family preservation program that targets juvenile offenders who are at imminent risk for out-of-home placement. Based on the Homebuilders model (Kinney, Haapala, & Booth, 1991), the program was initially created in 1989 by the New York Department of Juvenile Justice in Brooklyn Family Court and has since been expanded to other family courts in Manhattan, the Bronx, and Queens (New York Department of Juvenile Justice, 1990a; Robison & Binder, 1993; Soler, 1992).

Family Ties includes individualized ecological interventions that are intensive, flexible, time limited, and goal oriented. If the youth is eligible and the family agrees to participate, a family preservationist is assigned to work with the family for a minimum of 10 to 15 hours per week, over a period of 4 to 6 weeks. Each family preservationist has a caseload of two families and is expected to provide case coverage 24-hours a day, 7-days a week. Treatment is delivered in natural settings (home, school, or neighborhood) and usually includes individual and family counseling with the offenders and their parents to manage stress, resolve extant crises, and improve parental monitoring. Interventions are also provided to address concrete needs related to child care, education, employment, and housing. At the end of treatment, a judge evaluates the progress of the youth and family and decides whether the youth should be placed on probation or in a New York State Division for Youth facility.

Initial studies indicated that approximately 70% of the graduates of the Family Ties program had avoided subsequent institutional placement, which represented an annual cost savings of about $62,500 per youth (New York Department of Juvenile Justice, 1990a, 1990b; Robison & Binder, 1993). Although these initial findings are encouraging, it would be misleading to draw more than tentative conclusions about the effectiveness of the Family Ties program in the absence of supporting evidence from controlled (i.e., using random assignment to treatment conditions) clinical trials. Indeed, controlled studies with samples of behavior problem and delinquent adolescents have failed to support the long-term efficacy of the Homebuilders model (the prototype for Family Ties) as compared to traditional community services (for a review, see Fraser, Nelson, & Rivard, 1997). Thus, claims of program effectiveness must be viewed cautiously.

Multisystemic Therapy

Multisystemic Therapy (MST; Borduin & Henggeler, 1990; Henggeler & Borduin, 1990) is an intensive, time-limited treatment approach that is predicated on a social-ecological (Bronfenbrenner, 1979) view of behavior, in which criminal behavior is maintained by characteristics of the individual youth and the key social systems in which youths are embedded (i.e., family, peer, school, neighborhood). Importantly, MST interventions are consistent with findings from causal models of serious antisocial behavior and, as such, are designed to address a broad range of factors that may contribute to identified problems. Using treatment strategies derived from strategic family therapy (Haley, 1987), structural family therapy (Minuchin, 1974), behavioral parent training (Schaefer & Briesmeister, 1989), and cognitive-behavioral therapy (Braswell & Bloomquist, 1991), MST directly addresses intrapersonal, familial, and extrafamilial factors that are known to be associated with adolescent criminality and violence. Because different combinations of these factors are relevant for different adolescents, MST interventions are individualized and highly flexible. Moreover, to optimize the ecological validity of interventions, MST is conducted directly in the natural ecologies (home, school, neighborhood) of the youth and family.

The nine treatment principles listed below serve as general guidelines for designing MST interventions. Detailed descriptions of these principles, and examples that illustrate the translation of these principles into specific intervention strategies, are provided in a clinical volume (Henggeler & Borduin, 1990) and a treatment manual (Henggeler, Schoenwald, Borduin, Rowland, & Cunningham, 1998).

1. The primary purpose of assessment is to understand the "fit" between the identified problems and their broader systemic context.
2. Therapeutic contacts emphasize the positive and use systemic strengths as levers for change.
3. Interventions are designed to promote responsible behavior and decrease irresponsible behavior among family members.
4. Interventions are present focused and action oriented, targeting specific and well-defined problems.
5. Interventions target sequences of behavior within or between multiple systems that maintain the identified problems.
6. Interventions are developmentally appropriate and fit the developmental needs of the youth.
7. Interventions are designed to require daily or weekly effort by family members.
8. Intervention effectiveness is evaluated continuously from multiple perspectives with providers assuming accountability for overcoming barriers to successful outcomes.
9. Interventions are designed to promote treatment generalization and long-term maintenance of therapeutic change by empowering caregivers to address family members' needs across multiple systemic contexts.

MST is usually delivered by a master's level therapist with a caseload of four to eight families. The MST therapist is a generalist who directly provides most mental health services and coordinates access to other important services (e.g., medical, educational, recreational), always monitoring quality control. Although the therapist is available to the family 24 hours a day, 7 days a week, therapeutic intensity is titrated to clinical need. In general, therapists spend more time with families in the initial weeks of therapy (daily, if indicated) and gradually taper off (as infrequently as once a week) during a 3- to 5-month course of treatment. Throughout treatment, the therapist guides and supports the parents as primary change agents and helps them to develop a natural social support network to increase the likelihood that changes will be maintained after treatment ends.

Intensive training and supervision of therapists are important ingredients for favorable outcomes in MST (see Henggeler, Melton, Brondino, Scherer, & Hanley, 1997). Treatment fidelity is maintained by weekly group supervision meetings involving a team of three to four therapists and a doctoral level clinical supervisor. Importantly, the team accepts responsibility for engaging families in treatment and for effecting therapeutic change. Thus, when obstacles to successful engagement or to therapeutic change are identified, the team develops strategies to address those obstacles and to promote success.

To date, MST has received the most empirical support as an effective treatment for serious antisocial behavior in adolescents (for reviews, see Levesque, 1996; Tate, Reppucci, & Mulvey, 1995). In an initial outcome study conducted with inner-city juvenile offenders (Henggeler et al., 1986), many of whom were violent, MST was effective in improving key correlates of juvenile offending (e.g., decreased behavior problems, improved family relations, decreased association with deviant peers). In a study of adolescent sexual offenders (Borduin, Henggeler, Blaske, & Stein, 1990), MST was relatively effective at reducing recidivism at a 3-year follow-up for both sexual offenses and nonsexual crimes. Likewise, Henggeler et al. (1991) found that serious juvenile offenders who participated in MST had a lower rate of recidivism for drug-related crimes. In a subsequent study, Henggeler, Melton, and Smith (1992) established the effectiveness of MST in the treatment of serious and violent adolescent offenders with regard to key measures of ultimate outcome (i.e., rearrests, self-reported delinquency, time incarcerated) at a 59-week follow-up; results from a 2-year follow-up (Henggeler, Melton, Smith, Schoenwald, & Hanley, 1993) further supported the long-term efficacy of MST. Similarly, Borduin et al. (1995; see also Mann et al., 1990) demonstrated the relative effectiveness of MST across numerous outcomes in the treatment of violent and chronic juvenile offenders; most importantly, substantial between-groups differences in criminal behavior and violent offending were demonstrated at a 4-year follow-up. Thus, considerable evidence shows that MST can decrease rates of criminal activity and incarceration for serious juvenile offenders.

There is also evidence that MST is a cost-effective alternative to some of the other services provided to serious juvenile offenders. For example, in their study of serious and violent juvenile offenders, Henggeler et al. (1992) reported that the average cost per youth for treatment in the MST group was about $2,800, whereas the average cost in the usual services group was about $16,300. Moreover, these figures do not reflect the substantial cost savings (e.g., in victim medical care or property damage or loss; see Miller et al., 1993) associated with decreased criminal activity among MST participants relative to the usual services participants. More recently, a report from the Washington State Institute for Public Policy (1998) showed that MST was the most cost-effective of a wide variety of treatments to reduce serious criminal activity by adolescents. Indeed, the average net gain for MST in comparison with boot camps was $29,000 per case in decreased program and victim costs. Such savings point to the potential cost savings and cost-effectiveness of promising community-based treament models such as MST, especially when used with youths at high risk of out-of-home placement.

SUMMARY AND CONCLUSIONS

Interventions for serious antisocial behavior in adolescents have had little success historically. Since the 1980s, however, some promising community-based models of treatment for adolescent offenders have been developed, including BPT; FFT; wraparound services, as exemplified by the AYI; the Homebuilders model, as exemplified by Family Ties; and MST. Although each of these models is well conceptualized and has wide appeal, they differ in their demonstrated effectiveness in reducing long-term rates of serious antisocial behavior in adolescents. Indeed, to date, MST is the only treatment that has demonstrated both short- and long-term success in randomized, controlled clinical trials with violent and chronic juvenile offenders and their families.

The findings reviewed previously and the conclusions of numerous reviewers (e.g., Borduin & Schaeffer, 1998; Henggeler, 1989; Levesque, 1996; Tate et al., 1995) suggest that to effectively reduce serious antisocial behavior, treatment models must share at least three broad qualities:

1. In light of the multiple determinants of antisocial behavior in youths' naturally occurring systems (family, peer, school, neighborhood), treatment must be comprehensive enough to address problems within and between these systems. Wraparound services, Family Ties, and MST assume (implicitly or explicitly) a social-ecological view of behavior problems and provide a comprehensive approach to treatment.

2. Because different combinations of psychosocial factors can contribute to antisocial behavior in adolescents, the nature and intensity of interventions should be individualized and flexible. Again, only wraparound services, Family Ties, and MST attempt to provide individualized, yet comprehensive, treatment.

3. To enhance the probability of treatment generalization (i.e., ecological validity), interventions should be delivered directly within the youth's natural environments (home, school, neighborhood). All of the treatment models except BPT are delivered with ecological validity, although FFT does not deliver interventions in community settings outside of the home.

Although treatments must address the multiple determinants of antisocial behavior in an individualized and ecologically valid fashion, other complex issues must be successfully addressed before an effective treatment can be disseminated (Schoenwald & Henggeler, in press). For example, the treatment model must be specified (operationalized) in enough detail for a therapist to implement the model with integrity, assuming appropriate training and supervision. BPT, FFT, and MST are examples of well-specified treatment models, whereas specification of wraparound services and Family Ties is lacking.

Successful dissemination of an effective treatment model, such as MST, to a public or private provider organization requires intensive training and ongoing consultation in the model to promote treatment fidelity (see Henggeler et al., 1997). Moreover, the provider organization (including key administrators, supervisors, and therapists) must be fully committed to the philosophical (e.g., definition of the mental health professional's role) and empirical (e.g., accountability for clinical outcomes) framework of the treatment model. Substantial changes in agency policies and in staff members' work routines are often required to successfully implement an ecologically oriented (i.e., home- and community-based) treatment model, and concrete support should be evident from the administration of the service organization (e.g., implementing flex time and comp time policies for staff, scheduling regular supervision and consultation times, providing highly competitive salaries).

In summary, we believe that comprehensive, flexible, and ecologically valid treatment models, like several of those discussed here, hold the most promise in reducing long-term rates of criminal activity and violent offending in adolescents. Of course, extensive validation and replication are needed for even the most promising treatment approaches. Nevertheless, given the significant problems that adolescent offenders present for our society, as well as the questionable ethics of providing these adolescents with mental health services that do not produce durable changes, it is time that priority be placed on the evaluation of promising treatment models for serious antisocial behavior in adolescents.

REFERENCES

Akhtar, N., & Bradley, E. J. (1991). Social information processing deficits of aggressive children: Present findings and implications for social skills training. *Clinical Psychology Review, 11,* 621–644.

Alexander, J. F., Holtzworth-Munroe, A., & Jameson, P. B. (1994). The process and outcome of marital and family therapy research: Review and evaluation. In A. E. Bergin & S. L. Garfield (Eds.), *Handbook of psychotherapy and behavior change* (4th ed., pp. 595–630). New York: Wiley

Alexander, J. F., & Parsons, B. V. (1973). Short-term behavioral intervention with delinquent families: Impact on family process and recidivism. *Journal of Abnormal Psychology, 81,* 219–225.

Alexander, J. F., & Parsons, B. V. (1982). *Functional family therapy.* Monterey, CA: Brooks/Cole.

Arbuthnot, J., Gordon, D. A., & Jurkovic, G. J. (1987). Personality. In H. C. Quay (Ed.), *Handbook of juvenile delinquency* (pp. 139–183). New York: Wiley.

Astor, R. A., & Behre, W. J. (1997). Violent and nonviolent children's and parents' reasoning about family and peer violence. *Behavioral Disorders, 22,* 231–245.

Bank, L., Marlowe, J. H., Reid, J. B., Patterson, G. R., & Weinrott, M. R. (1991). A comparative evaluation of parent-training interventions for families of chronic delinquents. *Journal of Abnormal Child Psychology, 19,* 15–33.

Barton, C., Alexander, J. F., Waldron, H., Turner, C. W., & Warburton, J. (1985). Generalizing treatment effects of functional family therapy: Three replications. *American Journal of Family Therapy, 13,* 16–26.

Berrueta-Clement, J. R., Schweinhart, L. J., Barnett, W. S., & Weikart, D. P. (1987). The effects of early educational intervention on crime and delinquency in adolescence and early adulthood. In J. D. Burchard & S. N. Burchard (Eds.), *Prevention and delinquent behavior* (pp. 220–240). Newbury Park, CA: Sage.

Bickett, L. R., Milich, R., & Brown, R. T. (1996). Attributional styles of aggressive boys and their mothers. *Journal of Abnormal Child Psychology, 24,* 457–472.

Blaske, D. M., Borduin, C. M., Henggeler, S. W., & Mann, B. J. (1989). Individual, family, and peer characteristics of adolescent sex offenders and assaultive offenders. *Developmental Psychology, 25,* 846–855.

Borduin, C. M. (1994). Innovative models of treatment and service delivery in the juvenile justice system. *Journal of Clinical Child Psychology, 23* (Suppl.), 19–25.

Borduin, C. M., & Henggeler, S. W. (1987). Post-divorce mother–son relations of delinquent and well-adjusted adolescents. *Journal of Applied Developmental Psychology, 8,* 273–288.

Borduin, C. M., & Henggeler, S. W. (1990). A multisystemic approach to the treatment of serious delinquent behavior. In R. J. McMahon & R. Dev. Peters (Eds.), *Behavior disorders of adolescence: Research, intervention, and policy in clinical and school settings* (pp. 62–80). New York: Plenum.

Borduin, C. M., Henggeler, S. W., Blaske, D. M., & Stein, R. (1990). Multisystemic treatment of adolescent sexual offenders. *International Journal of Offender Therapy and Comparative Criminology, 34,* 105–113.

Borduin, C. M., Mann, B. J., Cone, L., Henggeler, S. W., Fucci, B. R., Blaske, D. M., & Williams, R. A. (1995). Multisystemic treatment of serious juvenile offenders: Long-term prevention of criminality and violence. *Journal of Consulting and Clinical Psychology, 63,* 569–578.

Borduin, C. M., Pruitt, J. A., & Henggeler, S. W. (1986). Family interactions in Black, lower-class families with delinquent and nondelinquent adolescent boys. *Journal of Genetic Psychology, 147,* 333–342.

Borduin, C. M., & Schaeffer, C. M. (1998). Violent offending in adolescence: Epidemiology, correlates, outcomes, and treatment. In T. P. Gullotta, G. R. Adams, & R. Montemayor (Eds.), *Delinquent violent youth: Theory and interventions* (pp. 144–174). Newbury Park, CA: Sage.

Braswell, L., & Bloomquist, M. L. (1991). *Cognitive-behavioral therapy with ADHD children: Child, family, and school interventions.* New York: Guilford.

Bronfenbrenner, U. (1979). *The ecology of human development: Experiments by nature and design.* Cambridge, MA: Harvard University Press.

Burchard, J., Burchard, S., Sewell, R., & VanDenBerg, J. (1993). *One kid at a time-The Alaska Youth Initiative: A demonstration of individualized services.* Washington, DC: Georgetown University Press.

Burchard, J., & Clarke, R. (1990). The role of individualized care in a service delivery system for children and adolescents with severely maladjusted behavior. *Journal of Mental Health Administration, 17,* 48–60.

Burkstein, O. G. (1994). Substance abuse. In M. Hersen, R. T. Ammerman, & L. A. Sisson (Eds.), *Handbook of aggressive and destructive behavior in psychiatric patients* (pp. 445–468). New York: Plenum.

Chavez, E. L., Oetting, E. R., & Swaim, R. C. (1994). Dropout and delinquency: Mexican-American and Caucasian non-Hispanic youth. *Journal of Clinical Child Psychology, 23,* 47–55.

Child Welfare League of America. (1992). *Sharing innovations: The program exchange compendium.* Washington, DC: Author.

Clarke, H. B., & Clarke, R. T. (1996). Research on the wraparound process and individualized services for children with multi-system needs. *Journal of Child and Family Studies, 5,* 1–5.

Cornell, D. G., & Wilson, L. A. (1992). The PIQ>VIQ discrepancy in violent and nonviolent delinquents. *Journal of Clinical Psychology, 48,* 256–261.

Crick, N. R., & Dodge, K. A. (1994). A review and reformulation of social information processing mechanisms in children's social adjustment. *Psychological Bulletin, 115,* 74–101.

Dishion, T. J., Eddy, J. M., Haas, E., Li, F., & Spracklen, K. (1997). Friendships and violent behavior during adolescence. *Social Development, 6,* 207–223.

Dishion, T. J., Patterson, G. R., Stoolmiller, M., & Skinner, M. L. (1991). Family, school, and behavioral antecedents to early adolescent involvement with antisocial peers. *Developmental Psychology, 27,* 172–180.

Dix, T., & Lochman, J. E. (1990). Social cognition and negative reactions to children: A comparison of mothers of aggressive and nonaggressive boys. *Journal of Social and Clinical Psychology, 9,* 418–438.

Dodge, K. A., Price, J. M., Bachorowski, J., & Newman, J. M. (1990). Hostile attributional biases in severely aggressive adolescents. *Journal of Abnormal Psychology, 99,* 385–392.

Dunn, S. E., Lochman, J. E., & Colder, C. R. (1997). Social problem-solving skills in boys with conduct and oppositional defiant disorders. *Aggressive Behavior, 23,* 457–469.

DuRant, R. H., Cadenhead, C., Pendergrast, R. A., Slavens, G., & Linder, C. W. (1994). Factors associated with the use of violence among urban Black adolescents. *American Journal of Public Health, 84,* 612–617.

Elliot, D. S. (1994). Serious violent offenders: Onset, developmental course, and termination. *Criminology, 32,* 1–21.

Elliot, D. S., Dunford, F. W., & Huizinga, D. (1987). The identification and prediction of career offenders using self-reported and official data. In J. D. Burchard & S. N. Burchard (Eds.), *Prevention of delinquent behavior* (pp. 90–121). Newbury Park, CA: Sage.

Elliot, D. S., Huizinga, D., & Ageton, S. S. (1985). *Explaining delinquency and drug use.* Beverly Hills, CA: Sage.

Elliot, D. S., & Voss, H. (1974). *Delinquency and dropout.* Lexington, MA: Heath.

Emler, N., Reicher, S., & Ross, A. (1987). The social context of delinquent conduct. *Journal of Child Psychology and Psychiatry, 28,* 99–109.

Farrell, A. D., & Bruce, S. E. (1997). Impact and exposure to community violence on violent behavior and emotional distress among urban adolescents. *Journal of Child Clinical Psychology, 26,* 2–14.

Farrington, D. P. (1989). Early predictors of adolescent aggression and adult violence. *Violence and Victims, 4,* 79–100.

Farrington, D. P., Ohlin, L., & Wilson, J. Q. (1986). *Understanding and controlling crime.* New York: Springer-Verlag.

Federal Bureau of Investigation. (1996). *Uniform crime reports.* Washington, DC: U.S. Government Printing Office.

Fitzpatrick, K. M., & Boldizar, J. P. (1993). The prevalence and consequences of exposure to violence among African-American youth. *Journal of the American Academy of Child and Adolescent Psychiatry, 32,* 424–430.

Forehand R., & Kotchick, B. A. (1996). Cultural diversity: A wake-up call for parent training. *Behavioral Therapy, 27,* 187–206.

Fraser, M. W., Nelson, K. E., & Rivard, J. C. (1997). Effectiveness of family preservation services. *Social Work Research, 21,* 138–153.

Gordon, D. A., Arbuthnot, J., Gustafson, K. E., & McGreen, P. (1988). Home-based behavioral systems family therapy with disadvantaged juvenile delinquents. *American Journal of Family Therapy, 16,* 243–255.

Gordon, D. A., Graves, K., & Arbuthnot, J. (1995). The effect of functional family therapy for delinquents on adult criminal behavior. *Criminal Justice and Behavior, 22,* 60–73.

Gorman-Smith, D., Tolan, P. H., Zelli, A., & Huesmann, L. R. (1996). The relation of family functioning to violence among inner city minority youth. *Journal of Family Psychology, 10,* 115–129.

Gottfredson, G. D. (1989). The experiences of violent and serious victimization. In N. A. Weiner & M. E. Wolfgang (Eds.), *Pathways to criminal violence* (pp. 202–234). Newbury Park, CA: Sage.

Graham, S., Hudley, C., & Williams, E. (1992). Attributional and emotional determinants of aggression among African-American and Latino young adolescents. *Developmental Psychology, 28,* 731–740.

Haapasalo, J., & Tremblay, R. E. (1994). Physically aggressive boys from ages 6 to 12: Family background, parenting behavior, and prediction of delinquency. *Journal of Consulting and Clinical Psychology, 62,* 1044–1052.

Haley, J. (1987). *Problem-solving therapy* (2nd ed.). San Francisco: Jossey-Bass.

Hanson, C. L., Henggeler, S. W., Haefele, W. F., & Rodick, J. D. (1984). Demographic, individual, and family relationship correlates of serious and repeated crime among adolescents and their siblings. *Journal of Consulting and Clinical Psychology, 52,* 528–538.

Hawkins, D. J., & Lamb, T. (1987). Teacher practices, social development, and delinquency. In J. D. Burchard & S. N. Burchard (Eds.), *Prevention of delinquent behavior* (pp. 241–274). Newbury Park, CA: Sage.

Hellman, D. A., & Beaton, S. (1986). The pattern of violence in urban public schools: The influence of school and community. *Journal of Research in Crime and Delinquency, 23,* 102–127.

Henggeler, S. W. (1989). *Delinquency in adolescence.* Newbury Park, CA: Sage.

Henggeler, S. W., & Borduin, C. M. (1990). *Family therapy and beyond: A multisystemic approach to treating the behavior problems of children and adolescents.* Pacific Grove, CA: Brooks/Cole.

Henggeler, S. W., Borduin, C. M., Melton, G. B., Mann, B. J., Smith, L. A., Hall, J. A., Cone, L., & Fucci, B. R. (1991). Effects of multisystemic therapy on drug use and abuse in serious juvenile offenders: A progress report from two outcome studies. *Family Dynamics of Addiction Quarterly, 1,* 40–51.

Henggeler, S. W., Edwards, J., Borduin, C. M. (1987). Family relations of female juvenile delinquents. *Journal of Abnormal Child Psychology, 15,* 199–209.

Henggeler, S. W., Melton, G. B., Brondino, M. J., Scherer, D. G., & Hanley, J. H. (1997). Multisystemic therapy with violent and chronic juvenile offenders and their families: The role of treatment fidelity in successful dissemination. *Journal of Consulting and Clinical Psychology, 65,* 821–833.

Henggeler, S. W., Melton, G. B., & Smith, L. A. (1992). Family preservation using multisystemic therapy: An effective alternative to incarcerating serious juvenile offenders. *Journal of Consulting and Clinical Psychology, 60,* 953–961.

Henggeler, S. W., Melton, G. B., Smith, L. A., Schoenwald, S., & Hanley, J. H. (1993). Family preservation using multisystemic treatment: Long-term follow-up to a clinical trial with serious juvenile offenders. *Journal of Child and Family Studies, 2,* 83–93.

Henggeler, S. W., Rodick, J. D., Borduin, C. M., Hanson, C. L., Watson, S. M., & Urey, J. R. (1986). Multisystemic treatment of juvenile offenders: Effects on adolescent behavior and family interaction. *Developmental Psychology, 22,* 132–141.

Henggeler, S. W., Schoenwald, S. K., Borduin, C. M., Rowland, M. D., & Cunningham, P. B. (1998). *Multisystemic treatment of antisocial behavior in children and adolescents.* New York: Guilford.

Hinshaw, S. P. (1992). Externalizing behavior problems and academic underachievement in childhood and adolescence: Causal relationships and underlying mechanisms. *Psychological Bulletin, 111,* 127–155.

Huesmann, L. R., Lefkowitz, M. M., Eron, L. D., & Walder, L. O. (1984). Stability and aggression over time and generations. *Developmental Psychology, 20,* 1120–1134.

Jouriles, E. N., Bourg, W. J., & Farris, A. M. (1991). Marital adjustment and child conduct problems: A comparison of the correlation across samples. *Journal of Consulting and Clinical Psychology, 59,* 354–357.

Kazdin, A. E. (1995). *Conduct disorders in childhood and adolescence* (2nd ed.). Thousand Oaks, CA: Sage.

Kazdin, A. E. (1997). Practitioner review: Psychosocial treatments for conduct disorder in children. *Journal of Child Psychology and Psychiatry, 38,* 161–178.

Kazdin, A. E. (1998). Parent management training: Evidence, outcomes, and issues. *Journal of the American Academy of Child and Adolescent Psychiatry, 36,* 1349–1356.

Kinney, J., Haapala, D. A., & Booth, C. (1991). *Keeping families together: The homebuilders model.* New York: Aldine de Gruyter.

Kratzer, L., & Hodgins, S. (1997). Adult outcomes of child conduct problems: A cohort study. *Journal of Abnormal Child Psychology, 25,* 65–81.

LaGrange, R. L., & White, H. R. (1985). Age differences in delinquency: A test of theory. *Criminology, 23,* 19–45.

Levesque, R. J. R. (1996). Is there still a place for violent youth in juvenile justice? *Aggression and Violent Behavior, 1,* 69–79.

Lipsey, M. W. (1992). Juvenile delinquency treatment: A meta-analytic inquiry into the variability of effects. In T. D. Cook, H. Cooper, D. S. Cordray, H. Hartman, L. V. Hedgges, R. J. Light, T. A. Louis, & F. Mosteller (Eds.), *Meta-analysis for explanation: A casebook* (pp. 83–127). New York: Russell Sage Foundation.

Loeber, R. (1982). The stability of antisocial and delinquent child behavior: A review. *Child Development, 53,* 1431–1446.

Loeber, R., Farrington, D. P., & Waschbusch, D. A. (1998). Serious and violent juvenile offenders. In R. Loeber & D. P. Farrington (Eds.), *Serious and violent juvenile offenders: Risk factors and successful interventions* (pp. 13–29). Thousand Oaks, CA: Sage.

Loeber, R., & Schmaling, K. B. (1985). Empirical evidence for overt and covert patterns of antisocial conduct problems: A meta-analysis. *Journal of Abnormal Child Psychology, 13,* 315–336.

Lourie, I. S., Katz-Leavy, J., & Stroul, B. A. (1996). Individualized services in a system of care. In B. A. Stroul (Ed.), *Children's mental health: Creating systems of care in a changing society* (pp. 429–452). Baltimore, MD: Brookes.

Lynam, D., Moffitt, T., & Stouthamer-Loeber, M. (1993). Explaining the relation between IQ and delinquency: Class, race, test motivation, or self-control? *Journal of Abnormal Psychology, 102,* 187–196.

Lyon, J. M., Henggeler, S. W., & Hall, J. A. (1992). The family relations, peer relations, and criminal activities of Caucasian and Hispanic-American gang members. *Journal of Abnormal Child Psychology, 20,* 439–449.

Lytton, H. (1990). Child and parent effects in boys' conduct disorder: A reinterpretation. *Developmental Psychology, 26,* 683–697.

MacKinnon-Lewis, C., Volling, B. L., Lamb, M. E., Dechman, K., Rabiner, D., & Curtner, M. E. (1994). A cross-contextual analysis of boys' social competence: From family to school. *Developmental Psychology, 30,* 325–333.

Malik, S., Sorenson, S. B., & Aneshensel, C. S. (1997). Community and dating violence among adolescents: Perpetration and victimization. *Journal of Adolescent Health, 21,* 291–302.

Mann, B. J., Borduin, C. M., Henggeler, S. W., & Blaske, D. M. (1990). An investigation of systemic conceptualizations of parent–child coalitions and symptom change. *Journal of Consulting and Clinical Psychology, 58,* 336–344.

Maughan, B., Gray, G., & Rutter, M. (1985). Reading retardation and antisocial behavior: A follow-up into employment. *Journal of Child Psychology and Psychiatry, 26,* 741–758.

Mayer, G. R. (1995). Preventing antisocial behavior in the schools. *Journal of Applied Behavior Analysis, 28,* 467–478.

Melton, G. B., Lyons, P. M., & Spaulding, W. J. (1998). *No place to go: The civil commitment of minors.* Lincoln, NE: University of Nebraska Press.

Melton, G. B., & Pagliocca, P. M. (1992). Treatment in the juvenile justice system: Directions for policy and practice. In J. J. Cocozza (Ed.), *Responding to the mental health needs of youth in the juvenile justice system* (pp. 107–139). Seattle, WA: National Coalition for the Mentally Ill in the Criminal Justice System.

Miller, G. E., & Prinz, R. J. (1990). Enhancement of social learning family interventions for childhood conduct disorder. *Psychological Bulletin, 108,* 291–307.

Miller, T. R., Cohen, M. A., & Rossman, S. B. (1993). Victim costs of violent crime and resulting injuries. *Health Affairs, 12,* 186–197.

Minuchin, S. (1974). *Families and family therapy.* Cambridge, MA: Harvard University Press.

Moffit, E. P. (1993). Adolescence-limited and life-course-persistent antisocial behavior: A developmental taxonomy. *Psychological Review, 100,* 674–701.

Moss, H. B., & Kirisci, L. (1995). Aggressivity in adolescent alcohol abusers: Relationship with conduct disorder. *Alcoholism: Clinical and Experimental Research, 19,* 642–646.

Mulvey, E. P., Arthur, M. W., & Reppucci, N. D. (1993). The prevention and treatment of juvenile delinquency: A review of the research. *Clinical Psychology Review, 13,* 133–167.

New York Department of Juvenile Justice. (1990a). *Family ties.* New York: Author.

New York Department of Juvenile Justice. (1990b). *Listen to the dreams: Annual report 1990.* New York: Author.

Ollendick, T. H. (1996). Violence in youth: Where do we go from here? Behavior therapy's response. *Behavior Therapy, 27,* 485–514.

Olweus, D. (1980). Familial and temperamental determinants of aggressive behavior in adolescent boys: A causal analysis. *Developmental Psychology, 16,* 644–660.

Parsons, B. V., & Alexander, J. F. (1973). Short-term family intervention: A therapy outcome study. *Journal of Consulting and Clinical Psychology, 41,* 195–201.

Patterson, G. R. (1982). *Coercive family process.* Eugene, OR: Castalia.

Patterson, G. R., Reid, J. B., & Dishion, T. J. (1992). *Antisocial boys.* Eugene, OR: Castalia.

Patterson, G. R., & Stouthamer-Loeber, M. (1984). The correlation of family management practices and delinquency. *Child Development, 55,* 1299–1307.

Poole, E. D., & Rigoli, R. M. (1979). Parental support, delinquent friends, and delinquency: A test of interaction effects. *Journal of Criminal Law and Criminology, 70,* 188–193.

Quay, H. C. (1987). Intelligence. In H. C. Quay (Ed.), *Handbook of juvenile delinquency* (pp. 106–117). New York: Wiley.

Robins, L. N. (1981). Epidemiological approaches to natural history research: Antisocial disorders in children. *Journal of the American Academy of Child and Adolescent Psychiatry, 20,* 566–580.

Robison, S., & Binder, H. (1993). Building bridges for families. *Public Welfare, 51,* 14–20.

Rosenblatt, A. (1996). Bows and ribbons, tape and twine: Wrapping the wraparound process for children with multi-system needs. *Journal of Child and Family Studies, 5,* 101–116.

Rutter, M. (1994). Family discord and conduct disorder: Cause, consequence, or correlate? *Journal of Family Psychology, 8,* 170–186.

Schaefer, C. E., & Briesmeister, J. M. (Eds.). (1989). *Handbook of parent training: Parents as co-therapists for children's behavior problems.* New York: Wiley.

Schoenwald, S. K., & Henggeler, S. W. (in press). Services research and family based treatment. In H. Liddle, G. Diamond, R. Levant, & J. Bray (Eds.), *Family psychology intervention science.* Washington, DC: American Psychological Association.

Seguin, J. R., Pihl, R. O., Harden, P. W., Tremblay, R. E., & Boulerice, B. (1995). Cognitive and neuropsychological characteristics of physically aggressive boys. *Journal of Abnormal Psychology, 104,* 614–624.

Serketich, W. R., & Dumas, J. E. (1996). The effectiveness of behavioral parent training to modify antisocial behavior in children: A meta-analysis. *Behavior Therapy, 27,* 171–186.

Simcha-Fagan, O., & Schwartz, J. E. (1986). Neighborhoods and delinquency: An assessment of contextual effects. *Criminology, 24,* 667–703.

Simons, R. L., Johnson, C., Beaman, J., Conger, R. D., & Whitbeck, L. B. (1996). Parents and peer group as mediators of the effect of community structure on adolescent problem behavior. *American Journal of Community Psychology, 24,* 145–171.

Smith, C., & Thornberry, T. P. (1995). The relationship between childhood maltreatment and adolescent involvement in delinquency. *Criminology, 33,* 451–481.

Smith, D. A., Visher, C. A., & Jarjoura, C. R. (1991). Dimensions of delinquency: Exploring the correlates of participation, frequency, and persistence of delinquent behavior. *Journal of Research in Crime and Delinquency, 28*, 6–32.

Snyder, J., & Patterson, G. R. (1987). Family interaction and delinquent behavior. In H. C. Quay (Ed.), *Handbook of juvenile delinquency* (pp. 216–243). New York: Wiley.

Soler, M. (1992). Interagency services in juvenile justice systems. In I. M. Schwartz (Ed.), *Juvenile justice and public policy: Toward a national agenda* (pp. 134–150). New York: Lexington.

Stattin, H., & Klackenberg-Larsson, I. (1993). Early language and intelligence development and their relationship to future criminal behavior. *Journal of Abnormal Psychology, 102*, 369–378.

Stouthamer-Loeber, M., Loeber, R., & Thomas, C. (1992). Caretakers seeking help for boys with disruptive and delinquent behavior. *Comprehensive Mental Health Care, 2*, 159–178.

Strasburg, P. A. (1978). *Violent delinquents*. New York: Monarch.

Tarter, R. E., Hegedus, A. M., Alterman, A. I., & Katz-Garris, L. (1983). Cognitive capacities of juvenile violent, nonviolent, and sexual offenders. *Journal of Nervous and Mental Disease, 171*, 564–567.

Tate, D. C., Reppucci, N. D., & Mulvey, E. P. (1995). Violent juvenile delinquents: Treatment effectiveness and implications for future action. *American Psychologist, 50*, 777–781.

Thornberry, T. P., Huizinga, D., & Loeber, R. (1995). The prevention of serious delinquency and violence: Implications from the program of research on the causes and correlates of delinquency. In J. C. Howell, B. Krisberg, J. D. Hawkins, & J. J. Wilson (Eds.), *A sourcebook: Serious, violent, and chronic juvenile offenders* (pp. 213–237). Newbury Park, CA: Sage.

Thornberry, T. P., Moore, M., & Christenson, R. L. (1985). The effect of dropping out of high school on subsequent criminal behavior. *Criminology, 23*, 3–18.

Tolan, P. H., & Lorion, R. P. (1988). Multivariate approaches to the identification of delinquency-proneness in adolescent males. *American Journal of Community Psychology, 16*, 547–561.

Vuchinich, S., Bank, L., & Patterson, G. R. (1992). Parenting, peers, and the stability of antisocial behavior in preadolescent boys. *Developmental Psychology, 28*, 510–521.

Walsh, A., Petee, J. A., & Beyer, T. A. (1987). Intellectual imbalance and delinquency: Comparing high verbal and high performance IQ delinquents. *Criminal Justice and Behavior, 14*, 370–379.

Washington State Institute for Public Policy. (1998). *Watching the bottom line: Cost-effective interventions for reducing crime in Washington*. Olympia, WA: Evergreen State College.

Webster, D. W., Gainer, P. S., & Champion, H. R. (1993). Weapon carrying among inner-city junior high school students: Defensive behavior vs. aggressive delinquency. *American Journal of Public Health, 83*, 1604–1608.

Weiss, B., Dodge, K. A., Bates, J. E., & Pettit, G. S. (1992). Some consequences of early harsh discipline: Child aggression and a maladaptive social information processing style. *Child Development, 63,* 1321–1335.

White, H. R., Pandina, R. J., & LaGrange, R. L. (1987). Longitudinal predictors of serious substance use and delinquency. *Criminology, 25,* 715–740.

Widom, C. S. (1989). Does violence beget violence? A critical examination of the literature. *Psychological Bulletin, 106,* 2–28.

Yoe, J. T., Santarcangelo, S., Atkins, M., & Burchard, J. D. (1996). Wraparound care in Vermont: Program development, implementation, and evaluation of a statewide system of individualized services. *Journal of Child and Family Studies, 5,* 23–27.

7

Applications of Person–Environment Psychology to the Career Development and Vocational Behavior of Adolescents and Adults

Jane L. Swanson
Serena P. Chu
Southern Illinois University at Carbondale

The field of vocational psychology strives to explain and predict work-related activity throughout individuals' lives. Vocational psychologists study a number of important issues that occur most frequently during specific life stages, such as the formation of interest patterns in childhood and adolescence, exploration of career alternatives and commitment to an initial career choice in adolescence and young adulthood, entry into an occupational choice in young adulthood, career progress in middle adulthood, and transition to retirement in later adulthood. Moreover, vocational psychologists study issues that occur throughout the life span, regardless of specific life stage, such as development and refinement of one's vocational identity, the interaction of work and nonwork life roles, and continued adjustment to occupational circumstances.

Vocational psychology is built on the recognition that successful pursuit of work activities is crucial to psychological well-being throughout the life span; furthermore, that mental health issues and vocational issues reciprocally affect one another in individuals' lives (Betz & Corning, 1993; Blustein & Spengler, 1995; Spokane, 1989). Therefore, understanding vocational issues and assisting individuals in the choice and implementation of their career-related goals adds to the richness of understanding about mental health throughout the life span, and therefore serves to improve the quality of life in general.

The interrelationship between work and mental health has been clearly demonstrated. For example, career satisfaction is related to indicators of good mental health, such as higher self-esteem and lower levels of depression (Dawis & Lofquist, 1984; Swanson, 1992). Furthermore, Brown and Brooks (1985) recommended that mental health practitioners consider the work situation, rather than intrapsychic factors, as the source of clients' psychological symptoms. According to Spokane (1989), work and mental health issues are most likely to intersect when individuals are experiencing stress or undergoing some type of transition, suggesting an important convergence between these two domains.

Person–environment (P–E) psychology is grounded in the basic assumption that a reciprocal relationship exists between people and their environments; that is, people influence their environments, and environments influence people (Walsh, Price, & Craik, 1992). Perhaps nowhere has this fundamental idea been more thoroughly implemented than in the realm of vocational psychology; in fact, the history of vocational psychology as a scholarly field is intimately intertwined with the evolution of P–E models applied to career behavior. Although many other theories of career behavior have been formulated—such as developmental and social learning theories (Savickas & Lent, 1994)—theories of P–E fit form the bedrock of the field of vocational psychology. Moreover, these theories remain vital to an understanding of vocational behavior, and continue to influence conceptualizations of career development throughout the life span (Swanson, 1996).

The purpose of this chapter is to provide an overview of the application of P–E psychology to a consideration of career development and vocational behavior. We begin with an outline of two theories of P–E fit, followed by a description of how these theories might be applied throughout the life span via programmatic or individually oriented interventions. We then present two case examples to illustrate how the theories may be used to understand and intervene in individuals' career and mental health concerns.

THEORIES OF PERSON–ENVIRONMENT
VOCATIONAL FIT

Two contemporary models of P–E fit occupy a prominent role in vocational psychology: Holland's (1997) theory of vocational personalities and work environments, and Dawis and Lofquist's (1984) theory of work adjustment (TWA). Both theories represent evolutionary extensions of earlier trait-and-factor counseling (Chartrand, 1991; Rounds & Tracey, 1990), which, in turn, had its roots in a social reform movement at the turn of the 20th century (Parsons, 1909/1989).

Both theories of P–E fit incorporate mechanisms to describe individuals and environments, and to quantify the degree of fit between person and environment. Both Holland's theory and TWA contain dimensions that can be used to describe either people or environments. Although these two theories are quite similar in many respects, Holland's theory places greater emphasis on vocational choice whereas TWA emphasizes vocational adjustment (Dawis, 1994), thus providing complementary rather than competing views (Swanson & Fouad, 1999).

Holland's Model of Vocational Personalities
and Work Environments

Holland's theory of P–E fit has been an influential force in vocational psychology since its introduction in the 1960s. Part of the theory's appeal is due to the simple and intuitively meaningful premises on which it is based. Holland posited that career choice is an extension of one's personality. Thus, an individual's choice of occupation can be viewed as a reflection of that person's motivation, knowledge of occupations, and understanding of personal abilities (Spokane, 1996). A related premise is that individuals choose to enter occupational environments that are congruent with their personality: People "search for environments that will let them exercise their skills and abilities, express their attitudes and values, and take on agreeable problems and roles" (Holland, 1997, p. 4). Such a fit between personality and environment is believed to result in satisfaction and tenure in the occupation.

There are several basic assumptions to the theory. First, individuals are said to resemble one or more personality types. Types are defined as a collection of personal attributes, including interests and abilities, that describe individuals. Holland postulated six basic personality types: realistic, investigative, artistic, social, enterprising, and conventional. Each of these types is characterized by a constellation of interests, values, and skills, as outlined in Table 7.1. Second, these same six types can be used in a parallel fashion to characterize environments. The dominant personality type in a given environment is said to define that environment (Walsh & Holland, 1992). Thus, an environment is characterized by the individuals that occupy it. However, an individual (or an environment) is rarely a single pure type; rather, individuals (and environments) are more likely to be a combination of several types. The three highest types are typically used to describe individuals and environments. This three-point code often is used in interventions and in research.

Third, Holland's theory outlines specific and predictable ways in which the types are interrelated. The six types are arranged in a hexagonal structure, with the types adjacent to one another sharing more in common than the types that are opposing in the hexagon; for example, realistic types are more like investigative types than they are like social types (see Fig. 7.1).

Furthermore, Holland postulated four additional constructs to describe the interrelation of types within people or environments, and between people and their environments: congruence, differentiation, consistency, and identity. The concept of *congruence* occupies a central role in Holland's theory. Congruence refers to the match between a person and his or her environment, in terms of the six types specified by the theory. An enterprising individual working in an enterprising environment is considered a highly congruent situation, as compared to the same individual working within an investigative environment. As mentioned earlier, congruence is hypothesized to be related to important work-related outcomes, such as job satisfaction and job tenure. Conversely, incongruent P–E situations are hypothesized to result in behavioral change; individuals will either change the environment they are in or change their perceptions.

Differentiation pertains to the degree of definition or crystallization of an individual's interests; interests are considered more

Table 7.1

Characteristics of Holland's Six Personality and Environmental Types

Type	Self-Concept and Values	Potential Competencies	Typical Work Activities and Environments
Realistic	Emotionally stable, reliable	Mechanical ability and ingenuity	Job with tangible results
	Practical, thrifty, persistent	Problem solving with tools, machines	Operating heavy equipment
	Shy, modest	Psychomotor skills	Using tools
	Uncomfortable talking about self	Physical strength	Physical demands
	Traditional values		Fixing, building, repairing
Investigative	Independent, self-motivated	Scientific ability	Ambiguous or abstract tasks
	Reserved, introspective	Analytical skills	Solving problems through thinking
	Analytical, curious	Mathematical skills	Working independently
	Task-oriented	Writing skills	Scientific or laboratory settings
	Original, creative, nonconforming	Perseverance	Collecting and organizing data
Artistic	Independent, nonconforming	Creativity, imagination	Creating artwork or performing
	Self-expressive	Verbal-linguistic skills	Working independently
	Intuitive, sensitive, emotional	Musical ability	Unstructured, flexible environments that allow self-expression

(Continues)

TABLE 7.1 (Continued)

Type	Self-Concept and Values	Potential Competencies	Typial Work Activities and Environments
	Impulsive	Artistic ability	
	Drawn to aesthetic qualities		
Social	Humanistic, idealistic, ethical	Social and interpersonal skills	Teaching, explaining, guiding
	Concerned for welfare of others	Verbal ability	Solving problems, leading discussions
	Tactful, cooperative, generous	Teaching skills	Educational, social service and mental health organizations
	Kind, friendly, cheerful	Ability to empathize with and understand others	
	Understanding, insightful		
Enterprising	Status conscious	Verbal skills related to speaking, persuading, selling	Selling, purchasing, leading
	Ambitious, competitive		Managing people and projects
	Sociable, talkative	Leadership skills	Giving speeches and presentations
	Optimistic, energetic, popular	Resilience, high energy, optimism	Financial, government and political organizations
	Aggressive, adventuresome	Social and interpersonal skills	

Conventional	Conscientious, persevering	Efficiency, organization	Organizing office procedures
	Practical, conservative	Management of systems and data	Keeping records and filing systems
	Orderly, systematic, precise, accurate	Mathematical skills	Writing reports, making charts
	Careful, controlled	Attention to detail, perfectionism	Structured organizations with well-ordered chains of command
		Operation of office machines	

Note. Adapted from Harmon et al. (1994) and Sharf (1997)

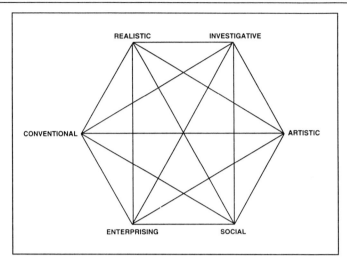

FIG. 7.1. Holland's hexagon of six types and their interrelations. SOURCE: Holland (1997). Reproduced by special permission of the publisher, Psychological Assessment Resources, Inc., from Making Vocational Choices, Third Edition, copyright 1973, 1985, 1992, 1997 by Psychological Assessment Resources, Inc. All rights reserved.

well-differentiated when there is a clear distinction between what an individual likes and dislikes. Poor differentiation would be characterized by similar scores across the six types. One method of determining degree of differentiation within a summary code is to subtract the highest score from the lowest score.

Consistency is a reflection of the "internal coherence" (Spokane, 1996) of an individual's interests, in terms of the hexagonal arrangement; an individual with artistic and investigative interests would be considered to be more consistent than an individual with artistic and conventional interests. Thus, types located closer together on the hexagon are more consistent than types located further apart.

Finally, *identity* relates to a sense of clarity for personal goals and interests. That is, a strong sense of identity would be characterized by high levels of differentiation and consistency (Spokane, 1996).

These four additional constructs are useful for making predictions about vocational outcomes. More specifically, individuals who are congruent, differentiated, and consistent are predicted to be more satisfied and better adjusted than individuals who are incongruent, undifferentiated, and inconsistent. For example, a well-differentiated social individual with secondary artistic interests working in a social environment would be happier and more productive than if this same individual were in a realistic environment.

Holland's theory of vocational personalities and work environments is the most widely researched P–E theory; and, in fact, is the most widely researched theory within vocational psychology as a whole. The ease with which the theory's constructs may be operationalized is one reason why Holland's theory has been extensively researched. For example, several interest inventories provide measures of the Holland typology, such as the Vocational Preference Inventory (Holland, 1985), the Self-Directed Search (Holland, Powell, & Fritzsche, 1994), and the Strong Interest Inventory (Harmon, Hansen, Borgen, & Hammer, 1994). The Holland typology also has been integrated into career guidance and information systems such as DISCOVER. Techniques and instruments such as the Position Classification Inventory (Gottfredson & Holland, 1991) also have been developed to determine the Holland types of specific environments (Walsh & Holland, 1992).

Since the introduction of Holland's theory, much of the relevant research has resulted in findings supportive of the reliability and validity of Holland's core concepts (Swanson & Gore, 1999). Overall, the findings suggest that individuals choose to be in environments that are congruent with their personality types (Holland, 1985; Spokane, 1985). Additionally, P–E congruence has been found to be related to personal and vocational adjustment (Walsh & Holland, 1992). However, research supportii g the relationship of consistency and differentiation with career outcomes has been less affirmative (Spokane, 1996), and researchers disagree about the extent to which congruent person–environment matches are related to job satisfaction (Assouline & Meir, 1987; Holland & Gottfredson, 1976; Tranberg, Slane, & Ekeberg, 1993).

Theory of Work Adjustment and Person–Environment Correspondence Counseling

The TWA consists of 17 formal propositions and their corollaries that address the process of adjustment to work (Dawis, 1996; Dawis & Lofquist, 1984). These propositions specify aspects of the individual and the work environment that predict job tenure and satisfaction. According to TWA, individuals "inherently seek to achieve and to maintain correspondence with their environments" (Lofquist & Dawis, 1991, p. 18), where correspondence is defined as a "harmonious relationship between the individual and the environment" (p. 22).

As noted earlier, theories of P–E fit incorporate mechanisms to describe the correspondence between individuals and environments. Whereas Holland postulated six types of persons or environments, TWA takes a different approach. Dawis and Lofquist (1984) described two sets of common dimensions: (a) an individual's abilities and those required by his or her job, and (b) an individual's values and the reinforcers available on the job. These two dimensions translate into the concept of *satisfaction*, or the correspondence between and individual's values and what the job offers, and the concept of *satisfactoriness*, or how well an individual's abilities and skills meet what the job or organization requires (see Fig. 7.2).

A central feature of TWA is that both satisfaction and satisfactoriness are equally important components in the prediction of work adjustment: "When each party is able to meet the other's requirements—when they are in correspondence—both parties experience and express *satisfaction*" (Dawis, 1996, p. 81). Despite the dual focus on person and environment, TWA clearly emphasizes what the person experiences, and uses the word *satisfaction* for an individual's satisfaction with his or her job, and the word *satisfactoriness* for the individual with whom the work environment is satisfied. Therefore, correspondence occurs when an individual is both satisfied and satisfactory (Dawis, 1996).

The 17 formal propositions address the precursors and outcomes of the degree of satisfaction and satisfactoriness. Satisfaction is predicted from the correspondence between an individual's values and the reinforcers available in the environment, and is negatively related to the probability of an individual quitting a job. Satisfactoriness is predicted from the correspondence between an individual's abilities and the abilities required by the environment, and is negatively related to an individual being fired from a job. Work adjustment, or job tenure, is the result of an individual's level of satisfaction and satisfactoriness at a specific time. Moreover, the variables of satisfaction and satisfactoriness each influence the prediction of the other variable, and the stylistic variables of flexibility and perseverance moderate the prediction of satisfaction, satisfactoriness, and work adjustment.

Furthermore, TWA postulates that four personality style variables are important in characterizing how an individual interacts with the environment: celerity, pace, rhythm, and endurance. *Celerity* refers to

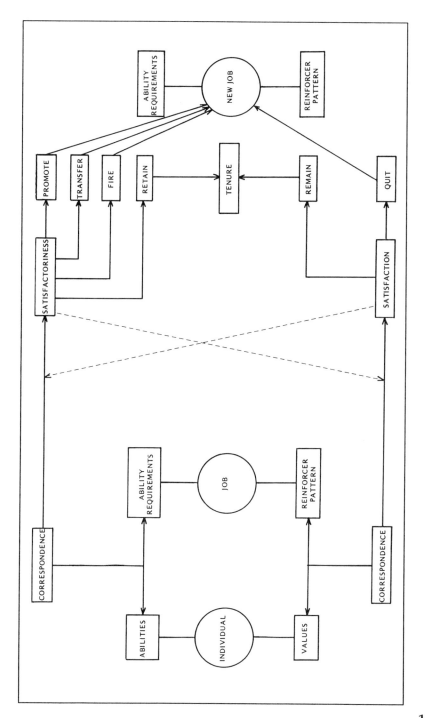

FIG. 7.2. The theory of work adjustment. SOURCE: Dawis and Lofquist (1984). Used with permission.

153

the speed by which an individual initiates interaction with his or her environment. *Pace* indicates the intensity or activity level of one's interaction with the environment. *Rhythm* is the pattern of the pace of interaction with the environment (steady, cyclical, or erratic). *Endurance* refers to the sustaining of interaction with the environment. These variables help explain why individuals with similar abilities and values may behave in different ways within a given work environment. Moreover, these constructs can be used to describe environments as well as people, and environments differ from one another in terms of celerity, pace, rhythm, and endurance.

Dissatisfaction serves a central motivational role according to TWA. Dissatisfaction on the part of either the person or the environment represents disequilibrium in the system, and is the impetus for adjustment to occur. "Satisfaction motivates 'maintenance' behavior; dissatisfaction motivates adjustment behavior" (Dawis, 1996, p. 87).

Adjustment can occur in two different modes. In the *active mode*, the individual attempts to change the work environment to reduce the amount of discorrespondence, by changing the requirements required by the environment or the reinforcers available in the environment. For example, in response to feeling overworked, an employee could ask for a reduction in job assignments, or ask for a raise or promotion. In the *reactive mode*, the individual attempts to change him- or herself to reduce discorrespondence, by changing his or her work skills or the importance attached to needs. In the previous example, an employee could learn time management skills to increase efficiency, or shift priorities so that less focus is placed on work. Thus, adjustment behavior can be aimed at one of four targets: the individual's skills or need requirements and the environment's available reinforcers and ability requirements.

Individuals vary in how much discorrespondence they can tolerate in their work environment before becoming dissatisfied; the term *flexibility* is used to describe the degree of tolerance (see Fig. 7.3). Individuals low in flexibility have less tolerance than do those high in flexibility. Both individuals and work environments can be characterized in terms of the degree of flexibility they exhibit.

Adjustment behavior, whether active or reactive, may continue for some time even if it is not successful. Eventually, however, if the adjustment behavior is not successful, the individual will withdraw from the environment. How long an individual continues with ad-

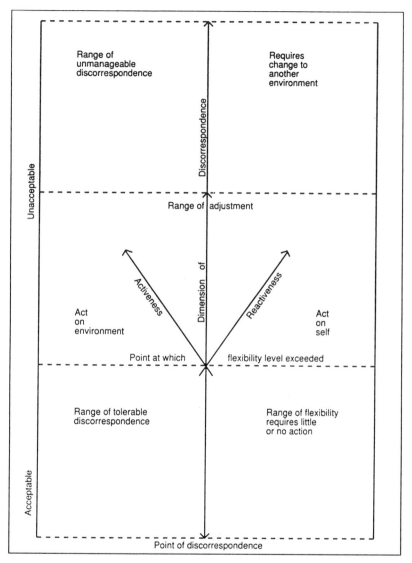

FIG. 7.3. Adjustment to person–environment discorrespondence.
SOURCE: Dawis and Lofquist (1984). Used with permission.

justment behavior is referred to as his or her *perseverance*. Individuals low in perseverance are likely to quit a job (or quit their attempts at adjustment) more quickly than are those high in perseverance. As with other constructs in TWA, perseverance can be used to characterize either individuals or environments.

The concepts of active and reactive modes, and of flexibility and perseverance, thus are important predictors of what an individual is likely to do if they are dissatisfied (or if the environment is dissatisfied with the individual's behavior). These concepts also are important considerations from a broader perspective: An individual develops a characteristic *adjustment style* over time, which is useful information in career counseling.

Finally, three general stages of development are outlined within TWA. *Differentiation* occurs in the first 20 years, in which abilities, skills, values, needs, and personality style are forming. *Stability* corresponds to the majority of adulthood, and is characterized by relative constancy of abilities and values, although specific skills and needs might vary. *Decline* is characterized by physiological changes that alter one's abilities, values, and style. The transitions between the three stages—between differentiation and stability, and between stability and decline—are "the critical points at which adjustment problems are expected to peak" (Dawis, 1996, p. 97).

The TWA has received a moderate amount of research attention, primarily by the theory's authors through the Work Adjustment Project at the University of Minnesota (Osipow & Fitzgerald, 1996; Tinsley, 1993). The majority of evidence supports the propositions of the theory (Betz, Fitzgerald, & Hill, 1989; Swanson & Gore, 1999), although because of the number and complexity of the propositions, it has not been tested in its entirety.

The development of the TWA has been accompanied by continued attention to instrumentation and measurement of the central constructs. For example, the Minnesota Importance Questionnaire (Rounds, Henley, Dawis, Lofquist, & Weiss, 1981) was developed to measure work values and needs, and the Minnesota Satisfaction Questionnaire (Weiss, Dawis, England, & Lofquist, 1967) was developed to measure job satisfaction. Moreover, considerable data has been assembled to establish the patterns of reinforcers characterizing different occupations.

Summary of Theories

There are three central assumptions that underlie these theories of P–E fit (Chartrand, 1991; Rounds & Hesketh, 1994; Rounds & Tracey, 1990; Swanson, 1996). First, individuals seek out environments that match their characteristics, whether defined as correspondence in TWA or as congruence in Holland's theory. Second, the degree of P–E fit is associated with important outcomes for both the person and the environment. The degree of P–E fit can be viewed along a continuum. Congruence or correspondence between person and environment is related to important outcomes, such as satisfaction, achievement, performance, stability, retention, and tenure. Each of these outcomes benefits the person and the environment, and each is more likely to occur as the degree of fit increases. Conversely, poor P–E fit is more likely to lead to negative outcomes, such as dissatisfaction, poor performance, and job turnover. Dissatisfaction or incongruence serves as a motivational force, in that it represents disequilibrium in the system and is the impetus for adjustment or change to occur.

The third and final assumption underlying these two theories is that the process of P–E fit is reciprocal, in that the person shapes the environment and the environment shapes the person. Just as people search for environments that allow them to use their abilities and express their values, so too environments search for people, such as through recruitment and selection practices. Furthermore, the reciprocal nature of P–E fit reflects a systems perspective, whereby change in one element influences the other elements in the system by creating a homeostatic imbalance.

APPLICATIONS OF PERSON–ENVIRONMENT FIT THEORIES

Theories of P–E fit are relevant to career development and vocational behavior across the lifespan, although the particular issues encountered will differ according to life stage. These theories also are relevant to different modes of career intervention. In this section, we outline two types of interventions: those that are delivered in a programmatic or systemic way, and those that occur on an individual basis such as within career counseling.

Programmatic Interventions

A number of interventions may be used to assist individuals in resolving their career concerns. The rubric of career interventions includes a wide variety of content areas and modes of delivery. For example, types of career interventions include audio- or videotaped materials, printed career materials, self-administered career instruments, and computer-based guidance programs. Moreover, career interventions may be delivered in a variety of ways, including career information libraries and integrated programs or curricula in elementary and secondary schools, community-based vocational guidance centers, and, increasingly, via the Internet.

An example of a programmatic intervention is reflected in efforts to address the transition from school to work for noncollege-bound students. The school-to-work movement represents an extensive intervention in the way that adolescents prepare to enter the world of work, which could "directly affect the vocational outcomes of potentially 75% or more of youth" (Worthington & Juntunen, 1997, p. 323). School-to-work programs received their impetus from federal funding available through the 1994 School-to-Work Opportunity Act. School-to-work programs typically incorporate partnerships between school systems and local employers, and focus on assisting middle- and secondary school students in developing relevant and transferable job skills, and in offering hands-on job experience.

School-to-work programs could benefit from the infusion of vocational psychology, and, particularly, theories of P–E fit (Swanson, 1997). These theories offer a superb method of facilitating the initial choices that adolescents feel compelled to make regarding their vocational futures, by providing a framework and a language for describing the match between individuals and work environments.

Individual Interventions

As just noted, considerable diversity exists in types of available career interventions. However, individual career counseling is arguably one of the most popular and effective types of interventions used. Career counseling involves an ongoing, direct interaction between counselor and client in which career- or work-related issues are the primary focus (Swanson, 1995). Thus, the activities that take place in career counseling occur within the context of a relationship between counselor and client (Swanson, 1995).

Career counseling serves several purposes. In general, career counseling professionals are interested in helping clients develop a better understanding of their interests and abilities. In addition to improving personal knowledge, career counselors also are interested in assisting clients in gaining more information about the world of work. These two aims clearly are related to the framework of P–E psychology. It is important to note that the approaches and goals of career counseling are largely dependent on the client's presenting issue. For example, Brown (1996) suggested that there are three different types of career clients. The first group of clients may be defined as those in need of help in making planned decisions, such as deciding on a college major or training program. The second group of clients consists of those that need help with making unplanned career decisions, such as finding another job after experiencing an unexpected lay-off. The final group consists of clients who are dealing with mental or physical health-related problems, in addition to their career issues. Thus, the course of career counseling is influenced by the client's current situation.

The approach taken in career counseling also depends on the counselor's theoretical orientation. For example, a developmental approach may emphasize the exploration of vocational development tasks, whereas a learning approach may stress the need to learn new skills (Savickas & Walsh, 1996). When using a P–E fit orientation, the first goal of career counseling is the enhancement of self-knowledge (Dawis, 1996). This can be achieved through examining the client's abilities, values, and interests. A related issue involves determining whether the client is satisfactoriness-oriented (i.e., achievement orientation) or satisfaction-oriented (i.e., concerned with self-fulfillment). It also is important to explore the client's present or future work environment. Counselors can help clients examine the degree of fit between their personality characteristics and talents and the work environment's characteristics and requirements. If the degree of fit is questionable, the counselor may assess the strategies available for work adjustment, such as change in the person, the environment, or both (Dawis, 1996; Swanson & Fouad, 1999).

CASE EXAMPLES

The two cases presented in this section were chosen to illustrate the ways in which P–E fit theories may be used to understand career development and to intervene in vocational difficulties. The two theories described in this chapter both offer useful conceptualizations of vocational behavior throughout the life span; we will apply Holland's theory to an individual exploring and choosing an initial career direction, and TWA to an individual experiencing difficulties in his current job.

Applying Holland's Theory to Initial Vocational Choice: The Case of Maria

Maria, a 15-year-old Latina high school sophomore, met with the school counselor to discuss her future career plans. She is currently working as a clerical assistant at a bank, a job assigned to her through her school's work experience program. Her main job responsibilities include answering the telephone, typing documents, and making photocopies. Maria has begun to feel bored with her clerical duties and this lack of interest has negatively impacted her job performance.

Maria is an academically gifted student, especially in the areas of math and science. Her favorite class is biology and her least favorite classes are English and history. She has taken a number of advanced placement classes and has performed well enough in these classes to earn college credit.

According to Holland's theory, the incongruence between Maria's personality type and her work environment is the cause of her current job dissatisfaction. Given Maria's penchant for biology, she is likely to be characterized primarily as an investigative type. She also has interests in social and realistic activities (ISR). In contrast, her current work environment may be characterized as primarily conventional, followed by social and enterprising (CSE). Her type (ISR) does not represent a good fit with her current work environment (CSE). Thus, working as a clerical assistant does not allow Maria to express her investigative interests. For example, investigative types tend to enjoy engaging in research and analytic activities. Conversely, a conventional environment requires conformity and inflexibility. Maria is likely to feel that her intellectual curiosity is being stifled in her constrictive work environment.

In addition to causing job dissatisfaction, this incongruence between personality type and work environment offers an explanation for Maria's poor job performance. According to Holland's theory, incongruent situations lead to a decrease in work productivity and achievement.

The school counselor in this situation could address Maria's job dissatisfaction in several ways. Incongruency can be resolved by changing to a new and more congruent environment (Spokane, 1985). Thus, the counselor could assist Maria in finding an investigative job. For example, she could work as a lab or research assistant. Another option would be to help Maria find a clerical job that requires the use of investigative skills; for example, working as a paralegal or as a secretary in a research lab.

Incongruency can also be resolved through changing one's personal behavior and perceptions about the current environment (Spokane, 1985). Using this approach, the counselor could help Maria explore ways of using investigative skills in her current job duties. For example, she could request job assignments that involve the use of research or analytic skills, or that allow her to learn new skills. The counselor also could assist Maria in changing her job-related perceptions. For example, she could learn to focus on the positive aspects of her job. Because this approach does not directly resolve the incongruence between personality type and work environment, it should be reserved for situations that have limited options (i.e., the person is unable to change jobs).

In addition to experiencing difficulty in her current job situation, Maria also is uncertain about her future academic plans. She has thought about going to college, but is not sure what she would choose as a major. Furthermore, her parents, who immigrated from Mexico, do not think it is necessary for Maria to earn a college degree. They believe that a woman should put her family before her career. Thus, it is more important that Maria find a "good husband" to take care of her. Given her family's limited financial resources, her parents also believe that it is more important to invest in a college degree for her brother because he "will be responsible for supporting his family in the future."

When addressing her uncertainty for future educational and career plans, the counselor could use interventions that capitalize on Maria's investigative skills. For example, a homework assignment for Maria might involve going to the library to research different careers. She could then analyze this information by looking at the advantages and disadvantages of various career options. Given her family's tight financial situation, she also could conduct research on the options available for financing a college education (e.g., scholarships, federal or state aid).

If Maria attends college, she is likely to choose a "hard sciences" major because of her current success in this area of study. Nevertheless, the counselor may want to gain more information about Maria's interests in this area to assess whether this would be a wise choice, or a good fit, for her. As previously mentioned, personality types are influenced by one's abilities and interests. Maria may be attracted to science and math courses because she is able to excel academically in these areas. However, she may experience very little enjoyment in studying the subject matter. If this is the case, the counselor may want to help Maria find a more suitable area of study, one that she can both enjoy and perform well.

When counseling Maria, it is important to consider how her ethnicity and gender may impact her career satisfaction and tenure. Holland posited that work environments are characterized by the people that occupy them. Individuals enter into specific work environments because of their interests and personalities, and stay in these occupations because interactions with the environment are reinforcing and satisfying. The underrepresentation of ethnic minorities and women in scientific fields may cause Maria to feel very dissimilar to her coworkers. This may make it more difficult for Maria to experience her environment as reinforcing and satisfying.

Finally, the counselor also should explore how Maria's family will impact her future goals. For example, it is possible that her parents' beliefs that women should not seek higher education will be a decisive factor in whether Maria decides to attend college. Maria also may feel pressured by her parents to choose a career that is compatible with getting married and having a family.

Applying TWA to Vocational Adjustment: The Case of Roy

Roy is a 54-year-old White male requesting counseling services at a community mental health agency at the urging of his wife. Roy reports feeling "tense and under a lot of stress," and is having difficulty sleeping. In addition, his wife reports that he is irritable and withdrawn when he comes home from work, and she is concerned about the amount that he is drinking.

Roy describes experiencing job-related stress due to his company's recent decision to downsize. He has been working as a middle manager at a long distance telephone company for more than 20 years. He was mainly responsible for hiring employees, assigning job duties, and coordinating projects with other departments. Roy felt very satisfied with these duties and enjoyed interacting on a close personal level with his employees. He was very popular among his coworkers and employees because of his easygoing and friendly personality. Roy excelled in his job performance. He received a number of accolades for his productivity and contributions to the company.

According to TWA, the stability of Roy's 20-year job tenure can be viewed as the result of achieving work adjustment. Work adjustment, in turn, is the product of two types of correspondence: Roy's satisfaction with the work environment, in terms of his values and needs that are met on the job, and the work environment's satisfaction with Roy, in terms of the abilities and skills that he has to offer the organization. Roy valued the close personal interactions he had with his employees, and gained a sense of accomplishment from hiring good employees and helping them develop within their jobs after they were hired. His interpersonal skills and personnel management abilities were a good match for the requirements of his job, and his supervisor was pleased with Roy's performance.

With the recent downsizing, Roy has been given the additional responsibilities of budgeting and updating computer files. His dislike for these job duties has negatively impacted his work and home life. Roy feels bored and incompetent with his additional duties and he often waits until the end of the day before doing them. On some occasions, Roy does not perform the necessary budgeting and computer work and this causes disruption and lost productivity in his department. The frequency with which he does not finish his additional duties has increased in recent weeks. Because of the changes at work, Roy often feels unhappy and tense, and his coworkers and employees no longer find him to be an enjoyable person to be around.

The changes in Roy's work environment—his job duties and the expectations that the organization has for him—have led to substantial discorrespondence according to the TWA. Again, two types of correspondence (or, in this case, discorrespondence) are relevant to an understanding of work adjustment—the amount of satisfaction that Roy experiences in his job, and the degree of satisfactoriness that Roy offers his employer. First, Roy clearly feels less satisfied with his work environment. Because of his new job duties, he no longer has as much direct contact with employees, and when he takes time to interact with employees, he cannot complete the tasks that his supervisor expects him to do. He has lost the aspects of his job that provided the most reinforcement for him, and, he has taken on new responsibilities that he does not find rewarding. Second, Roy is less satisfactory to his employer: he is not yet skilled at his new responsibilities, and he is not completing them well nor on time. In fact, his supervisor is worried about whether Roy will succeed in this new position, and has begun to make pointed comments to Roy about his performance.

According to TWA, dissatisfaction serves a motivational role. On Roy's part, he has been considering whether he should ask for a transfer to a new position, or quit his job. He is concerned, however, about the riskiness of doing either given the downsizing of his company and economic conditions in general. His decision to seek counseling at this time also can be seen as motivated by the dissatisfaction he is currently experiencing. On the work environment's part, Roy's supervisor has been contemplating what to do about Roy's job performance, and he has considered firing him.

A counselor might use TWA as a framework to consider the options available to Roy. On the person side of the equation, Roy has two overarching options: to stay in his job, or to quit. These two options, however, represent a considerably wider range of possibilities to explore in counseling. First, the counselor can help Roy systematically examine his current job situation, to identify what he might find rewarding about his new job responsibilities, and in what areas he would do well to pursue further training. This step seems crucial given Roy's affective reactions to his current job situation: His irritability and tension is accompanied by anger and hostility toward his supervisor and the organization because he perceives them as "taking away the things I do best." These affective reactions also are manifested in his behavior on and off the job, such as avoiding talking with his supervisor about his new responsibilities. The counselor can help Roy prepare to talk with his supervisor by role-playing in session.

Second, the counselor can help Roy realistically assess his options for leaving his current job. Such an assessment would include a thorough consideration of Roy's skills and work experience, his motivation to take on a job search, and the degree to which a new position might provide better correspondence. Other factors to consider include the local job market, his willingness to relocate, and how much his current affective reactions are influencing his thoughts of quitting.

On the environment side, Roy's decreased satisfactoriness also may lead to two overarching options: to keep him in his current position, or to remove him from the position. The latter might be accomplished by firing, promotion, or transfer. All of these options can be considered within counseling, and the counselor can help Roy explore each of these possibilities. Although neither Roy nor his counselor has direct control over the work environment, it is highly possible to influence the outcome or decisions that his supervisor will make regarding Roy. For example, if Roy would like to stay in his current position, he may need to request additional training from his employer, and communicate his commitment to learn and develop on the job. An alternative is for Roy to discuss the possibility of a transfer within the organization.

SUMMARY
AND CONCLUSION

In this chapter, we presented two theories of vocational behavior that are grounded in P–E psychology. These theories provide a framework for understanding the work-related activities of individuals over the life span, and are useful in acknowledging the important role that the environmental context plays in shaping career behavior. We illustrated the utility of the theories by applying them to two case examples, and discussed how a career counseling professional might use the theories in conceptualizing these clients' current difficulties.

These two theories demonstrate the influential role that P–E psychology has had on the development of theories of vocational psychology. The theories also serve to remind practitioners of the need to consider both person and environment—and their interaction—when designing interventions to assist individuals in achieving a satisfying career choice.

REFERENCES

Assouline, M., & Meir, E. I. (1987). Meta-analysis of the relationship between congruence well-being measures. *Journal of Vocational Behavior, 31,* 319–332.

Betz, N. E., & Corning, A. F. (1993). The inseparability of "career" and "personal" counseling. *Career Development Quarterly, 42,* 137–142.

Betz, N. E., Fitzgerald, L. F., & Hill, R. E. (1989). Trait factor theories: Traditional cornerstone of career theory. In M. D. Arthur, D. T. Hall, & B. S. Lawrence (Eds.), *Handbook of career theory* (pp. 26–40). New York: Cambridge University Press.

Blustein, D. L., & Spengler, P. M. (1995). Personal adjustment: Career counseling and psychotherapy. In W. B. Walsh & S. H. Osipow (Eds.), *Handbook of vocational psychology* (2nd ed., pp. 295–329). Mahwah, NJ: Lawrence Erlbaum Associates.

Brown, D. (1996). Brown's values-based, holistic model of career and life-role choices and satisfaction. In D. Brown, L. Brooks, & Associates (Eds.), *Career choice and development* (3rd ed., pp. 337–372). San Francisco: Jossey-Bass.

Brown, D., & Brooks, L. (1985). Career counseling as a mental health intervention. *Professional Psychology: Research and Practice, 16,* 860–867.

Chartrand, J. M. (1991). The evolution of trait-and-factor career counseling: A person X environment fit approach. *Journal of Counseling and Development, 69,* 518–524.

Dawis, R. V. (1994). The Theory of Work Adjustment as convergent theory. In M. L. Savickas & R. W. Lent (Eds.), *Convergence in career development theories* (pp. 33–43). Palo Alto, CA: Consulting Psychologists Press.

Dawis, R. V. (1996). The Theory of Work Adjustment and Person–Environment-Correspondence Counseling. In D. Brown, L. Brooks, & Associates (Eds.), *Career choice and development* (3rd ed., pp. 75–120). San Francisco: Jossey-Bass.

Dawis, R. V., & Lofquist, L. (1984). *A psychological theory of work adjustment.* Minneapolis: University of Minnesota Press.

Gottfredson, G. D., & Holland, J. L. (1991). *Position Classification Inventory: Professional manual.* Odessa, FL: Psychological Assessment Resources.

Harmon, L. W., Hansen, J. C., Borgen, F. H., & Hammer, A. L. (1994). *Strong Interest Inventory: Applications and technical guide.* Palo Alto, CA: Consulting Psychologists Press.

Holland, J. L. (1985). *Manual for the Vocational Preference Inventory.* Odessa, FL: Psychological Assessment Resources.

Holland, J. L. (1997). *Making vocational choices: A theory of vocational and work environments.* Odessa, FL: Psychological Assessment Resources.

Holland, J. L., & Gottfredson, G. D. (1976). Using a typology of persons and environments to explain careers: Some extensions and clarifications. *The Counseling Psychologist, 6,* 20–29.

Holland, J. L., Powell, A. B., & Fritzsche, B. A. (1994). *The Self-Directed Search professional user's guide.* Odessa, FL: Psychological Assessment Resources.

Lofquist, L., & Dawis, R. V. (1991). *Essentials of person–environment-correspondence counseling*. Minneapolis: University of Minnesota Press.

Osipow, S. H., & Fitzgerald, L. F. (1996). *Theories of career development* (4th ed.). Boston: Allyn & Bacon.

Parsons, F. (1989). *Choosing a vocation*. Garrett Park, MD: Garrett Park Press. (Original work published 1909)

Rounds, J. B., Henley, G. A., Dawis, R. V., Lofquist, L. H., & Weiss, D. J. (1981). *Manual for the Minnesota Importance Questionnaire*. Minneapolis: University of Minnesota, Psychology Department, Work Adjustment Project.

Rounds, J. B., & Hesketh, B. (1994). The Theory of Work Adjustment: Unifying principles and concepts. In M. L. Savickas & R. W. Lent (Eds.), *Convergence in career development theories* (pp. 177–186). Palo Alto, CA: Consulting Psychologists Press.

Rounds, J. B., & Tracey, T. J. (1990). From trait-and-factor to person–environment fit counseling: Theory and process. In W. B. Walsh & S. H. Osipow (Eds.), *Career counseling* (pp. 1–44). Mahwah, NJ: Lawrence Erlbaum Associates.

Savickas, M. L., & Lent, R. W. (Eds.). (1994). *Convergence in career development theories*. Palo Alto, CA: Consulting Psychologists Press.

Savickas, M. L., & Walsh, W. B. (Eds.). (1996). *Handbook of career counseling theory and practice*. Palo Alto, CA: Davies- Black Publishers.

Sharf, R. S. (1997). *Applying career development theory to counseling* (2nd ed.). Pacific Grove, CA: Brooks/Cole.

Spokane, A. R. (1985). A review of research on person–environment congruence in Holland's theory of careers. *Journal of Vocational Behavior, 26*, 306–343.

Spokane, A. R. (1989). Are there psychological and mental health consequences of difficult career decisions? *Journal of Career Development, 16*, 19–23.

Spokane, A. R. (1996). Holland's theory. In D. Brown, L. Brooks, and Associates (Eds.), *Career choice and development* (3rd ed., pp. 33–74). San Francisco: Jossey-Bass.

Swanson, J. L. (1992). Vocational behavior, 1989–1991: Life-span career development and reciprocal interaction of work and nonwork. *Journal of Vocational Behavior, 41*, 101–161.

Swanson, J. L. (1995). The process and outcome of career counseling. In W. B. Walsh & S. H. Osipow (Eds.), *Handbook of vocational psychology* (2nd ed., pp. 217–259). Mahwah, NJ: Lawrence Erlbaum Associates.

Swanson, J. L. (1996). The theory is the practice: Trait-and-factor/Person–environment fit counseling. In M. L. Savickas & W. B. Walsh (Eds.), *Handbook of career counseling theory and practice* (pp. 93–108). Palo Alto, CA: Davies-Black Publishers.

Swanson, J. L. (1997, August). What do theories of person–environment fit offer? In R. L. Worthington & R. W. Lent (Chairs), *Applying vocational psychology theories to the school-to-work transition*. Symposium presented at the annual meeting of the American Psychological Association, Chicago.

Swanson, J. L., & Fouad, N. A. (1999). *Career theory and practice: Learning through case studies*. Thousand Oaks, CA: Sage.

Swanson, J. L., & Gore, P. A., Jr. (1999). Advances in career development theory and research. In S. D. Brown & R. W. Lent (Eds.), *Handbook of counseling psychology* (3rd ed.). New York: Wiley.

Tinsley, H. E. A. (1993). Special issue on the Theory of Work Adjustment. *Journal of Vocational Behavior, 43,* 1–4.

Tranberg, M., Slane, S., & Ekeberg, S. E. (1993). The relation between interest congruence and satisfaction: A meta-analysis. *Journal of Vocational Behavior, 42,* 253–264.

Walsh, W. B., & Holland, J. L. (1992). A theory of personality types and work environments. In W. B. Walsh, K. H. Craik, & R. H. Price (Eds.), *Person–environment psychology: Models and perspectives* (pp. 35–69). Mahwah, NJ: Lawrence Erlbaum Associates.

Walsh, W. B., Price, R. H., & Craik, K. H. (1992). Person–environment psychology: An introduction. In W. B. Walsh, K. H. Craik, & R. H. Price (Eds.), *Person–environment psychology: Models and perspectives* (pp. vii–xi). Mahwah, NJ: Lawrence Erlbaum Associates.

Weiss, D. J., Dawis, R. V., England, G. W., & Lofquist, L. H. (1967). Manual for the Minnesota Satisfaction Questionnaire. *Minnesota Studies In Vocational Rehabilitation,* XXII.

Worthington, R. L., & Juntunen, C. L. (1997). The vocational development of non-college-bound youth: Counseling psychology and the school-to-work transition movement. *The Counseling Psychologist, 25,* 323–363.

Culture as an Essential Aspect of Person–Environment Fit

Jody L. Swartz-Kulstad
University of Wisconsin Superior
William E. Martin, Jr.
Northern Arizona University

For the past several deca des, mental health professionals (MHPs) have been cautioned, no, challenged to make their provision of ser- vices more culturally relevant. Until more recent years, this meant that the MHP relied on either preconceived notions of what was construed as culturally relevant and appropriate service provision or they looked on their current practice and said "I provide services that are sensitive to all, regardless of their background." Somewhere between these two positions lies the current practice of culturally sensitive and relevant counseling in today's mental health field.

Neither stereotyping the client, nor failing to recognize the role of ethnocultural background, current practice is moving in the direc- tion of recognizing that culture is a part of all of our lives; dynamic and encompassing. Along with this newer, more inclusive position, comes the acceptance that as culture surrounds each of us, like all en- vironmental factors, it affects us in different ways. No two individu- als internalize culture in the same way (Ho, 1995). Social factors (e.g., age, class, gender, region) and acculturation processes directly and indirectly influence the construction of subcultures of ethnoculture (Guarnaccia & Rodriguez, 1997); and these subcultures interact with unique factors of the individual such that understanding how we became who we are and how we "fit" with our world lies within the complex interaction between our person and the multisystem nature of our environment. As such, perhaps the most effective way of understanding how culture affects each individual is through the person–environment (P–E) perspective.

Past State of Culturally Appropriate Services

Hermans and Kempen (1998) maintained that "in an increasingly interconnected world society, the concept of independent, coherent, and stable cultures becomes increasingly irrelevant" (p. 1111). For too long, researchers and practitioners have viewed culture as an independent variable, able to be categorized or grouped, treating diverse individuals as a single entity (Ho, 1995). Gaining steam in the early 1970s, numerous articles, books, and reports explored the "right" way to provide services to the Asian client, Hispanic client, and so forth. In 1996, Patterson decried the state of culturally appropriate services, suggesting that attempting to categorize our clients based on such an approach ignores the human characteristics of the individual, the shared characteristics that transcend cultural boundaries and contribute to diversity among members in ethnocultural groups. According to Vontress (1999), decades of focusing on difference only served to create a chasm between cultural groups that obscured similarities germane and basic to all individuals.

In his recent exposition on the integrative model in counseling and psychotherapy, Leong (1996, referring to Kluckhohn & Murray's, 1950, work) summarized Kluckhohn and Murray's position regarding determinants of personality formation—each person is to some extent like all other people, like some other people, and like no other person. This position lends support for the need to go beyond group-level and universal-level approaches to embrace the multidimensionality of human experience. According to Leong (1996), this position, coupled with a need to understand the influence of the client's ethnocultural experience, requires the culturally competent counselor to continually monitor where the client is in relation to universal, group, and individual variables. In the past, culture has been considered a group level variable. Models to understand how an individual's ethnocultural and contextual experience influences his or her current functioning have been inherently limited by a narrow focus on culture as a group-level variable (i.e., acculturation models, racial or ethnic identity models; Leong, 1996). Although an improvement over previously unidimensional models of human functioning (i.e., artificial distinctions based on such aspects as ethnicity, race, or religion), they do not consider the interactive and dynamic aspects of universal or individual level variables. As Miller (1997) noted, more attention needs to be paid to the heterogeneity of cultural practices and meanings among subgroups of populations, and, we might add, to the shared practices and meanings among all individuals.

Understanding the complexities of the individual requires inclusion of, rather than classification by, ethnocultural and contextual factors in the psychological assessment and intervention process (Swartz & Martin, 1999). Indeed, we must remember that all individuals are unique. According to Ho (1995), each individual possesses differing combinations of cultural characteristics, regardless of reference group membership, such that even people from the same group manifest their culture in very different ways. As such, clinicians must remember, indeed expect, that they will work "with clients who have characteristics that are idiosyncratic and atypical of persons of their culture ... this definition applies to any group that has shared learned behavior for the purpose of adjustment, adaptation, and growth" (Ridley, Li, & Hill, 1998, pp. 834–835).

On a service delivery level, according to Guarnaccia and Rodriguez (1997), past programs based their evaluation of whether they were providing culturally appropriate services on narrow definitions of culture, static (anthropological) definitions of culture most commonly based on ethnic identity (e.g., were there professionals on staff of same ethnic classification as the client?), language (e.g., were there professionals who could conduct services in the language of the client?), and signs and symbols (e.g., were there physical indicators that suggested who belonged, who was in charge, and who the services were geared toward).

Culture cannot be captured by such approaches alone, it is far too complex, far too influenced by intricate social and acculturative processes that are altered primarily by time. As Guarnaccia and Rodriguez (1997) noted, "culture is both a product of group values, norms, and experiences and of *individual innovations and life histories* [Italics added]" (p. 2). Histories are the product of what once was our today, dynamic indeed. As such, rather than viewing culture as an independent variable, culture should be viewed as an outcome—dynamic and complex. It must be viewed as existing within the individual and within the environment.

Person–Environment Theory

Person–environment theory, as a whole, addresses the need to view a client's concerns as originating at a point in-between the individual and the environment, in the interaction between the two (Swartz & Martin, 1997). Premised on the notion that a greater understanding of individual and environmental characteristics are essential to determination of the match between the two, P–E theory provides the necessary constructs and methodology for measuring this potential fit. Although much of the past research on the utility of a P–E approach has been conducted in work and educational settings, the basic position that discrepancies in P–E fit lead to strain on the individual has great implications for the broader mental health field.

Given that aspects of the environment that influence behavior are determined by how the individual interacts with the environment, each individual's unique constellation of traits serves to create different environments such that no two people experience the environment in the same way (Bandura, 1985). According to Kendler (1986), understanding an individual's actions relies on knowledge of the context in which the behavior occurs. In the same way, understanding the process of psychosocial adaptation for any individual relies on knowledge of the how and whether an individual's competencies and characteristics meet the requirements of the different contexts in which the person exists.

Three primary P–E models (ecological approach, French's P–E model, and Theory of Work Adjustment [TWA]) provide the necessary constructs for understanding the role of culture and context in the person's mental health.

French's Person–Environment Model

The first model, proposed by French and Harrison (Harrison, 1978), views mental health difficulties as originating from a discrepancy in either the objective and subjective environment or the objective and subjective person. In other words, is the individual objectively able to meet the demands of the environment (e.g., does the individual's behavior fit the "norm" for the environment—does the person "look, talk, act" like others) and does the individual feel as though he or she "fits in" (e.g., are there others similar to the individual within the environment, does the individual have a sense of belonging). Two additional concepts are of importance in this model: contact with reality and accuracy of self-assessment and the individual's objective and subjective fit with the environment. In the former, the person's realistic appraisal of self and environment are based on accuracy of the individual's perception—does the individual have a realistic view of him- or herself and the environment. In the latter case, fit with the environment—two processes take place, the environment's ability to meet the needs of the individual and the individual's ability to meet the demands of the environment (later explained by Theory of Work Adjustment). (For a review of research related to French's contributions to P–E, see Caplan & Van Harrison, 1993.)

Theory of Work Adjustment

According to Lofquist and Dawis (1969, 1972, 1991; Dawis & Lofquist, 1984) the TWA is premised on the assumption that individuals seek to achieve correspondence with their environment. Accordingly, TWA can be described in terms of its central constructs: work personality, reinforcement, correspondence, and satisfaction/satisfactoriness. The constructs of interest in regard to adaptation and adjustment are satisfaction/satisfactoriness and correspondence. Satisfaction and satisfactoriness relate to an evaluation of the extent that an individual and the environment meet each other's needs (Bizot & Goldman, 1993). Specifically, satisfaction is an individual's internal evaluation regarding the extent to which an environment provides requisite reinforcement. Correspondingly, satisfactoriness is the external evaluation of the individual's ability to satisfy the requirements of the work environment. Correspondence occurs when an individual fulfills the demands of the environment and the environment meets the needs of the individual. For example, if a Native American female has lived in a small city near her tribe's reservation for the greater part of her life and she moves to city 100 miles away for a job, she may find that although she has only minor difficulty meeting the demands of the environment (she is able to speak the language and has the skills and competencies necessary for success in her chosen career), she may experience a lack of correspondence due to being away from her close knit extended family and other support systems, inability to participate in cultural traditions and celebrations, and inflexibility in her work schedule to travel home as desired. Indeed, correspondence is a dynamic process characterized by a reciprocal relationship where the individual and the environment change to meet each other's needs.

Lack of correspondence, or discorrespondence (as described more completely by Dawis, chap. 5 , this volume), elicits change, most likely on the part of the person in the form of adaptation. Where cultural issues are concerned, this change is referred to as acculturation, and each time two cultures come into contact, change occurs (Ho, 1995). As Dawis notes, change typically occurs at the surface level, in terms of skills and needs, rather than source traits of values and inborn abilities. In relation to working with clients this is an important distinction, to suggest a client needs to change the core of who he or she is as a cultural being would be unethical (reference here), but to suggest a client learn to function more effectively in his or her environment is a valid goal of treatment.

Ecological Models

Although ecological models are typically referred to as models of P–E fit, discussions of P–E psychology often neglect to include these very important models in their discussion of developments in P–E theory. What ecological models add, that is missing from basic P–E perspectives, is dimensionality, that is, they provide a greater understanding of the multiple systems in which the individual functions and the principles that govern these interactions. Ecological models recognize that individuals do not exist or act in isolation, rather they function within an interrelated system of relationships that are unique and integral to understanding the person (Wicker, 1979). The following four principles (for a complete description see Toro, Trickett, Wall, & Salem, 1991) undergird the ecological approach. The first principle, *adaptation*, focuses on the interaction between the individual and the social environment. An understanding of the individual's adaptation requires exploration of the sociocultural influences, norms, rules, attitudes, supportive structures, and beliefs surrounding problem definition that are present in the multileveled social context, as well as knowledge of the active processes the individual employs to cope with these requirements and opportunities. The *cycling of resources* principle, on the other hand, refers to the need to identify and build on strengths that are inherent to the individual and the systems (i.e., individual, familial, interpersonal, community, and cultural) in which he or she functions; these are strengths or resources that can facilitate adaptation and may be present to a greater or lesser extent at any of the five systems levels. The third principle, *interdependence*, suggests that when there is change (or a threat of change) at one level, the other components of the system will be affected (Fine, 1985; Toro, Trickett, Wall, & Salem, 1991; Wicker, 1979). The interdependence principle states that the system is comprised of interdependent parts, which separately and collectively strive to maintain homeostasis. When individuals experience challenges to their adaptation, both expected and unintended consequences occur. Moreover, changes in systems are expected to occur. That is, according to the *principle of succession*, "systems are in a constant state of flux" (Toro et al., 1991, p. 1213). To this end, the individual's current adaptation process is a result of historical and contextual influences. Consequently, when working with clients who are experiencing adaptation difficulties, it is necessary to explore not only what they are experiencing now, but also where they have been.

Conoley and Haynes (1992) maintain that "discordance may be defined as a disparity between an individual's abilities and the demands or expectations of the environments—a failure of match" (p. 180). This failure of match may simultaneously relate to the individual's past history or lack of history in similar environments as well as the person's current experience in other systems and to the contextual variables that may impair the individual's ability to function effectively in the environment. As such, intervention focuses on increasing the match, e.g., this may mean learning more effective communication skills and social skills, or building effective support networks and community resources.

One thing that must be kept in mind is that people exist within multiple systems, at the most direct level microsystems at the most removed, yet no less influential, macrosystem (Bronfenbrenner, 1979, 1995).

Microsystem: comprised of the intimate aspects of the individual's development including goal directed behavior, interpersonal relationships, and system-defined roles and experience. For example, for a child, the school, the home, and peers are all microsystems.

Mesosystem: consists of the link between and among the individual's multiple microsystems. For example, this would include the interrelationship of the work and home environments such that events at work would impact home functioning.

Exosystem: comprised of events that do not directly affect or are not directly affected by the individual. For example, these may include governmental agencies, institutions, and media.

Macrosystem: consists of the cultural and societal belief systems and underlying ideologies that may be present at the other levels but inherently influence the individual's functioning within their microsystem.

Culture and the Person–Environment Interaction

Borrowing from Bronfenbrenner's (1979) conception of ecological structures, Ahia (1991) asserted that cultural impact on mental health must be viewed from an ecological perspective. Factors to consider range from those closest to the person such as biological factors (i.e., genetic endowment, individual variabilities, prenatal experiences) to those that are more removed that are psychogenic factors (i.e., environmental or social conditions, familial relationships, learning of an individual), and those most removed are cosmogenic factors (i.e., factors influencing the understanding, explanation, and prediction of behavior such as worldview or stereotypes).

Likewise, Arredondo and Glauner (1992; Arredondo, Toporek, et al., 1996) proposed a person-in-culture model whose dimensions of personal identity are modeled after Bronfenbrenner's nested structures. According to Arredondo and colleagues, the person can be viewed as being impacted by three dimensions: Dimension A: primarily fixed characteristics that are evidenced by all people (age, sex, ethnicity, culture, physical disability); Dimension B: characteristics that are changeable and impacted by the fixed characteristics of Dimension A and the contextual characteristics of Dimension C (e.g., educational background, marital status, work experience, recreational interests, geographic location); and Dimension C: contextual characteristics defined by sociopolitical, political, and environmental events. From an ecological perspective, Dimension B is a result of the interaction between Dimensions A and C.

Subsumed within ecological approaches is the assumption of homeostasis. As individuals structure, change, and organize their environments (Moos, 1980), their environments work to do the same. Culture can be viewed as an individual's medium of adaptation to the demands of the environment such that an individual must simultaneously incorporate information based on what is occurring in his or her immediate context and those environments that surround it (Cole, 1991). Where culture is concerned, the environment may call on the individual to possess, to some degree, certain attributes that will alleviate or ease the psychosocial adaptation process. These attributes, whether biological, psychological, or cultural in origin, may or may not be part of the individual's repertoire of behaviors, and as such, may result in a mismatch between the individual and the environment.

Person–Environment Fit, Adaptation, and Mental Health

Where mental health is concerned, it is not specific group membership that allows for a greater or lesser degree of psychosocial adaptation, but the way individuals learn to function in the context of their cultural environment. At the most basic, adaptation is a contextually driven behavioral response in that the individual is required to mold his or her behavior to fit the current environment (Wandersman, Murday, Wadsworth, 1979). Additionally, it is a psychosocial process, a synthesis of the psychological and internal with the social and external, where mental health is inextricably intertwined with inner and outer experiences (Kivnick, 1993). From a social-ecological framework, "there is an interdependence of factors in the environment and the strong motivation of individuals and systems to act in ways that foster their own survival" (Rosado & Elias, 1993, p. 455). According to Kivnick, everyday mental health may be described as an attempt to live meaningfully, in a particular set of social and environmental circumstances, relying on a particular collection of resources and supports, where one exercises existing strengths and uses personal strategies to balance out personal weaknesses and environmental deficits. This becomes even more complex given that individuals function in a variety of diverse environments, with often conflicting demands.

According to theories of P–E fit, individuals seek environments where they may express their unique personality and, consequently, where they will succeed. Success, as defined by the environment, is gained through skills and abilities of the individual and by the ability of the environment to meet the needs of the individual; neither exists in isolation of the other. Thus, where there is a discrepancy (i.e., the person is experiencing a difficulty in adaptation), both person and environment variables must be considered as a potential explanation for the lack of fit.

Culture's Impact on Person–Environment Fit and Psychosocial Adaptation

At the most basic, viewing the individual from a person–environment perspective enables the MHP to separate characteristics of individuals from the wider cultural group to which they belong; viewing the person as a unique individual. However, extraction of characteristics does not suggest that individuals be treated without regard for the world around them. Adding to the notion that environmental or contextual variables shape an individual's behavior, is the idea that the various systems in which the individual functions differentially impact the individual's level of psychosocial adaptation.

In this same vein, there are factors that result in positive psychosocial adaptation. For example, certain skills will assist the individual in functioning effectively, essentially promoting a good fit, without changing the source traits of the individual. As such, culturally competent provision of psychological services requires the MHP "to encourage the individual to learn how to function in a larger culture and, at the same time, appreciate his or her own culture and social constitution" (McFadden, 1996, p. 235).

Psychosocial and cultural characteristics are important in developing adaptive and maladaptive behavior (Sethi, 1989). Some situations will be familiar to the individual and performance will be based on prior knowledge and experience, others may be somewhat unfamiliar and adjustment of performance and understanding will lead to individual growth, while still others may exact resources not known to the individual and may lead to frustration and distress (Trimble, 1989). Moreover, as Ridley et al. noted, "stressors a client experiences are seen as culturally contextualized; that is, whether ... more dispositionally based, more environmentally based, or a combination ... they are always expressed through the client's cultural lenses" (p. 858, 1998). Exposure to a new cultural environment can challenge the very "rock" on which an individual bases his or her way of knowing, understanding, and being (Cross, 1995). For example, as an individual spends more time in the host culture, there are more opportunities for the two cultures to come into contact and thus the more the individual is influenced by the host culture's processes (Suinn, Khoo, & Ahuna, 1995). As the individual is undergoing changes, a significant amount of stress occurs (Portes, 1996). According to Sandhu, Portes, and McPhee (1996), the individual may experience threats to ethnocultural identity, feelings of powerlessness, inferiority, and alienation as well as a sense of marginality and hostility. Moreover, it is important to remember that not all individuals (e.g., adolescents, refugees, economically displaced persons) have the freedom to select their environments; thus, for these individuals, a greater challenge in attaining fit may be present.

To this end, Berry, Kim, and Boski (1986) suggested that, when confronted with unknown or somewhat unfamiliar situations, achievement of successful psychosocial adaptation requires the individual to change his or her psychological characteristics, change the surrounding context, or change the amount of contact. In selecting one or more of these directions, the clinician must have a thorough understanding of where the discrepancies are and what is necessary to remedy them. For clinicians, this increased understanding of cultural and contextual factors underlying psychosocial adaptation will assist in helping clients optimize their functioning in their environment (McFadden, 1996).

A Person–Environment Model for Cultural and Contextual Variables

So what are those variables related to culture and context that impact the P–E fit? Our (Swartz, 1996) qualitative and quantitative exploration of the cultural and contextual factors related to psychosocial adaptation yielded a five-domain qualitative model and a three-factor quantitative model. Derived from a content analysis of the psychological literature dating back to 1962, the qualitative model included five primary domains (cultural orientation, family environment, community environment, communication style, and language). These domains are briefly defined here:

Cultural Orientation. Although individuals may perceive their environment through a specific filter, as they come into contact with individuals from other cultures, their filters change (Ho, 1995); sometimes imperceptibly, sometimes completely. These filters constitute the individual's ethnocultural orientation, a multidimensional domain that includes mode and style of acculturation; beliefs related to health and healing; value orientations (and worldview); norms associated with social and gender-role behavior; information on the individual's participation in native cultural and dominant culture activities such as traditions and ceremonies; and characteristic coping style.

Family. Grieger and Ponterotto (1995) stated that "comprehensive assessment entails viewing the client as a unique individual, as a social unit within a family, and as a member of a cultural group" (p. 357). For many cultural groups outside the mainstream U.S., family plays a central role in the person's ability to function effectively. Indeed, family lifestyles, as microcosms of ethnocultural heritage, can, to a greater or lesser degree, attenuate the effects of psychosocial problems through structure and support as well as by providing a foundation from which individuals can learn and develop an understanding of themselves and others (Fukuyama, 1990). However, family is not always a support, in some cases it can serve as an environmental demand that leads to significant psychological distress (e.g., conflict between roles in community or social and family, intergenerational conflict, changing communication styles; Swartz, 1996). This is particularly true as the individual begins to expand the number of microsystems in which he or she functions such as school or work, home, peers, community, marital relationships, and activities.

Community Environment. Individuals are participants, either directly or indirectly, in distinct and overlapping psychosocial environments and these environments to a greater or lesser degree not only impact the individual's ability to adapt to life's demands but make demands on the individual that directly affect the person's psychosocial functioning (Coleman, 1995; Swartz & Martin, 1997a). The community environment can promote mental health by providing networks that buffer the individual from the stressors inherent in the structure of the community and provide support for the demands implicit in daily life. Although support systems are on the whole positive, they can exact demands on the individual that lead to stress and discomfort. Specifically, social support networks have expectations that lead to norms and the development of roles. Individuals tend to think of themselves in terms of their learned roles in interpersonal relationships (Westermeyer, 1993) and evaluate their competence against what is expected in the environment (Coleman, 1995). Research suggests that the failure to meet these requirements can lead to psychological discomfort (Sandhu et al., 1996). For example, Sandhu et al. found that feelings of a pressure to conform to cultural standards and feelings of living a dual life were related to psychological pain and distress whereas feelings of adequate functioning were related to positive adaptation.

Communication Style. When individuals enter environments, they are expected to meet the competency demands of the environment, part of those competency demands relate to communication style. The reality is that, for some individuals, the message sent is not the same as the one received. Variables related to interactional style (e.g., hierarchical, direct, linear) as well as aspects of nonverbal communication style (e.g., attitudes toward physical contact, eye contact, physical gestures, facial expressions, movement synchrony, and proxemics) and verbal communication style (speech or conversational patterns, speech rate, tone, voice level, language switching, verbal tracking, and wait time). The psychological difficulties inherent in living within a society where you are not understood are exacerbated when differences in communication exist. Miscommunication is particularly detrimental in the clinical relationship; as noted in Martin (1995), whenever there are differences between the counselor and client, a potential for miscommunication exists. According to Suzuki and Kugler (1995), differences in communication style can lead to inadvertently misjudging and stereotyping of the individual.

Language. More limiting views of culture and the cultural adaptation process pointed to language usage (in most cases English) as the primary means of determining the individual's acculturation level and consequently whether an individual would experience difficulty in his or her environment. However, it is now clear that language usage is just one factor in a multidimensional, dynamic process. Santiago-Rivera (1995) asserted that it is possible for the individual to continue to adhere to certain culturally sanctioned processes while losing the ability to speak his or her native language fluently. Consideration must be given to information about what language the individual uses in the home, work/school, and social settings, as well as to specific aspects of language that, taken together, provide a comprehensive picture of the individual's use of language; information about language usage such as language proficiency, comprehension, preference, and developmental history of language provide a context in which current language usage can be understood. According to the literature, when individuals lack the basic ability to verbally communicate in their environment, this places added stress on their ability to function effectively, in effect, hindering their adaptation process (Anda, 1984).

(For a more thorough description of the domains and their associated subdomains, see Swartz & Martin, 1999).

Cultural and Contextual Correspondence

The five domains provided a multidimensional model of culture and context, but still fell short of explaining the relationship between psychosocial adaptation and culture and context. To examine this relationship, we (Stolle, 1998; Swartz, 1996; Swartz & Martin, 1997) conducted a series of factor analyses using the Psychosocial Adaptation for Cultural and Contextual Correspondence–Research Form, (PACCC–R; Martin & Swartz, 1996), a research instrument derived from the domain and subdomains of the qualitative study. What emerged was a three-factor structure, corresponding somewhat to the model proposed by Dawis and Lofquist to explain P–E fit. The factor accounting for the most amount of variance, as would be expected in a model describing cultural and contextual factors, described how the person sees her or himself as a cultural being (unique internalization of culture). The second factor addressed issues of contextual satisfaction; how the individual perceives his or her cultural environment. The final factor is comprised of items pertaining to contextual satisfactoriness; whether the individual possesses the abilities to meet the expectations of the environment. Following are more complete descriptions of the factors.

Cultural Orientation. The cultural orientation factor assesses the individualized experience of cultural orientation. Cultural orientation emerged as a multidimensional, multicontextual, cross-temporal process that cannot be measured simply by knowing an individual's ethnic background, language usage, or value orientation. Variables such as participation in activities, practices, and processes related to the native culture have traditionally defined cultural orientation (Dana, 1993; Oetting & Beauvais, 1991; Ryan & Ryan, 1989). This factor extends beyond the traditional variables to encompass a psychosocial approach to cultural orientation that includes the salient influences of family and social system. This approach is consistent with the direction of research initially suggested by Ruiz (1981), situational acculturation, which was further elucidated and extended by Keefe and Padilla (1987).

Contextual Satisfaction. The second factor addresses issues of an individual's needs within his or her psychosocial environment. For the most part, these needs relate to the presence and use of instrumental and expressive supports by family, peers, and community networks. This is consistent with past research suggesting the need for balance within and among the individual's ecosystems (e.g., Sandhu et al., 1996; Santiago-Rivera, 1995; Toro et al., 1991; Ulrich & Bradsher, 1993). For example, research by Ulrich and Bradsher (1993) found that presence of multiple support systems promotes coping in African American women. More recently, Santiago-Rivera's (1995) model for including culture in counseling emphasized the necessity of examining the individual's requirements for optimal mental health, which included informal resources. Similarly, Sandhu et al.'s (1996) examination of the factor structure of psychological pain related to adaptation revealed that individuals who perceive themselves as not having their needs met experienced feelings of alienation, loneliness, pressure, and inferiority. According to Coleman (1995), this experience of distress can be ameliorated or avoided when the individual em-

ploys strategies (see next factor) that accentuate the congruence between the individual and his or her environment. The difficulty,
however, is that individuals rely on reinforcement, through social
supports, for employment of the coping strategies. One would
think, then, that the second and third factor would show a significant correlation. This, however, was not the case.

   Contextual Satisfactoriness. The third factor suggests that
there are certain contextual requirements that, when not met, can
lead to poor psychosocial functioning. This is consistent with
McFadden's current work on transcultural counseling. Specifically,
McFadden asserted that individuals need to be provided with opportunities to learn the requisite skills for functioning effectively in
their environment. This is not to say that they must reject or neglect
their ties to their native culture; rather, they can learn to function in
their psychosocial environment while continuing to respect and
garner support from their native culture. Similarly, Coleman proposed that individuals must develop methods of coping with the
demands of their environment. Failure to do so results in psychological distress (Coleman, 1995).

   It is interesting to note that although there appeared to be some
overlap between the factors, particularly two and three, statistically
the factors had little relationship to one another. Conceptually, however, there is a relationship between contextual satisfaction and contextual satisfactoriness. Specifically, mental health is conceived as a
congruence between the individual's needs and abilities and the resources and requirements of the environment (O'Connor, 1977). Environments require individuals to recycle resources. That is, when
the requirements of the environment exceed the present strengths of
the individual, consideration must be given to ways in which the resources can be expanded or recycled. In order to help clients achieve
congruence, there is a need for clinicians to identify and build on
strengths or resources that are inherent to the individual and the systems in which he or she functions (Toro et al., 1991).

CULTURE AND PERSON–ENVIRONMENT: APPLICATION TO PRACTICE

Realistically, individual differences are vast and growing. Patterson
(1996) posited that the multiplicity of combinations of group mem-

berships for one individual renders the notion that it is possible to "fit" theory, assessment, or counseling approaches to a specific group, implausible. Although currently the field of ethnocultural psychology is moving toward a greater recognition of individual differences, considerable debate continues to exist regarding the provision of services to individuals from varied ethnocultural backgrounds. Perhaps rather than likening the United States to a melting pot, as MHPs we profit more by seeing our metaculture and the process of enculturation as one similar to making a stew, the ingredients flavor each other, but a carrot is still a carrot.

Emphasizing the integral nature of the P–E interaction in behavioral expression and perception of mental health may not be enough. This emphasis does not ameliorate the present concern when practitioners and researchers apply stereotypically derived conceptions of the individual based on a wholesale perception of cultural dissimilarity. Implicit in the concept of providing culturally responsive psychological services is that to optimize the individual's treatment process, requires conceptualization of the client according to his or her individualized experience as a cultural being (Ridley, Mendoza, Kanitz, Angermeier, & Zenk, 1994). Specifically, Martin (1995) asserted that "Culture is evidenced in differential ways .... Environmental factors and specific characteristics of individuals interplay with culture to create persons who are unique (p. 246)." No ethnographic description of a cultural group matches directly to the psychological characteristics of the client (Das, 1995). Moreover, Wallen (1992) and Betancourt and Lopez (1993) argued against the belief that practicing in a culturally appropriate manner is restricted to services with minority or ethnically different individuals. Wallen indicated that "the notion of cultural appropriateness ... is one that can benefit all clients, whether or not they are minorities, because it reflects a perspective that values client's perceptions and needs" (p. 294).

For decades we have recognized the need to attend to culture in the application of mental health assessment and intervention, the conundrum comes when considering how to put all our "awareness" into practice. Lee (1997) reflected this sentiment when noting that application is one of the pitfalls of culturally responsive counseling, it is not as if this has been ignored, but that the ambiguity that surrounds culture limits its integration into practice. Perhaps, the reason this has been so difficult is twofold: First, as Vontress (1999) noted, we spend much of our time stressing the differences between cultural groups that may create an unnecessary apprehension on the part of both the client and the counselor on entering the therapeutic relationship; second, we have treated culture as though it is a stand-alone variable rather than something that is woven into the very fabric of who the person is, much like we consider personality dynamics or the role schemas play in depression.

Genetic predisposition and involvement in multiple overlapping systems (e.g., family, peers, school, community) affect the acquisition and maintenance of unique behavioral repertoires (Bronfenbrenner, 1995). In large part, it is this behavioral repertoire that enables the individual to "fit" into the environment. Therein lies the conundrum for MHPs. On the one hand, approaching the P–E fit "problem" from the perspective of changing the person is little different from mental health services of decades ago. On the other hand, changing the environment to be more culturally responsive takes time, often too much time to be of benefit for the client. Like personality, or schemas for that matter, clinically speaking, culture makes little sense when considered outside the context of the individual and the multiple systems in which the individual functions. Application of assessment and intervention strategies with individuals from varied ethnocultural backgrounds relies on the interplay among the unique aspects of individuals, their history of learning experiences, and the environmental situations in which they function (Johnson, Swartz, & Martin, 1995). Taken together, all of the information about the person provides a picture of how the individual is functioning in his or her environment. Indeed, accurate conceptualization is the cornerstone of good treatment planning.

Planning Culturally Responsive Services

The psychological encounter is based on the recognition that there are both similarities and differences across and within cultures. Furthermore, either minimization or overemphasis on the similarities or differences without regard for the other would result in harm to the psychological intervention process (Pedersen, 1996). Pedersen acknowledged that although there may be an overemphasis on cultural diversity, failure to consider differences is equally problematic.

Instead, Pedersen (1991) suggested that MHPs simultaneously recognize diversity and explore areas of culture that link individuals from varied ethnocultural backgrounds together.

Before we discuss assessment and intervention, an overarching issue must be highlighted. A necessary step and continuous part of the assessment and intervention process is entering the client's system (Chung & Pardeck, 1998; Ridley et al., 1998). When this is achieved, the MHP has a far better chance of truly understanding the client's subjective experience of him or herself and his or her environment. In addition, it is here that the MHP can elicit information on the client's cultural orientation, contextual satisfaction, and his or her perception of contextual satisfactoriness.

Assessment.   As with any therapeutic encounter, assessment is the cornerstone of the treatment process. Dynamic and ongoing, assessment offers the MHP information on where clients have been, where they are now, and where they may need to go. Rather than assuming that an individual is experiencing a P–E mismatch as a result of cultural background, the MHP must ascertain the level at which the cultural and contextual characteristics are manifested along a continuum and how these characteristics lead to a discrepancy in correspondence between the individual and the environment (Swartz & Martin, 1999). According to Ridley et al. (1998), assessment is best understood as a process of progressive decision-making. Questions such as "What data are culturally relevant and what are idiosyncratic?" "Which stressors are dispositional and which are environmental?" "What data are clinically significant and which are insignificant?" and "What is my working hypothesis?" are some of the decision points the clinician can use to narrow the obtained assessment information into a working hypothesis. In the past, cultural data was far too broad a term. Information from the clinical interview often neglected a full exploration of culture, and culturally oriented interviews were far too time consuming to be of use in the managed care environment in which we now practice. Moreover, MHPs were unclear on what to do with the information once it was obtained.

Today, we have several new models (e.g., Chung & Pardeck, 1997; Ridley et al., 1998; Santiago-Rivera, 1995), one of which is the Cultural and Contextual Guide (CCG) process (Martin & Swartz, 1995; for an expanded description of the CCG process, see Swartz & Martin, in press). The CCG uses cultural and contextual factors to differentially examine the individual's correspondence with his or her environment. Determinations of correspondence are derived from an individual's satisfaction (i.e., internal evaluation regarding the extent to which an environment provides their requisite reinforcement) with the environment and an individual's satisfactoriness (i.e., external evaluation of the individual's ability to satisfy the requirements of the environment; Bizot & Goldman, 1993; Dawis & Lofquist, 1993). Premised on the notion that an individual's cultural and contextual adaptation can best be assessed through examination of the satisfactoriness of his or her psychosocial adaptation, the CCG endeavors to determine the discrepancy of correspondence present for the individual and the environment. The individual's discrepancy is mapped along the five domains, cultural orientation, family environment, community environment, communication, and language, to determine where matches and discrepancies exist. Central to the construct of correspondence is the notion that temporal indicators of the individual's position along the continuum help determine their level of discrepancy.

According to Anastasi and Urbina (1997), an individual's movement along this continuum is mediated by the length of time the individual has been in the environment, a term Dawis (chap. 5, this volume) refers to as tenure. Moreover, as an individual's psychosocial adaptation is determined as a function of the several different environments (or subsystems) in which the individual operates, it is necessary to consider the contribution of these potential discrepancies when determining their level of satisfactoriness. In other words, the MHP needs to assess the client's functioning in all salient environments (e.g., work or school, home, community, social); in essence mapping the client's ecology by describing the various systems in which the client functions and the people and events that are a part of those systems. According to Chung and Pardeck (1997), this allows the clinician to determine where and to what degree person–environment discrepancies exist in all relevant environments, not just the one(s) noted in the initial encounter.

The CCG serves as a guiding framework for understanding cultural data obtained in the initial session. This initial assessment of the client's concerns sets the tone for the remaining sessions (Budman, Hoyt, & Friedman, 1992; Walborn, 1996), allowing the MHP to convey a respect for the total person of the client. By adding the CCG process, this allows for a richer and more descriptive examination of the individual's experience as a unique ethnocultural being and a greater understanding of the context in which the client's concerns exist. This is particularly useful as a means of building rapport in the relationship as well as providing the counselor with a framework for assessing an individual's ethnocultural and contextual characteristics. Within this, in conjunction with cultural and contextual decision paths (Martin & Farris, 1994), MHPs can determine if and to what degree the assessment process needs to be altered to better capture an accurate understanding of what the individual is experiencing. Use of a framework for assessment can decrease the potential for missed data and help guide the counselor through the process of linking important concepts and integrating findings into a functional and comprehensive picture of the individual.

Information obtained from the CCG is subsequently used in two ways, to determine the impact that cultural and contextual variables may have on the therapeutic process (e.g., can the sessions be conducted in not only a common language but a language that is preferred by the client; is the treatment approach consistent with the client's belief system related to healing) and to evaluate where intervention may need to be directed and what resources can be capitalized on to assist the client in achieving a good fit.

Intervention.   We must remember that we are treating the client, not the problem; bottom line, it is the client with whom we are working. Patterson (1996) suggested the past overemphasis on techniques has overshadowed the importance of developing a sound therapeutic relationship. Vontress (1999) noted that too often we enter the clinical encounter assuming that we need to address cultural issues, when in reality cultural issues should be emphasized only when they are relevant to the client's concern. Cultural and contextual issues are not items to be checked off, but integrated into our understanding of the person, and, like other parts of the person, only addressed when they directly bear on the problem at hand or they are germane to the provision of services. When it appears that the client may be experiencing some cultural or contextual conflict (i.e., P–E mismatch), these issues are brought out and explored as part of the treatment process.

According to Fischer, Jome, and Atkinson (1998), counselors no longer need to choose between the two camps, ignoring cultural and contextual issues or focusing narrowly on them. Rather, services that follow the guiding principles of a common factors framework allow for the inclusion of culture as a determining factor in service planning and delivery. The four common factors—the therapeutic relationship, shared worldview, client expectations, ritual or intervention—are present in all psychotherapy. In recent years, several authors have proposed models of assessment and treatment with individuals from varied ethnocultural backgrounds (e.g., Atkinson, Thompson, & Grant, 1993; Helms, 1995; Leong, 1996; Smith, 1985; Trevino, 1996). What many of these models share is a departure from the ethnic group- treatment approach match; rather, they share aspects of the common factors approach. Fischer et al. noted that the common factors requires the counselor to "continually hypothesize what he or she can do within the context of the client's unique culture, to enhance the therapeutic relationship, to facilitate the convergence in worldview raise the clients expectations, and implement culturally relevant interventions" (p. 566).

CONCLUSION

The uniqueness of individuals is the most basic of psychological concepts (Tyler, 1965). Differences resulting from the inherent uniqueness of the individual are shaped by learning experiences as provided by opportunities in the environment. Processes of attention, guided by symbolic and motivational influences, determine which situational factors of the environment to attend to, and which to incorporate into their behavioral repertoire (Bandura, 1985). Following a cyclical path, these differences serve to change the environment such that each person creates their own environment from which opportunities and subsequent behavior arise (Bandura, 1977; Moos, 1980). Matsumoto stated that "as each culture must meet different demands of the environment, each culture will develop differences in the way it impacts on the people within it" (1994, p. 5). Culture is one of the many aspects of the environment that is impacted by and subsequently affects acquisition of new behavior. It follows, then, that the relation between culture and behavior can be conceived of as one of continuous interaction, each working to shape the other (Ho, 1995).

The time to change is now. Change how we view culture and context as separate from the P–E, as something to be singularly recognized in the counseling session apart from who the client is. It is time for this to change. It is time for mental health professionals to gain an awareness and sensitivity to the unique individual, including cultural and contextual issues. Moreover, it is a time to recognize similarities; for too long researchers, clinicians, and the media have treated cultural groups as though they are islands, separate from other land. It is time to build bridges between those islands. Recognize people for who they are, sharing many basic characteristics, with each person using his or her best abilities to cope effectively with the environmental demands around them; hence, attempting to attain a P–E fit.

REFERENCES

Ahia, C. E. (1991). Cultural contextualization of diagnostic signs, symptoms, and symbols in international mental health. *Journal of College Student Psychotherapy*, 6(1), 37–51.

Anastasi, A., & Urbina, S. (1997). *Psychological testing* (7th ed.). New York: Prentice-Hall.

Anda, D. (1984, March-April). Bicultural socialization: Factors affecting the minority experience. *Social Work*, 101–107.

Arredondo, P., & Glauner, T. (1992). *Personal dimensions of identity model*. Boston: Empowerment Workshops.

Arrendondo. P., Toporek, R., Brown, S. P., Jones, J., Locke, D. C., Sanchez, J., & Stadler, H. (1996). Operationalization of the multicultural counseling competencies. *Journal of Multicultural Counseling and Development*, 24, 42–78.

Atkinson, D. R., Thompson, C. E., & Grant, S. K. (1993). A three dimensional model for counseling racial/ethnic minorities. *The Counseling Psychologist*, 21, 257–277.

Bandura, A. (1977). *Social learning theory*. Englewood Cliffs, NJ: Prentice-Hall.

Bandura, A. (1985). Model causality in social learning theory. In M. J. Mahoney & A. Freeman (Eds.), *Cognition and psychotherapy* (pp. 81–99). New York: Plenum.

Berry, J. W., Kim, U., & Boski, P. (1986). Acculturation and psychological adaptation. In Y. Y. Kim & W. B. Gudykunst (Eds.), *Current studies in cross-cultural adaptation* (Vol. II of Intercultural Communication Annual). London: Sage.

Betancourt, H., & Lopez, S. R. (1993). The study of culture, ethnicity, and race in American psychology. *American Psychologist*, 48, 629–637.

Bizot, E. B., & Goldman, S. H. (1993). Prediction of satisfaction: An 8-year follow up. *Journal of Vocational Behavior*, 4, 19–29.

Bronfenbrenner, U. (1979). *The ecology of human developmen*. Cambridge, MA: Harvard University Press.

Bronfenbrenner, U. (1995). Developmental ecology through space and time: A future perspective. In P. Moen, G. H. Elder, Jr., & K. Luscher (Eds.), *Examining lives in context* (pp. 619–647). Washington, DC: American Psychological Association.

Budman, S. H., Hoyt, M. F., & Friedman, S. (1992). First words on first sessions. In S. H. Budman, M. F. Hoyt, & S. Friedman (Eds.), *The first session in brief therapy* (pp. 3–6). New York: Guilford Press.

Caplan, R. D., & Van Harrison, R. (1993). Person–environment fit theory: Some history, recent developments, and future directions. *Journal of Social Issues, 253–276.*

Chung, W. S., & Pardeck, J. T. (1997). Treating powerless minorities through an ecosystem approach. *Adolescence, 32,* 625–635.

Cole, M. (1991). A cultural theory of development: What does it imply about the application of scientific research. *Learning and Instruction, 1,* 187–200.

Coleman, H. L. K. (1995). Strategies for coping with cultural diversity. *The Counseling Psychologist, 2,* 722–740.

Conoley, J. C., & Haynes, G. (1992). An ecological approach to intervention. In R. C. D'Amato & B. A. Rothlisberg (Eds.), *Psychological perspectives on intervention: A case study approach to prescriptions for change.* New York: Longman.

Cross, S. E. (1995). Self-construals, coping, and stress in cross-cultural adaptation. *Journal of Cross-Cultural Psychology, 26,* 673–698.

Dana, R. H. (1993). *Multicultural assessment perspectives for professional psychology.* Needham Heights, MA: Allyn & Bacon.

Das, A. K. (1995). Rethinking multicultural counseling: Implication for counselor education. *Journal of Counseling & Development, 74,* 45–52.

Dawis, R. V., & Lofquist, L. H. (1984). *A psychological theory of work adjustment.* Minneapolis, MN: University of Minnesota Press.

Dawis, R. V., & Lofquist, L. H. (1993). Rejoinder: From TWA to PEC. *Journal of Vocational Behavior, 43,* 113–121.

Fine, M. J. (1985). Intervention form an ecological perspective. *Professional Psychology: Research and Practice, 16,* 262–270.

Fischer, A. R., Jome, L. M., & Atkinson, D. R. (1998). Reconceptualizing multicultural counseling: Universal healing conditions in a culturally specific context. *The Counseling Psychologist, 26,* 525;208;588.

Fukuyama, M. A. (1990). Taking a universal approach to multicultural counseling. *Counselor Education and Supervision, 30,* 6–17.

Grieger, I., & Ponterotto, J. G. (1995). A framework for assessment in multicultural counseling. In J. G. Ponterotto, J. M. Casas, L. A. Suzuki, C. M. Alexander (Eds.), *Handbook of multicultural counseling* (pp. 357–374). Thousand Oaks, CA: Sage.

Guarnaccia, P. J., & Rodriguez, O. (1997). Concepts of culture and their role in the development of culturally competent mental health services. *Hispanic Journal of Behavioral Sciences, 18,* 419–444.

Harrison, R. V. (1978). Person–environment fit and job stress. In C. L. Cooper & R. Payne (Eds.), *Stress at work* (pp. 175–205). New York: Wiley.

Helms, J. E., (1995). An update of Helmsí White and People of Color racial identity models. In J. G. Ponterotto, J. M. Casas, L. A. Suzuki, & C. M. Alexander (Eds.), *Handbook of multicultural counseling* (pp. 181–198). Thousand Oaks, CA: Sage.

Hermans, H. J. M. , & Kempen, H. J. G. (1998). Moving cultures: The perilous problems of cultural dichotomies in a globalizing society. *American Psychologist, 53,* 1111–1120.

Ho, D. Y. F. (1995). Internalized culture, culturocentrism, and transcendence. *The Counseling Psychologist, 23*(1), 4–24.

Johnson, M. J., Swartz, J. L., & Martin, W. E., Jr. (1995). Application of psychological theories for career development with native Americans. In F. T. L. Leong (Ed.), *Career development and vocational behavior among ethnic minorities* (pp. 103–133). Hillsdale, NJ: Lawrence Erlbaum Associates.

Keefe, S. E., & Padilla, A. M. (1987). *Chicano ethnicity.* Albuquerque: University of New Mexico Press.

Kendler, T. S. (1986). Worldviews and the concept of development: A reply to Lerner and Kauffman. *Developmental Review, 6,* 80–95.

Kivnick, H. Q. (1993). Everyday mental health: A guide to assessing life strengths. *Generation, 17*(1), 13–20.

Kluckhohn, C., & Murry, H. A. (1950). Personality formation: The determinants. In C. Kluckhohn & H. A. Murray (Eds.), *Personality in nature, society, and culture* (pp. 35–48). New York, Alfred A. Knopf.

Lee, C. C. (1997). The promise and pitfalls of multicultural counseling. In C. C. Lee (Ed.), *Multicultural issues in counseling* (2nd ed., pp. 3–13). Alexandria, VA: American Counseling Association.

Leong, F. T. L. (1996). Toward an integrative model for cross-cultural counseling and psychotherapy. *Applied & Preventative Psychology, 5,* 189–209.

Loftquist, L. H., & Dawis, R. V. (1969). *Adjustment to work: A psychological view of man's problems in a work-oriented societ.* New York: Appleton-Century-Crofts.

Lofquist, L. H., & Dawis, R. V. (1991). *Essentials of person–environment correspondence counselin.* Minneapolis: University of Minnesota Press.

Martin, W. E., Jr. (1995). Career development assessment and intervention strategies with American Indians. In F. T. L. Leong (Ed.), *Career development and vocational behavior among ethnic minorities* (pp. 227–248). Hillsdale, NJ: Lawrence Erlbaum Associates.

Martin, W. E., Jr., & Farris, K. K. (1994). A cultural and contextual decision path approach to career assessment with Native Americans: A psychological perspective. *Journal of Career Assessment, 2,* 258–275.

Martin, W. E., Jr., & Swartz, J. L. (1995). *Cultural and contextual guide process.* Unpublished assessment instrument.

Matsumoto, D. R. (1994). *People: Psychology from a culturl perspective.* Pacific Grove, CA: Brooks/Cole.

McFadden, J. (1996). A transcultural perspective: Reaction to C. H. Patterson's "Multucultural counseling: From diversity to universality." *Journal of Counseling & Development, 74,* 232–235.

Miller, J. G. (1997). Theoretical issues in cultural psychology. In J. W. Berry, Y. H. Poortinga, & J. Pandy (Eds.), *Handbook of cross cultural psychology* (Vol. 1, pp. 85–128). Boston: Allyn & Bacon.

Moos, R. H. (1980). Major features of a social ecological perspective. *APA Division of Community Psychology Newsletter, 13,* 1.

O'Connor, W. A. (1977). Ecosystems theory and clinical mental health. *Psychiatric Annals, 7,* 363–372.

Oetting, E. R., & Beauvais, F. (1991). Orthogonal cultural identification theory: The cultural identification of minority adolescents. *The International Journal of the Addictions, 2,* 655–685.

Patterson, C. H. (1996). Multicultural counseling: From diversity to universality. *Journal of Counseling & Development, 74,* 227–231.

Pedersen, P. B. (1991). Multiculturalism as a generic approach to counseling. *Journal of Counseling & Development, 70,* 6–12.

Pedersen, P. B. (1996). The importance of both similarities and differences in multicultural counseling: Reaction to C. H. Patterson. *Journal of Counseling & Development, 74,* 236–237.

Portes, P. R. (1996). Ethnicity in education and psychology. In D. Berlinger & R. Calfee (Eds.), *The handbook of educational psychology* (pp. 331–358). New York: Macmillan.

Ridley, C. R., Li, L. C., & Hill, C. L. (1998). Multicultural assessment: Reexamination, reconceptualization, and practical application. *The Counseling Psychologist, 26,* 827–910.

Ridley, C. R., Mendoza, D. W., Kanitz, B. E., Angermeier, L., & Zenk, R. (1994). Cultural sensitivity in multicultural counseling: A perceptual schema model. *Journal of Counseling Psychology, 41,* 125–136.

Rosado, J. W., Jr., & Elias, M. J. (1993). Ecological and psychocultural mediators in the delivery of services for urban, culturally diverse Hispanic clients. *Professional Psychology: Research and Practice, 24,* 450–459.

Ruiz, R. A. (1981). Cultural and historical perspectives in counseling Hispanics. In D. W. Sue (Ed.), *Counseling the culturally different* (pp. 186–215). New York: Wiley.

Ryan, R. A., & Ryan, L. (1989). *Multicultural aspects of chemical dependency treatment: An American Indian perspective.* Unpublished manuscript, Turnaround Adolescent Treatment Program, Vancouver, WA.

Sandhu, D. S., Portes, P. R., & McPhee, S. A. (1996). Assessing cultural adaptation: Psychometric properties of the Cultural Adaptation Pain Scale. *Journal of Multicultural Counseling and Development, 24,* 15–25.

Santiago-Rivera, A. L. (1995). Developing a culturally sensitive treatment modality for bilingual Spanish-speaking clients: Incorporating language and culture in counseling. *Journal of Counseling & Development, 74,* 12–17.

Sethi, B. (1989). Family as a potent therapeutic force. *Indian Journal of Psychiatry, 31,* 22–30.

Smith, E. M. J. (1985). Ethnic minorities: Life stress, social support, and mental health issues. *The Counseling Psychologist, 13,* 537–579.

Stolle, D. W. (1998). *Construct validity of the Psychosocial Adaptation for Cultural and Contextual Correspondence-Research Version.* Unpublished doctoral dissertation, Northern Arizona University, Flagstaff, AZ.

Suinn, R., Khoo, G., & Ahuna, C. (1995). The Suinn-Lew Asian Self Identity Acculturation Scale: Cross-cultural information. *Journal of Multicultural Counseling and Development, 23,* 139–148.

Suzuki, L. A., & Kugler, J. F. (1995). Intelligence and personality assessment: Multicultural perspectives. In J. G. Ponterotto, J. M. Casas, L. A. Suzuki, & C. M. Alexander (Eds.), *Handbook of multicultural counseling* (pp. 493–515). Thousand Oaks, CA: Sage.

Swartz, J. L. (1996). *Factor analytic identification of cultural and contextual components of mental health: Application to psychological services.* Unpublished doctoral dissertation, Northern Arizona University, Flagstaff.

Swartz, J. L., & Martin, W. E., Jr. (1996). *Psychosocial Adaptation for Cultural and Contextual Correspondence-Research Version.* Unpublished instrument, Northern Arizona University, Flagstaff, AZ.

Swartz, J. L., & Martin, W. E., Jr. (1997). Ecological psychology theory: Historical overview and application to educational ecosystems. In J. L. Swartz & W. E. Martin, Jr. (Eds.), *Applied ecological psychology in schools and communities: Assessment and intervention* (pp. 3–27). Mahwah, NJ: Lawrence Erlbaum Associates.

Swartz, J. L., & Martin, Jr., W. E. (in press). Impact of culture and context on psychosocial adaptation: Person-environment correspondence. *Journal of Counseling and Development.*

Toro, P. A., Trickett, E. J., Wall, D. D., & Salem, D. A. (1991). Homelessness in the United States: An ecological perspective. *American Psychologist, 46,* 1208–1218.

Trevino, J. G. (1996). World view and change in cross-cultural counseling. *The Counseling Psychologist, 24,* 198–215.

Trimble, J. (1989). Multilinearity of acculturation: Person–situation interactions. In D. M. Keats, D. Munro, & L. Mann (Eds.), *Heterogeneity in cross-cultural psychology* (pp. 173–186). Rockland, MD: Swets & Zeitlinger.

Tyler, L. E. (1965). *The psychology of human differences* (3rd ed.). New York: Appleton-Century-Crofts.

Ulrich, P. M., & Bradsher, J. E. (1993). Perceived support, help-seeking, and adaptation to stress among older Black and white women living alone. *Journal of Aging and Health, 5,* 365–386.

Vontress, C. E. (1999, February). Culture and counseling. *Counseling Today,* pp. 8, 18.

Walborn, F. S. (1996). *Process variables: Four common elements in counseling and psychotherapy.* Pacific Grove, CA: Brooks/Cole.

Wallen, J. (1992). Providing culturally appropriate mental health services for minorities. *The Journal of Mental Health Administration, 19,* 288–295.

Wandersman, A., Murday, D., & Wadsworth, J. C. (1979). The environment-behavior-person relationship: Implications for research. *Environmental Design Research Association, 10,* 162–174.

Westermeyer, J. (1993). Cross-cultural psychiatric assessment. In A. C. Gaw (Ed.), *Culture, ethnicity, and mental illness* (pp. 125–144). Washington, DC: American Psychiatric Press.

Wicker, A. W. (1979). *An introduction to ecological psychology.* Monterey, CA: Brooks/Cole.

IV

Conclusion

Focal Points for Person–Environment Psychology: Ecological Validity, Systems Orientation, Fit, and Efficacy

William E. Martin, Jr.
Northern Arizona University
Jody L. Swartz-Kulstad
University of Wisconsin-Superior

Theory, research, and practice are three integral components to enduring change. Change, which moves the focus of the problem from the individual to the person–environment (P–E) interaction, calls for innovation in the very way we approach our work with clients. In contrast to theories that focus primarily on the individual, incorporation of P–E concepts allows for a more comprehensive and indepth analysis of sources contributing to the individual's ability to adapt to his or her psychosocial environment. As individuals age, this task becomes more complex, with P–E interactions increasing, not only in number but in complexity. For the mental health professional who is working with adolescents and adults, the previous eight chapters provide a guide for effective practice.

The contributing authors have highlighted key directions in P–E psychology. Four important focal points emerged that not only reflect themes of P–E psychology but also reflect uniqueness and strengths of a P–E orientation to successfully develop effective mental health assessment and intervention strategies applied to adolescents and adults. The four focal points discussed next are: (a) ecological validity and P–E assessments and interventions, (b) systems orientation to P–E assessment and intervention, (c) P–E fit—the matching process, and (d) efficacy of P–E assessments and interventions

ECOLOGICAL VALIDITY AND P–E ASSESSMENTS AND INTERVENTIONS

A functional outcome advantage of P–E approaches over more clinical orientations is the importance of conducting assessments and interventions within the natural settings of individuals to enhance the probability of assessment and treatment generalization. For example, Borduin et al. (chap. 6, this volume) stressed that a major reason for current ineffective interventions for serious antisocial behavior in adolescents is that "treatments are generally individually oriented and delivered in settings that bare little relation to the problems being addressed (e. g., group home, training school, psychiatric hospital;" (p. 114). One major criticism of current methods is that we expect systems to change when we do no intervention with them or in other words, we work with an individual and he or she returns to an environment in which the behavior or concern was developed, maintained, or exacerbated and we fail to assist the individual in altering those factors. The result is the system "forces" the individual back to where he or she was before, either reinstating or making worse the earlier problem. Furthermore, the authors identified the optimization of ecological validity for interventions as one of their three criteria in selecting promising models of community-based treatment. In fact, all of the treatment models that Borduin et al. presented, except for behavioral parent training, are delivered with ecological validity. They point out that ecologically valid treatments must include careful operationalization, intensive provider training, and ongoing consultation to promote treatment fidelity. Moreover, the entire provider organization must commit fully to the changes that follow a shift to ecologically based interventions.

Horton and Bucy (chap. 3, this volume) stressed the importance of gaining assessment information about the contexts in which an adolescent functions in concert with the adolescent's personal characteristics to find the "fit" between the two. This process that is basic to P–E methods, is often overlooked due to the effort and time required to gain an accurate picture. Indeed, a difficulty arises when realizing that commensurate measures are not readily available for this task outside of vocational or educational psychology. Horton and Bucy, although, provide some creative and useful ways of exploring the P–E match. The key is for the mental health professional to be active in his or her strategies for gathering information. One often overlooked area is interviews with relevant participants in the individual's life. The authors recommended interviewing significant others in the life of an adolescent including family members and teachers. These are the people who see the concerns, are part of the concerns and can assist one in gaining a clearer picture of the context in which the concern can be understood. Furthermore, the authors discussed the Family Interaction Tasks approach that is an analogue observation method used to reveal family conflict patterns. These types of tasks can give the mental health professional a "birds-eye-view" into the communication functioning of the context in which the individual spends a great deal of his or her time. Similarly, naturally occurring incidents (enactments) during counseling sessions were identified that can be used to provide a glimpse of behavior at home. This also provides a snapshot of the client's behavior with peers, how the client relates to you as a person, the feelings and perceptions that arise as part of your work with the client can assist you in understanding how others relate to this person.

Munger (chap. 2, this volume) frames the necessity of ecological validity within an individualized, community-based delivery system that examines all of the domains in the child's environment to discover the social ecology of the child's behavior. Munger highlights the methods of ecologically valid assessment and treatment by discussing how four life space patterns (i.e., time, space [places], activities, and people) form the core of ecological environmental intervention. Using Moo's concept of Environmental Status Examination, Munger illustrates the value of ecologically valid assessment through the work of two field-based researchers. For example, Gump (1984) concluded that a young woman client was not "sick" so much as her lifestyle when he used the strategy to learn about the woman's behavior over a typical weekend. This points out that it is not most accurate to find the genesis of the problem within the individual, although it certainly is more convenient. Likewise, Csikszentmihalyi and Larson (1984) emphasized that knowledge of various disorders requires knowledge gained from a "thick description" of an individual's daily life.

Koehly and Shivy (chap. 4, this volume) established the position that professional researchers and clinicians in psychology have most often attended to the intraindividual variables that comprise a person's behavior. Although knowledge of the person is certainly important, the authors suggested that more meaningful aspects of an individual's life may be the frequency, affective intensity, and duration of interactions within their personal communities. Koehly and Shivy developed the use of social network analysis that clearly reflects the importance of ecological validity by stressing the study of individuals' interactions as they take place naturally, with their "personal communities."

What we can glean from these chapters is that the future of research and practice within P–E psychology needs to be oriented to exploring more effective and practical methods optimizing ecological validity. As researchers, we need to be asking, what variables, both intraindividual and extraindividual, will promote generalization. As mental health professionals, we need to be asking ourselves the question, sure this person is functioning well in my office, group home, hospital but how can I be sure that he or she will function well in his or her natural environment?

SYSTEMS ORIENTATION TO P–E ASSESSMENT AND INTERVENTION

Fundamental to P–E psychology is the notion that behavior exhibited at any given time is the result of a complex set of interactions within and between intraindividual systems and extraindividual systems. These interactions are reciprocal whereas an individual's behavior can alter intraindividual and extraindividual systems and the systems can alter the individual's behavior. Additionally, an individual's behavior is dynamic suggesting that it may be different given a seemingly similar set of interactions. (However, if there were not consistency in an individual's exhibited behavior for which we can predict future behavior from, there would be no need to pursue a P–E theory in psychology or, for that matter, applied psychology). Furthermore, we can conduct P–E systems assessments and interventions using an individual's and others perceptions of behavior, approximations of behavior in real settings, contexts of behavior, and settings of behavior.

Intra- and Extra-Individual Systems and P–E Assessments

Horton and Bucy (chap. 3, this volume) identified the need to assess intraindividual systems that include cognitive, affective, and behavioral attributes. The extraindividual systems they identify are parents, peers, school, and work. They discuss intraindividual assessment techniques (some are also used for extraindividual assessments) to measure an adolescent's perceptions that include interviews, eco-maps, self-report objective measures (Family Environment Scale, The Life Stressors and Social Resources Inventory–Youth Form), projective measures (Adolescent Apperception Cards and Family Apperception Test). Horton and Bucy also discuss approximation of behavior techniques that are Family Interaction Techniques and Enactments.

In their discussion of adolescents who exhibit serious antisocial behavior, Borduin et al. (chap. 6, this volume) focused on the individual characteristics of IQ and sociocognitive deficits. They discussed family relations, peer relations, school and academic performance, and neighborhood context as extraindividual systems. Four of the five promising models for working with adolescents who exhibit serious antisocial behavior identified by Borduin et al. combine both assessment and intervention techniques within the contexts of behavior. The fifth model, behavioral parent training, focuses on assessments and interventions that approximate behavior in actual settings.

As part of a comprehensive, needs-based approach for adolescents, Munger (chap. 2, this volume) stresses that we cannot understand child behavior in isolation from its context. Although, he did identify characteristics at the individual level that have distinct implications for the understanding of behavior that are genetically determined tendencies, biological variables, intellectual ability, medical conditions, neuropsychological influences, pharmacological agents, intrapsychic forces, cognitions, reinforcement contingencies, gender-role development, and affective states. Intraindividual systems that Munger discussed are family level, peer level, school level, and neighborhood/community level. Munger's community-based needs approach covers a full range of perceptions, approximations, contexts, and settings of behavior.

The complexities associated with understanding P–E interactions over time can be so overwhelming that it becomes easier to faithfully acknowledge them while at the same time kindly ignoring them; only to proceed to focus on more unidimensional explanations of behavior. Clearly, psychology needs to step out of the office and lab and enter the environment of the individual. This is a daunting task and no one is denying that this takes more time and effort. The payoff, however, is when an individual achieves a modicum of fit with his or her environment, they will be functioning effectively enough not to need our services or the services of the social services system, justice system, and so forth.

PERSON–ENVIRONMENT FIT: THE MATCHING PROCESS

An underlying purpose of P–E psychology, as illustrated in several theoretical applications, is to ascertain how people with their individual characteristics fit to given environments with their associated attributes. Both Dawis (chap. 5, this volume) and Swanson and Chu (chap. 7, this volume) present a historical perspective on P–E fit and characteristics of successful P–E fit models. Dawis describes the P–E tradition in counseling psychology with a link to P–E fit originators like Parsons (1909), Lewin (1936), and Murray (1938). He recounts the development of measurement milestones that led to the successful applications of P–E fit methods. For example, Viteles (1936) introduced the "psychograph" which enabled measurement of the "goodness of match" using clinical judgment. Moreover, Dawis describes the influence of trait-factor and individual differences theory to the development of P–E psychology ranging from g (Spearman, 1904) to the Big Five in personality assessment (Digman, 1990).

Swanson and Chu detailed Holland's Model of Vocational Personalities and Work Environments and the theory of work adjustment (TWA), which are two of the most researched and used P–E psychology theoretical models. Holland's theory continues to demonstrate empirically that persons' vocational personalities and parallel characteristics of vocational environments can be measured and good matching can result in people finding satisfaction and tenure in occupations. Likewise, TWA is a successful empirically based P–E fit model that focuses on the process of adjustment to work. The TWA fit process entails individuals inherently seeking to achieve a harmonious relationship with their environments that involves the correspondence between an individual's values and what the job offers (satisfaction) and how well the individual's abilities and skills meet job and organizational requirements (satisfactoriness). Additionally, Dawis describes how TWA was generalized as person–environment correspondence (PEC) theory and applied to the counseling process.

Utilizing Dawis (1996) and Lofquist and Dawis (1991) theory, we (chap. 8, this volume) formulated a model to ascertain how well individuals fit culturally and contextually in the process of psychosocial adaptation to environments. We relate our P–E fit model to improving mental health practice by incorporating clients' cultural and contextual uniqueness into service delivery. Our approach generates assessment information that allows a clinician and client to determine the extent to which cultural and contextual factors influence the client's adaptation to given environments. If a lack of cultural and contextual correspondence exists between an individual and an environment, specific deficits are identified in the areas of cultural orientation, contextual satisfaction, and contextual satisfactoriness.

Those who first spoke of seeing the person in context broke new ground in psychology, but that has been nearly a century ago. Our theory base is still strong. Our understandings of the multidimensional nature of the person and the environment are growing, providing for exciting new directions for both research and practice. The P–E history is rich in theory, but our future needs to be paved by finding new more innovative ways of putting that theory into practice.

EFFICACY OF PERSON–ENVIRONMENT
ASSESSMENTS AND INTERVENTIONS

The only way that P–E methods will more fully influence applied psychology's successes in prevention and remediation of psychosocial problems is by continuing to demonstrate the efficacy of P–E assessments and interventions. There is a growing body of efficacy research that reflects both clinical field trials (Henggeler, 1997) and case studies that capitalize on the resources inherent in local ecologies (Trickett, 1997). This research is evident in several chapters in this book. For example, Borduin et al. (chap. 6, this volume) summarized the correlates and causes of serious antisocial behavior of adolescents pertaining to individual adolescent and key social systems. The authors identified associations between intraindividual characteristics including IQ and sociocognitive deficits with antisocial and aggressive behavior. Family relations correlates to antisocial behavior included low levels of family warmth and cohesion, marital and family conflict, lax and effective parental discipline, and witnessing or experiencing family violence. Research was reported showing the influence of peer support and acceptance on criminal activity. Borduin et al. also point out that negative peer influence can be mediated by positive family relations and prosocial peer support. The authors identified the consistent findings that poor school performance, dropping out, and school characteristics are consistently linked with serious antisocial behavior among adolescents. School characteristics include low student attendance, high student–teacher ratios, instability of the student population, poor academic quality, inconsistent discipline practices, and unfair school policies. The authors also report findings that show that the neighborhood context can influence criminal activity of adolescents. These neighborhood correlates include witnessing or being a victim of community violence, modeling criminal subculture behavior, and ready access to weapons and drugs. Finally, Borduin et al. discuss causal modeling research that attempts to overcome some of the inherent limitations of correlational research. For example, they cited a study by Elliott, Huizinga and Ageton (1985) who conducted a longitudinal study of 1, 725 adolescents that showed that serious delinquent behavior was directly correlated to involvement with delinquent peers and secondarily associated with family and school difficulties. The authors report other causal modeling studies that consistently show serious antisocial behavior is contributed directly or indirectly by individual, family, peer, school, and community variables.

Munger (chap. 2, this volume) also reports scientific literature showing the relationships between intraindividual and extraindividual characteristics to disturbed child and adolescent behavior. In addition to citing common studies that Borduin et al. summarize related to delinquency, Munger identifies precipitating factors of suicide that included family disruption, parental rejection, isolation, lack of support and depression. Furthermore, Munger reports evidence that psychosocial factors and family relations contribute to psychotic behavior.

CONCLUSION

With the increasing complexity of adolescent and adult lives, traditional person-focused methods fail to capture the true essence of the individual. As such, P–E methodology is especially alluring given its attention to ecological validity and a systemic orientation. It only makes sense to conduct intra- and extra-individual, systemic assessments and interventions within natural settings to enhance the probability of assessment and treatment generalization. With the growing influence of managed care, mental health professionals are having to show that what happens in the office can be applied to the home, school, work, or community. On the downside, however, is trying to make sense of the complexities associated with an individual's ecological niche.

Understanding who individuals are and how they function in their environment can be a daunting task. Certainly the better we understand the person and his or her world, the more ecologically valid our interventions will be. However, the more we begin to understand about ecological niches, the person's place in the great scheme of things, the more complex the issues become. This leads to a need for more sophisticated models of fit that account for the multiple systemic interactions that exist in individual's lives. Many approaches may seem onerous given the limited time mental health professionals really have to focus on any given client. In order to be effective, assessment needs to address both subjective and objective aspects of fit. We are working to make this process more practical.

In the preceding chapters we have had a glimpse of the future of the field, but we need to add to this progress. Our future research efforts need to be directed to identifying more efficient methods of assessment and intervention that can easily be used by all professionals. Moreover, there needs to be more attention paid to the programs that are already effective and learning how to move those methods into a more widely used approach to benefit all clients. Mental health concerns of adolescents and adults are not going to become less complex. With this in mind, we must agree the future is now.

REFERENCES

Csikszentmihalyi, M., & Larson, R. (1984). *Being Adolescent: Conflict and growth in the teenage years.* New York, Basic Books.

Dawis, R. V. (1996). The theory of work adjustment and person–environment-correspondence counseling. In D. Brown & L. Brooks (Eds.) *Career choice and development* (3rd ed., pp. 75–120). San Francisco: Jossey-Bass.

Digman, J. M. (1990). Personality Structure: Emergence of the five-factor model. *Annual Review of Psychology, 41,* 417-440.

Elliot, D. S., Huizinga, D., & Ageton, S. S. (1985). *Explaining delinquency and drug use.* Beverly Hills, CA: Sage.

Gump, P. (1984). Ecological psychology and clinical mental health. In W. O'Connor & B. Lubin (Eds.), *Ecological approaches to clinical and community psychology* (pp. 57–71). New York, Wiley.

Henggeler, S. W. (1997). Future directions: Specification, validation, and funding of ecologically based interventions for schools within communities. In J. Swartz & W. Martin, Jr., *Applied ecological psychology for school within communities: Assessment and intervention* (pp. 221–223). Mahwah, NJ: Lawrence Erlbaum Associates.

Lewin, K. (1936). *Principles of topological psychology.* New York, McGraw-Hill.

Lofquist, L. H., & Dawis, R. V. (1991). *Essentials of person–environment-correspondence counseling.* Minneapolis: University of Minnesota.

Murray, H. A. (and collaborators). (1938). *Explorations in personality.* New York, Oxford.

Parsons, F. (1909). *Choosing a vocation.* Boston: Houghton Mifflin.

Spearman, C. (1904a). The proof and measurement of association between two things. *American Journal of Psychology, 15,* 72–101.

Trickett, E. J. (1997). Developing an ecological mind-set on school-community collaboration. In J. Swartz & W. Martin, Jr., *Applied ecological psychology for school within communities: Assessment and intervention* (pp. 139–163). Mahwah, NJ: Lawrence Erlbaum Associates.

Viteles, M. S. (1936). A dynamic criterion. *Occupations, 14,* 963–967.

About the Editors and Contributors

EDITORS

William E. Martin, Jr., EdD, is professor and chair of educational psychology at Northern Arizona University. Prior to this appointment, he was director of research for the American Indian Rehabilitation Research and Training Center. Dr. Martin's research activities relate to ethnocultural assessment, psychosocial adaptation, person–environment based prevention and intervention methods, and applied ecological psychology.

Jody S. Swartz-Kulsatd, EdD, is an assistant professor of counselor education and coordinator of the Community Counseling Program at the University of Wisconsin–Superior. She is also director of the Clinical Services Center, a clinical training facility of the Counselor Education Department. Dr. Swartz has emphasized the role of person–environment fit in her research, primarily through exploration of how cultural and contextual factors play a role in psychosocial adaptation.

CONTRIBUTORS

Charles M. Borduin, PhD, is professor of psychology at the University of Missouri–Columbia and director of the Missouri Delinquency Project. He received his doctorate in clinical psychology from the University of Memphis and interned at Rutgers Medical School. His research interests include adolescent violent and sexual offending, family dysfunction, and the development and refinement of multisystemic therapy for the treatment of serious antisocial behavior in adolescents. Dr. Borduin has published extensively in the areas of juvenile delinquency and adolescent psychopathology, and he has served as a consultant to numerous state and federal agencies on the reform of children's mental health services.

Jayne E. Bucy, PhD, is an assistant professor of psychology at Illinois State University in Normal, Illinois. She is a graduate of the University of North Carolina at Chapel Hill, earning her doctorate in school psychology with a specialization in early intervention with infants and toddlers. As a school psychologist, she has worked with children of all ages and their families since 1984.

Serena P. Chu, MA, is a doctoral candidate in counseling psychology at Southern Illinois University at Carbondale. She is the recipient of numerous undergraduate honors including the American Psychological Association Undergraduate Students of Excellence in Psychology Award in 1995. She has presented papers and interactive sessions on issues related to ethnic identity development at the annual meetings of the Midwestern Psychological Association and the Asian American Psychological Association.

René V. Dawis obtained his bachelor's degree in psychology in 1951 at the University of the Philippines and his master's and doctorate degrees in psychology, with Donald G. Paterson, in 1955 and 1956, respectively, at the University of Minnesota. After 1 year as assistant professor at the University of the Philippines, he returned to Minnesota to do research with Lloyd Lofquist, George England, and David Weiss in the Work Adjustment Project. Among other things, this project produced the Theory of Work Adjustment, the Minnesota Importance Questionnaire, the Minnesota Satisfaction Questionnaire, the Minnesota Satisfactoriness Scales, the Minnesota Job Description Questionnaire (with which 200 Occupational Reinforcer Patterns were developed), the Minnesota Occupational Classification System, and most recently, the Minnesota Ability Test Battery. In 1963, Dr. Dawis joined the faculty of Minnesota's Industrial Relations Department, and in 1968, transferred to the Department of Psychology. Dr. Dawis has taught a variety of courses, including Introductory Psychology, Psychological Measurement, Psychology of Individual Differences, Vocational Psychology, Personnel Psychology, and Counseling Psychology (History & Theories, Assessment, Research Methods); supervised the dissertation research of 77 PhDs;

authored or co-authored 6 books, 27 book chapters, and 103 journal articles and monographs. He has been a consultant for many organizations, including the U.S. Department of Labor, Veterans Administration, State of Minnesota, City of Minneapolis, Ford, Honeywell, Control Data, and the Ball Foundation. Dr. Dawis retired from the University of Minnesota in June 1997. He is now senior research fellow (part time) at the Ball Foundation, Glen Ellyn, Illinois. His research interests continue to be in vocational psychology, psychometric assessment, and individual differences.

Shelly A. Grabe, BA, is a doctoral student in the child specialty track of the clinical psychology program at the University of Missouri–Columbia. She received her bachelor's degree in psychology from Michigan State University. Her research interests include juvenile delinquency, parental social support networks, and family dysfunction.

Naamith Heiblum, MA, is a doctoral student in the clinical psychology program at the University of Missouri–Columbia. She received her master's degree in clinical psychology from the University of Missouri and her bachelor's degree from Stanford University. Her research interests include adolescent maltreatment, parental belief systems, and sexual deviancy in youth.

Connie Burrows Horton, PhD, is an associate professor in the Psychology Department at Illinois State University where she teaches in the school psychology program. She earned her PhD from the University of Texas at Austin. Her current research and clinical interests are in the area of child maltreatment.

Michael R. Jones, MA, is a doctoral student in the clinical psychology program at the University of Missouri–Columbia. He received his master's degree in clinical psychology from the University of Missouri–Columbia and his bachelor's degree from St. Mary's College of Maryland. His research interests include family therapy process and outcome, juvenile delinquency, and child physical abuse and neglect.

Laura M. Koehly, PhD, received her PhD in quantitative psychology from the University of Illinois in 1996, after which she completed postgraduate work at the University of Texas M.D. Anderson Cancer Center in the Division of Cancer Prevention. She is currently assistant professor of educational measurement and statistics in the College of Education at the University of Iowa. There she teaches courses in statistical methods, including analysis of variance, categorical data analysis, and social network analysis. Her research interests include the development and application of statistical models for social network data, particularly ego-centered networks and perceptual networks. Her substantive work focuses on the application of network methodology in health education, specifically in the areas of breast cancer screening, HIV prevention, and the impact of genetic testing on family dynamics.

Richard L. Munger, PhD, is a child psychologist practicing in Asheville, North Carolina. He received his doctorate in educational psychology from the University of Michigan in 1979. Most recently he served as chief of the Child and Adolescent Mental Health Division, Hawaii Department of Health and Associate Professor of Psychiatry at the John A. Burns School of Medicine. He has served on the clinical faculty in the Department of Psychiatry at Duke University, University of North Carolina, and the Medical University of South Carolina. He is the author of two professional books, *Child Mental Health Practice from the Ecological Perspective* and *The Ecology of Troubled Children*, and a book for parents, *Changing Children's Behavior Quickly*.

Victoria A. Shivy, PhD, is an assistant professor in the Department of Psychology at Virginia Commonwealth University where she teaches a graduate-level course in personality assessment, provides clinical supervision to counseling psychologists-in-training, and teaches an undergraduate course in research methods. She received her PhD in counseling psychology from the University at Albany, State University of New York, and completed a 2-year postdoctoral traineeship in Quantitative Psychology at the University of Illinois. Her research interests lie at the intersection of career development and decision making and psychological assessment.

Jane L. Swanson, PhD, is an associate professor of psychology at Southern Illinois University at Carbondale. She received her PhD from the University of Minnesota in 1986. She serves on the executive board of the Division of Counseling Psychology of the American Psychological Association, and is chair-elect of the Society for Vocational Psychology. She currently serves on editorial boards of *The Counseling Psychologist, Journal of Career Assessment,* and *Career Development Quarterly,* and has served on editorial boards of *Journal of Vocational Behavior* and *Journal of Counseling Psychology.* Her areas of research include career barriers, career counseling process, measurement of vocational interests, and career psychology of women.

Author Index

A

Ageton, S. S., 121, *135*, 206, *208*
Ahia, C. E., 176, *191*
Ahuna, C., 179, *194*
Akhtar, N., 116, *132*
Alexander, C. N., 74, *82*
Alexander, J. F., 123, 124, *132*, *133*, *139*
Alexander, W. P., 94, *108*
Allen, A., 92, *108*
Allport, G. W., 91, *108*
Alterman, A. I., 116, *140*
American Psychiatric Association, 60, *83*
Anastasi, A., 188, *191*
Anda, D., 182, *191*
Anderson, C. J., 80, *82*, *83*, *87*
Aneshensel, C. S., 120, *138*
Angermeier, L., 185, *194*
Ankarlo, G., 60, *86*
Anthonisse, J. M., 73, *83*
Arabie, P., 78, *83*
Arbuthnot, J., 116, 124, *132*, *135*
Archer, R. P., 66, *83*
Arredondo, P., 176, *191*
Arthur, M. W., 114, 115, *138*
Assouline, M., 104, *108*, 151, *166*
Astor, R. A., 116, *133*
Atkins, M., 125, 126, *141*
Atkinson, D. R., 190, *191*, *192*

B

Bachorowski, J., 116, *134*
Baker, N., 40, 48, 49, 54, *57*
Bandura, A., 172, 190, *191*
Bank, L., 117, 123, *133*, *140*

Banks, D., 67, *83*
Barker, R. G., 4, *7*
Barnett, W. S., 119, *133*
Barton, C., 124, *133*
Batchelder, W. H., 67, *85*
Bates, J. E., 117, *141*
Batsche, G. M., 46, *55*
Bauman, K. E., 44, *56*
Baumler, B., 60, *86*
Baumrind, D., 40, 41, 42, *55*
Beaman, J., 121, *139*
Beaton, S., 119, *136*
Beauchamp, M. A., 73, *83*
Beauvais, F., 183, *194*
Behre, W. J., 116, *133*
Bem, D. J., 92, *108*
Ben-Porath, Y. S., 66, *83*
Bennett, L. A., 42, 43, *55*, *58*
Berdie, R. F., 100, 101, *108*
Berkowitz, R., 13, *37*
Bernard, H. R., 63, *85*
Berrueta-Clement, J. R., 119, *133*
Berry, J. W., 179, *191*
Berscheid, E, 61, *82*, *85*
Betancourt, H., 185, *191*
Betz, N. E., 143, 156, *166*
Beyer, T. A., 116, *140*
Bickett, T. A., 116, *133*
Biggs, D. A., 99, 100, 101, *111*
Binder, H., 125, 126, 127, *139*
Binet, A., 95, *108*
Bizot, E. B., 173, 188, *191*
Blaske, D. M., 117, 129, *133*, *138*
Bloch, D., 26, *36*
Bloomquist, M. L., 127, *134*

Subject Index

A

Adaptation, 174–175, 177
  psychosocial adaptation, 179
Adolescence, 39–55, 113–132, 143–165
  academic performance, 119
  antisocial behavior
    causal models, 120–122
    correlates of, 115–120
    treatment of, see Treatment models,
      122–130
  alterations in process, 189
  career development, 160–162
  cognitive abilities, 116
  familty relations, 117–118
  intelligence (IQ), 115–116
  neighborhood context, 119–120
  parents, 40–43
    management training, 122
  peers, 43–45, 118
  school, 45–47, 119
  social skills, 116
  work, 47–48
Assessment, 14–26, 48–54
  activities, 22–23
  commensurate measurement, 96–98,
    105
    lambda coeffcient, 98
    occupational ability pattern, 96
    occupational scale (Strong), 97
    and validation in personnel selec-
      tion, 97
  comprehensive needs, 14
  culture, 182, 187–188
  enactments, 54
  family interaction tasks, 53
  family-level, 16–17
  individual-level, 16
  interviews, 48–51
    eco-maps, 51
  measuring social relations, 63, *see also*
    social network analysis, 62

  neighborhood-level, 18
  observation, 53
  and P–E psychology, 200–204
  peer-level, 17
  people, 24–25
  places, 21–22
  projectives, 52
  school-level, 17–18
  self-report measures, 51–52, *see also*
    psychological testing, 95–96
    Family Environment Scale (FES),
      51
    Family Adaptability and Cohesion
      Scale (FACES III), 52
  social network analysis, 60–82
  sociomatrix, 67
  specialized, 25–26
  strenth-based, 11
  systems, 188
Attributional bias, 116

C

Comprehensive Needs-Based Assessment
  Checklist, 27–35
Contexual satisfaction, 183–185, 188
Contextual satisfactoriness, 183–185, 188
Counseling from a P–E perspective,
  106–107
  choice of intervention, 106
  counselee satisfaction, 106, 107
  counseling process, models of
    106–107
  counselor satisfaction, 106, 107
  feedback systems, 107
  reinforcement, 107
Cultural and Contextual Correspondence,
  175, 178, 184
Cultural and Contextual Guide Process,
  179

225